# The West Virginia One~Day Trip Book

To my favorite chauffeurs
and road companions:
Peter, Dianna and Maureen.

S.L.


To my mother, Evelyn Metzger,
who patiently taught me appreciation
for the written word.

J.M.

# THE WEST VIRGINIA ONE~DAY TRIP BOOK

## Suzanne Lord
## Jon Metzger

EPM Publications
McLean, Virginia, 22101

Library of Congress Cataloging-in-Publication Data

Lord, Suzanne, 1941–
    The West Virginia one-day trip book : more than 150
jaunts in the Magic Mountain State / Suzanne Lord and Jon
Metzger.
        p.  cm.
    Includes index.
    ISBN 0-939009-70-6
    1. West Virginia—Tours.
I. Metzger, Jon.   II. Title.
F239.3.L67   1993
917.5404'43—dc20                                    93-16659
                                                       CIP

EPM Publications, Inc., 1003 Turkey Run Road,
    McLean, Virginia 22101
Printed in the United States of America

Cover and book design by Tom Huestis
Cover photos: Mountain bikers at Bear Rocks on Dolly Sods,
    Stephen J. Shaluta, Jr., WV Division of Tourism & Parks
    Inset: Glade Creek Mill, Babcock State Park, Larry Belcher,
    WV Division of Tourism & Parks
Back cover: *West Virginia Belle*, Stephen J. Shaluta, Jr.

# Contents

# THE WEST VIRGINIA ONE-DAY TRIP BOOK

# POTOMAC HIGHLANDS
## (EAST CENTRAL MOUNTAINS)

## ═══════════MOUNTAIN LAKES (CENTRAL)═══════════

## MOUNTAINEER COUNTRY
## ═══════════(NORTH CENTRAL)═══════════

## MID-OHIO VALLEY
### (WEST CENTRAL)

## NEW  RIVER /
## GREENBRIER  VALLEY

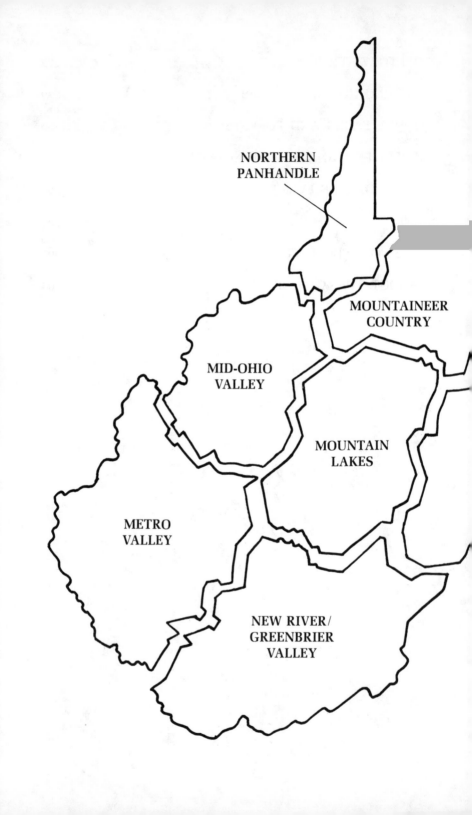

NORTHERN
PANHANDLE

MOUNTAINEER
COUNTRY

MID-OHIO
VALLEY

MOUNTAIN
LAKES

METRO
VALLEY

NEW RIVER/
GREENBRIER
VALLEY

# IT ALL COMES TOGETHER
# IN WEST VIRGINIA

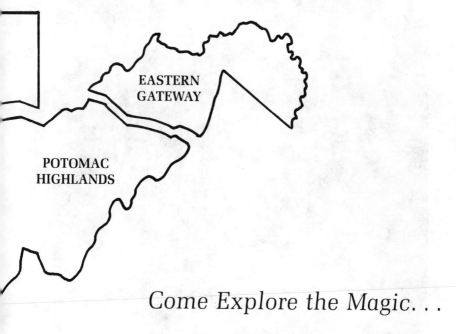

EASTERN
GATEWAY

POTOMAC
HIGHLANDS

Come Explore the Magic. . .

From the Potomac River
to the Mighty Ohio,
From the Appalachians
to the Central Lakes
and Western Valleys

Some of the 50 miles of hiking trails in Otter Creek Wilderness double in winter for cross-country skiing. STEPHEN J. SHALUTA, JR.

# Welcome to
# West Virginia

*"West Virginia's sons know her as a different land. To them she is not befouled by a commercial age. They know her as a land of peace, a land where blue waters serenely flow between the fragrant hills to make the valleys green. To them she is ever the same: white mists hanging over the waters, straight trees unblackened by smoke, shoals murmuring over rounded pebbles. . . the path of the moon on the waters! She is a land of dreams and of laughter and of love."*

Albert Benjamin Cunningham, *The Manse at Barren Rocks*

Welcome to some of the most beautiful scenery and the most genuine people anywhere. From the Potomac River to the mighty Ohio, from the Appalachians to the central lakes and western valleys, welcome to the power and poetry of one of the last stretches of wilderness east of the Mississippi.

This guide, the ninth in EPM's series of One-Day Trip Books, shares the magic of the Mountain State in these short, affordable excursions. Here are more than 150 day jaunts, organized geographically into eight regions (according to the format the WV Division of Tourism and Parks uses). Directions are given starting from central points—inter-state highways or large towns and cities—within each region (Wheeling in Northern Panhandle, Parkersburg in Mid-Ohio Valley, etc.), and most attractions can be combined easily with others in the same vicinity for a diverse and manageable one-day outing.

Since these are primarily day trips, we did not research overnight accommodations, whether campgrounds, inns or large resorts, unless day trippers are allowed to use their recreational facilities. Nor, with few exceptions, are we including restaurants—subject matter for yet another book.

In choosing and researching our destinations, we took the invaluable suggestions of the WV Division of Tourism and Parks and selected area Convention and Visitors Bureaus. We are greatly indebted to them. For the most part, we followed our noses and the advice of helpful hosts whom we met along the way, ferreting out sites that appeal to a wide span of interests and ages, rediscovering established favorites and often stumbling upon new ones. We found places you can visit by train, sternwheeler, canoe, raft, car, mini-tram, horseback and even in a hot-air balloon. Choose from historic mansions, Civil War battle-fields, animal parks, art and science museums, glass and china factories, theaters, craft and entertainment centers, gristmills, underground caverns, even a miniature Swiss village, a palace of gold, and one of the most sophisticated observatories for radio astronomy in the world. For the sports minded, we found ski slopes, whitewater rafting rivers, fishing holes, hiking trails, and places to hunt, climb rocks, watch birds, scuba dive, or just "hang out" outdoors. Special texts and lists in the back tell about ski resorts, hunting/fishing/rafting areas, and a Calendar of Events helps you plan ahead for special happenings.

Included in each description are the core facts you'll need to plan ahead: hours open to the public, directions, telephone num-bers, addresses and helpful tips. First-time visitors to the state are usually amazed to discover that most sites, public and pri-vate, do not charge an entrance fee. If there is an "Admission," it's listed after "Hours." Otherwise entrance is free.

Due to the severity of the weather in certain areas, some at-tractions are open only in summer or close early due to unpre-dictable, unseasonable snowfalls. So be sure to call ahead when in doubt to check hours and road conditions.

### State Parks

For the benefit of all travelers, West Virginia's jewel in the crown is its superb system of state parks (36) and forests (9). No other state we know of has prettier, more accessible, better managed parks that satisfy such a wide range of interests and incomes. Choose from resort-level lodges with championship golf courses to family campgrounds and shelters off remote mountain trails; from ski slopes to virgin hemlock forests, from crystal lakes to majestic rock cliffs. And the price is right: entrance to almost every park is free; overnight accommodations and use of tennis courts, pools, and sports facilities are very reasonably priced. Come for an hour or a week. Reservations for overnight accom-modations during peak seasons are a must. Call 1-800-CALL-WVA. Because of their size and number we have described only some of these parks in detail, those representing a broad spec-trum of facilities and attractions. They are all worth a visit; each is special in its own way. (See entry.)

### About Roads

West Virginia justifiably takes pride in the excellent maintenance of both primary and secondary roads. Pot holes are filled, guard rails repaired, land dividers painted, rock slides cleared when and where needed in short order. Even in bad storms, roads are cleared remarkably quickly, as much for the school buses as for other traffic. In winter a four-wheel drive vehicle is advisable almost anywhere and essential in the mountains and ski resorts.

Because of the nature of the terrain in certain regions, some mountain roads curve sharply or drop and climb at steep angles. Watch for and obey the yellow signs advising speed limits and warnings of treacherous spots, possible rock falls, dangerous passing zones and animal crossings. Signs are accurate and well spaced in advance of trouble spots. So pay them heed, particularly in cold weather when icy patches are difficult to predict.

Deer, partly due to their explosive population growth, are a particularly dangerous and common hazard statewide; thousands are killed by motorists every year. Be aware of cars behind and approaching when swerving to avoid collision or braking suddenly. Again, heed warning signs and, above all, drive slowly. Traveling in West Virginia is such a delight you don't want to hurry. Traffic jams and rush-hour gridlocks are unknowns in most areas; there's plenty of time to enjoy the important things. Adjust your mental clock to local time, a time that allows for digging ramps, casting a line into a stream and listening to songbirds along the way.

Reflecting on our year's travel on back roads and busy highways, mountain trails and river rapids some memorable images leap to mind: a sunrise on Dolly Sods, lady-slippers along the Greenbrier Trail, Blennerhassett Island emerging from the mist, the voices of chanting Krishna devotees echoing across the hills, a fawn following its mother through the snow in Canaan Valley, the bustle of Charleston's streets around the majestic capitol, the dark, cool intrigue underground at Beckley Exhibition Coal Mine, and watching from the deck at Canyon Rim Visitor Center the awe-inspiring New River wind through the gorge below.

We also remember getting lost and being rescued by gracious, patient strangers. Above all—and the image most enduring—is the warmth, wisdom, generosity, humor, charm and kindness of West Virginians we met in every part of the state. Thank you for sharing your proud heritage and beautiful state with us. Thank you for enriching our lives.

Finally, there are so many unexpected surprises, so many sensual and visual delights waiting around that next curve that no guide book—no matter how well intentioned, researched and written—can bring you the full experience of Wonderful West Virginia. You have to see it and "do" it yourself!

S.L. and J.M.

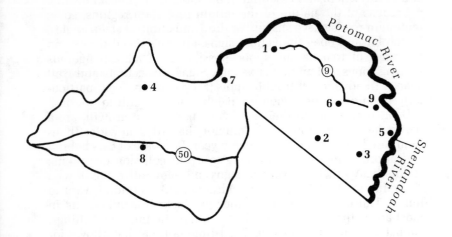

# EASTERN GATEWAY

1. **Berkeley Springs**
   Berkeley Springs State Park and
      Downtown
   Berkeley Castle
   Cacapon State Park

2. **Bunker Hill**
   Bunker Hill Flour Mill
   Morgan Cabin

3. **Charles Town**

4. **Fort Ashby**

5. **Harpers Ferry**

6. **Martinsburg**
   Blue Ridge Outlet Center
   Boarman House Art Center
   General Adam Stephen House and
      Triple Brick Museum

7. **Paw Paw Tunnel**

8. **Romney, The Potomac Eagle**

9. **Shepherdstown**
   The Entler Hotel
   James Rumsey Monument
   Thomas Shepherd Gristmill
   O'Hurley's General Store

# ═══Eastern Gateway═══

The Eastern Panhandle sticks into Pennsylvania and Maryland like a saddle-shaped piece from a jig-saw puzzle. Fate, in the aftermath of the Civil War, was kind to the Mountain State by granting her custody of this gorgeous geographic step-child, completing the profile that defines West Virginia's unique and unconventional identity. Rolling hills and rich farmland surround quaint towns. Scenic rivers flow through narrow gorges, where eagles nest, and merge to form rapids just right for recreational rafting.

But it is the history of the area that accounts for the area's popularity and fast-growing tourist trade. Over a half a million visitors a year come to relive John Brown's story and the Civil War at Harpers Ferry. Some churches and homes in Shepherdstown, Berkeley Springs and Charles Town go back farther, a few to when George Washington bathed in the mineral springs at Bath. Victorian mansions, now gracious inns, recall the industrial boom of the last century. Tree-lined streets, cute stone houses, and charming antique shops are a few minutes' drive from state parks, fishing streams, a championship golf course and even a racetrack. Whether your interest is in houses or horses, hiking or history, the Eastern Panhandle is a welcoming gateway to a great day's getaway.

For more information on the Eastern Gateway contact:

Travel Berkeley Springs, 304 Fairfax Street, Berkeley Springs, WV 25411, phone 1(800)447-8797 or (304)258-9147.

Jefferson County Convention and Visitor Bureau, PO Box A, Harpers Ferry, WV 25425, phone 1(800)848-TOUR or (304)535-2627.

Mineral County Convention and Visitors Center, 109 N. Davis St., Keyser, WV 26726, phone (304)788-2513.

## Berkeley Springs

Still officially the Town of Bath, Berkeley Springs has been famed for its curative warm mineral water since George Washington bathed here, seeking relief from rheumatic fever. A plaque on the self-guided walking tour documents his testimony to the springs' healing powers: "I myself benefitted by the water and am not without hope of their making a cure of me. . . ." In fact, Indians recognized the healthful properties of the waters centuries earlier. In the 18th century, Bath was reputedly America's premier spa, and, although the attractive setting, nestled in the Blue Ridge near the Cacapon and Potomac rivers, attracts outdoor enthusiasts, visitors still come here primarily for the therapeutic springs. The discharge, which has not faltered in recorded time, is 2,000 gallons per minute at the constant temperature of 74.3 degrees.

Before starting off on foot (the best way to see downtown attractions), stop at the Travel Berkeley Springs/Chamber of Commerce Office at 304 Fairfax Street weekdays between 9:00 A.M. and 5:00 P.M. and pick up brochures on local attractions and a walking tour map (1(800)447-8797 or (304)258-9147). You'll learn that the town was laid out by George Washington and his friends in 1776, one of the lots being designated for Washington's own house.

## Berkeley Springs State Park and Downtown

A good starting point is **Berkeley Springs State Park**, in the heart of town on Washington Street. Only seven acres in size, the park is a hub-bub of activity in warm months when the 1815 Roman Bath House, the museum inside and swimming pool are open. In the north corner the state-run Main Bath House is open year-round and offers both a Roman bath, (a small step-in pool), or the "relaxing bath" in an oversize bathtub. Water is brought in directly from the base of the mountains and heated to 102 degrees. The spa in the Main Bath House is a real bargain: a 45-minute bath, a shower and massage for $25. Open daily with the exception of Christmas and New Year's Day from 10:00 A.M. to 6:00 P.M. These baths are very popular, and you should make reservations at least two weeks in advance: 1(800)CALL-WVA or (304)258-2711.

Also on the park grounds is Lord Fairfax's public tap to which travelers come great distances to fill up their jugs with spring drinking water. You'll see a stone bathtub nearby, sitting in tribute to the baths' most famous patron, George Washington. In summer the park is a delightful backdrop for the summer concert series.

Downtown shopping opportunities abound. There are two antique malls jammed with furniture, glass, china and clothing within walking distance of the park. It's worth strolling on side streets like Fairfax Street and browsing through craft and novelty shops. If you are in town on the weekend and want to rub elbows with locals, don't pass up the movies at **STAR Theater**—an old fashioned experience. Sit in overstuffed couches that supplement conventional seats, chomp on buttered popcorn made in a 1947 machine, get your change from an antique cash register, buy candy for a few cents and see everybody in town worth knowing.

Down the street from the park at 201 Independence Street, **Maria's Garden and Inn** houses an inspiring array of religious objets d'art'. Dedicated to the Virgin Mary, the shrine-like mini-museum is hung with paintings and statues honoring the Madonna. Of particular interest are the Polish Madonna seeded in pearls, a grotto dedicated to Our Lady of Lourdes, Stations of the Cross hand-painted on copper, and outside, a garden replication of the appearance of Mary at Lourdes. Owner Peg Perry is willing to share her enthusiasm and unique collection with visitors who call for a tour. Off-dining hours are best: (304)258-2021.

## *Berkeley Castle*

Dominating the skyline above the park, Berkeley Castle looms over the town like a monstrous beast on guard. Built in 1885 from local hand-carved sandstone as a replica of Berkeley Castle in England, the structure was intended as a wedding gift from Colonel Samuel Taylor Suit to his much-younger bride. Its Victorian whimsy and romantic aura must have pleased her for she became a famous party-giver, running through her husband's fortune by extravagant entertaining. After decades of neglect the castle was purchased in 1954 and gradually restored by the current owner, Walter Bird. A direct descendant of James I of England and James IV of Scotland, Bird claims that his is the "only truly royal castle in America."

Three levels are open to the public. The grand entrance hall (or ballroom), draped in brocade, wood paneled and dominated by a massive stone fireplace, is used for dinner theater. Heirlooms and antique furniture belonging to the owner's family date from James I of Scotland. One velvet sofa is reputedly 1,000 years old. To the right of the dining room, note the miniature stone replica of the castle built by a young girl as a project for her art class. Recognizing her talent, an architectural firm offered her a $50,000 scholarship for education costs if she studied architecture and eventually joined their company—a modern fairy tale dream come true.

Of particular charm on the second level is the Children's Room with its miniature furniture and dainty bed. Here tea sets and Victorian toys scattered about look abandoned as if the children had just been called to supper. Stairs lead to the roof terrace and turret from which viewers reputedly can see four states and part of the Blue Ridge Mountains. The magnificent view of town makes you feel like the "king of the castle."

*German stonemasons were paid eight cents an hour to build the walls of Berkeley Castle three feet thick.* David Fattaleh

**Admission**: Adults $5.00, seniors $4.50, children 4 to 12 $2.00, under 3 free. Prices do not include a mandatory state tax.

**Hours**: 8:00 A.M. to 8:00 P.M. every day of the week, year-round. Many Friday and Saturday evenings the castle closes an hour earlier for dinner theater performances.

**Directions**: You can climb the steps in the back of the park up to the castle. For more information call (304)258-4000.

To reach Berkeley Springs Park from I-70 take US 522 eight miles south to the center of town, or from I-81, take US 522 north from Winchester about 34 miles. For more information write Berkeley Springs State Park, 121 S. Washington St, WV 25411. One of the most scenic spots in the area is **Prospect Peak** on Rt. 9 three miles west of Berkeley Castle. Look for the marker and pull-off at the side of the road. In good weather you can see Pennsylvania, Maryland and the Potomac and Cacapon rivers. The sign boasts that "The National Geographic rates this scene among America's outstanding beauty spots."

## Cacapon State Park

This gem of a park—one of the four state resort parks—is close enough to Berkeley Springs for town entertainment yet distanced enough to be enjoyed as a country escape. With 6,000 acres of mountain and valley terrain there is ample opportunity and space for a wide variety of activities. Nearly 30 miles of hiking and riding trails pass through forest to the top of Cacapon Mountain. The 18-hole championship golf course, designed by Robert Trent Jones, is considered one of the best in the country and can double in the winter for cross country skiing. A full-time pro is available for golf lessons. Guests may fish, swim and row on nearby Cacapon Lake. There are tennis courts, stables and picnic areas. In summer and spring guided trail rides are a popular way of getting exercise while sightseeing; overnight trips can be arranged.

To stay the night in one of the facilities, all reasonably priced, your options are: cottages scattered throughout the park fully equipped for light housekeeping; the 11-room Old Inn with its own private dining room (great for groups up to 25); the Lodge, a cozy, bright 50-room facility snuggled next to the golf course. Rooms are simple, clean and reasonable and the dining room looks out onto the fairway. The staff organizes special weekend activities such as square dancing, craft demonstrations and nature hikes on weekends. Cacapon is highly recommended for either day treks or over-night getaways. There's plenty of space for kids to run, shout and explore the mysteries of nature.

**Location**: Take Rt. 9 south from Berkeley Springs for about ten miles. Follow signs. For more information call (800)CALL-WVA or (304)258-1022 or write Cacapon Resort State Park, Berkeley Springs, WV 25411.

# Bunker Hill

## Bunker Hill Flour Mill

"I don't mind tourists coming here to paint the mill," says Paul Giles, smothering an ironic smile, "but they always bring such small brushes and lose interest when I give them the paint." It's no wonder he gets artists camping on his front yard with their canvases and oils.

This picturesque turn in the road marked by gurgling Mill Creek is dominated by the only gristmill with two waterwheels left in the state. Unfortunately, you will not see them in operation. The handsome five-story stone and wood structure has not functioned as a mill since 1964, but it is the hub of a busy livestock feed store that supplies neighboring farmers and doubles as a social center for chewing the fat around the wood stove.

Owner Giles, when not waiting on customers or swapping yarns with "the boys," is willing to explain the history and mechanics of the equipment, most of which dates from the 19th and early 20th century. The stone foundation, however, puts the original building in the 1700s. In the next century Bunker Hill was a thriving community, and no less than 13 mills operated along the creek. The colorful red wooden section was added in the 1880s to replace fire damage and provides the contrast with the gray rock that draws photographers and the painters with "small brushes."

Stacked with feed bags and old farm implements, the working area is usually congested with the comings and goings of farmers, dogs and cats—not an appropriate gathering spot for busloads of gawkers. However, Mr. Giles, an enthusiastic collector of local history, will accommodate small groups for prearranged tours. His own stately, solid brick home next door, built by Quaker farmers in 1851, is representative of L-shaped Federal-style houses that grace the West Virginia countryside.

**Hours**: Monday, Tuesday, Thursday and Friday 8:00 A.M. to 5:00 P.M. and Saturday 8:00 A.M. to NOON. Closed Sunday and Wednesday. To arrange a tour of the mill call (304)229-8707.

**Directions**: From I-81 take Rt. 11 south and turn east on Old Mill Rd. (Rt. 26). Go about a mile to the mill on your right. For more information write Bunker Hill Mill, Rt. 1, Box 300, Old Mill Rd., Bunker Hill, WV 25413.

## Morgan Cabin

Morgan Cabin, a simple cabin structure in farm country, is worth visiting if only to appreciate the frontier fortitude and ingenuity our forebears needed to survive in the wilderness of the 1730s. The present house, on the National Register of Historic Places, is reconstructed from the original logs, including one that opened for the owner to shoot at Indians. After choosing the site for its proximity to a stream, Colonel Morgan Morgan spent three years cutting wood for logs and quarrying stone for the base and chimney, completing the home for his family in 1734. The state of West Virginia considers him its first white settler. It was here at the cabin that, during the Revolution, one of Morgan's grandsons was caught by Tories and shot in front of his wife and children. Morgan County and Morgantown are named after this famous family, which included sons who fought in the French and Indian Wars and were prominent settlers.

Even in winter when the house is closed to the public, a quick stop is informative, as there is a push-button audio tape that tells the history, and you can look through the windows at the primitive lifestyle represented here. Morgan Cabin May Day Festival, an annual fundraiser, is held the first Sunday in May, featuring a full luncheon, crafts demonstrations and horse and buggy rides.

**Hours**: Open each Sunday May 5 through August 25 from 2:00 to 5:00 P.M. Group tours at other times may be arranged by calling (304)229-8946.

Less than three miles away is **Christ Church**, reputedly the site of the first church in the state (1740). The present brick structure in a Greek-revival style is the third to be constructed here and is only open for services once a month. But the cemetery is worth a stop since it is here that Colonel Morgan Morgan and his wife are buried.

Antique hunters can leap frog into another century by visiting the **Bunker Hill Antiques Associates** next to the church. Over 175 dealer spaces are housed in this restored 19th-century woolen mill, and displayed wares span nearly every interest: toys, clocks, furniture, jewelry, glass, chinaware, clothing, books and paintings. Unlike some antique malls that smell of mold, dust and moth balls, this building is clean, bright and spacious. An upstairs deli restaurant with a balcony overlooking a park offers refreshment for serious shoppers and patient spouses alike.

**Hours**: Open seven days a week 10:00 A.M. to 5:00 P.M. except Friday when it's open until 9:00 P.M. For further information call (304)229-0709.

**Directions**: From I-81 take Rt. 11. Turn right, going west onto Old Mill Rd. (Rt. 26). Christ Church is on your right, next to the antique mall. Continue from church 2.7 miles to Morgan Cabin on left.

## Charles Town

George Washington certainly knew a good piece of land when he surveyed it. Only 16 years old when he first took sightings of the wooded hills and valleys on this side of the Potomac, Washington—within just a few years—accumulated some 2,300 acres here alone and persuaded his kin to do likewise. His tip lead to the founding of the town by his youngest brother, Charles, in 1786 and the building of five homes by various members of the clan, some of which remain today, like Charles's "Happy Retreat." Is it any surprise that Main Street is called Washington Street, and cross streets George, Charles, Samuel, Lawrence?

The area continued making history by becoming the locale for the famous trial and subsequent hanging of abolitionist John Brown (see Harpers Ferry). During the Civil War its strategic position caused it much suffering and damage. You can spend the good part of a morning strolling the old sidewalks, admiring gracious, restored mansions and period gardens, visiting the county court house and poking around the Jefferson County Museum—all within easy walking distance of each other. Some of the private homes, representing Federal, Greek Revival and Victorian architecture are open to the public during the spring tour sponsored by the garden clubs of Berkeley and Jefferson counties—usually scheduled for the last weekend of April. Proceeds fund plantings in historic areas and along highways. For information write: Tour Director, PO Box 1166, Shepherdstown, WV 25443.

The Chamber of Commerce at the corner of Washington and Samuel streets provides an excellent map and description of the historic area in a pamphlet "Bicentennial Guide to 'Old' Charles Town." Stop here, call them at (304)725-2055 or write Jefferson County Chamber of Commerce, PO Box 426, Charles Town, WV 25414-0426. In addition to the residences, some of the highlights of your own self-guided tour should include the following.

In the same site as the Chamber of Commerce in the **Old Charles Town Civic Center** (Washington and Samuel streets) the **Jefferson County Museum** houses thousands of artifacts tracing the history of the area from Washington's original surveys to Brown's cot and the wagon that took him to the gallows, Confederate flags and Civil War weapons including a sword lost in 1885 and returned to the owner 50 years later. Open 10:00 A.M. to 4:00 P.M., Monday to Saturday, April to December. Call (304)725-8628.

Destroyed by fire, the original **Jefferson County Courthouse** (1803) was replaced by today's structure (1836) at Washington and George streets. Here Brown, lying wounded on his cot, was condemned to death in 1859. Used as a barracks and badly damaged during the Civil War and later restored, the two-story, red brick, columned courthouse with its clock tower is a stately example of Georgian Colonial design. The clock, purchased in 1872 from the Boston Watch Company, chimes on the hour. Open 9:00

A.M. to 5:00 P.M. Monday through Thursday and to 7:00 P.M. on Friday.

The 1912 **Old Opera House** (George and Liberty streets) with gracious curved balcony and seats for nearly 300, operates once again as a theater for performing arts after extensive renovations. For ticket information call (304)725-4420.

For an entirely different horse of another color, you can bet on an afternoon or evening of excitement at the famous **Charles Town Races**. If you are prudent—and lucky— the evening shouldn't cost more than a few dollars, including parking. Glass-enclosed and weatherized grandstand and clubhouse allow comfortable viewing of thoroughbred racing all year-long.

**Admission**: Between $2.00 and $5.00 depending on where you sit.

**Hours**: Early afternoon (around 1:00), evening (between 6:00 and 7:00). For a complete up-to-date schedule call (304)725-7001 or write Charles Town Races, PO Box 551, Charles Town, WV 25414.

**Directions**: About 6 miles west of Harpers Ferry on Rt. 340 via I-70 or I-270.

# Fort Ashby

When you arrive at Fort Ashby, don't bother looking out in back for cannons, stockades or a typical military garrison. The structure made from large, hand-hewn logs sitting close to the street *is* the fort and the only standing one of its kind. Built in 1755 on the orders of George Washington, as a chain of 69 Indian forts defending the Virginia frontier, Fort Ashby is a sober reminder of how vulnerable settlers were to Indian attack. Indeed, the man for whom the fort is named, Colonel John Ashby, reached safety here after escaping from Indians. He later commanded the fort. The structure centers around a massive chimney 14 feet wide and 4 feet thick. Much of the interior woodwork and wrought iron is original as are the hinges from the large doors and the fireplace mantel. The fort, after fulfilling its military purpose and being no longer needed for protection, served as a schoolhouse. Most of the articles on display are from the 19th century. Owned by the Daughters of the American Revolution since 1927, the fort was restored and opened to the public on July 4th, 1939.

**Admission**: Free but donations appreciated.

**Hours**: You must call one of these numbers ahead of arrival to arrange entrance: (304)298-3319, 3926, 3318 or 3722.

**Directions**: Coming east into the town of Fort Ashby from Kaiser on Rt. 46, go straight through the one traffic light in town and the fort will be on your left, less than ¼ mile. For further information, write: Fort Ashby, Box 233, Fort Ashby, WV 26719.

# Harpers Ferry National Historical Park

Harpers Ferry sits on a dramatic, storybook setting in the Blue Ridge foothills where three states (MD, VA and WV) and two rivers meet (Shenandoah and Potomac). Although one has the feeling of being in the mountains, the town is actually one of the lowest points in the state—275 feet above sea level. The views from several spots are magnificent in any season of the year and explain in part why the town, most of which is a national park, draws half a million visitors annually.

Early settlers ran a ferry service at the junction of the two rivers in the mid 1700s, among them Robert Harper, for whom the town is named. In 1790 President George Washington urged Congress to establish a national armory here because of the site's proximity to Washington, accessible water power and raw materials and a secure position. The armory and its gun production subsequently supported the town's economy and encouraged the growth of other small industries. With the construction of the C&O Canal along the Potomac and the B&O Railroad, the town grew to more than 3,000 inhabitants by the 1850s.

Then came the raid in 1859 by abolitionist John Brown, who tried to seize the armory and, with the confiscated guns, to incite a slave rebellion. Forces under Robert E. Lee—then with the U.S. Army—defeated the raiders, who are considered by some as among the first martyrs of the Emancipation effort. The Civil War that followed nearly a year and a half later was the main cause of the town's economic demise. Harpers Ferry was a strategic prize for both armies and suffered the consequences of changing hands eight times during the war.

Due to its riverside location—deceptively serene during a dry spell—the area has suffered continuous and devastating floods, several in the late 1800s that discouraged people from resettling here.

Under the management of the National Park Service, much of Harpers Ferry has been restored and today ranks number one as the state's most visited attraction. Because parking space is extremely limited in the town, particularly on weekends, the Park Service requests that visitors park at the Cavalier Heights Visitor Center and take the shuttle into town. Look for signs on Rt. 340 as you approach the turnoff for Harpers Ferry.

**The Information Center** on Shenandoah Street close to the shuttle drop-off area is a good place to start your visit. As you'll

*A young visitor gets a hands-on history lesson at Harpers Ferry's annual event, "Election Day—1860."*

HARPERS FERRY NATIONAL HISTORICAL PARK

see, the park emphasizes four main themes: industry, John Brown's raid, the Civil War and African-American history. Pick up an orientation map and ask which living-history walking tours will be conducted that day by park rangers (daily in summer and weekends in the fall and spring). From there stroll to the **John Brown Museum** to see a display on the history of the raiders and their fiery leader. Take in the slide show (10 minutes) on the background of the area and a 26-minute film, "To Do Battle in the Land" about the story of John Brown, whose valor in the cause of emancipation still stirs deep emotion. Then follow the map to John Brown's Fort and, a little distance beyond, enjoy the view of the rivers' confluence from "The Point." Retrace your steps back along Shenandoah Street to other restored 19th-century buildings like the Blacksmith Shop and the Dry Goods Store. Of particular interest is the replicated Philip Frankel & Co. clothing store. A park ranger explains evolution of clothing production from hand-sewn to machine made and its impact on daily life. You may be told that Victorian men wore up to eight layers of clothing (women, more) and that a pair of men's handmade shoes in the 1880s cost $1.00.

Across from the Information Center near the river bank, look for the high-water marks on the wall and the display showing the devastation from floods since 1859. The highest mark documents the river cresting at 36 feet above average in 1936.

Not part of the national park but an interesting stop is **John Brown's Wax Museum** on High Street, where 86 lifesize wax figures re-create the life story of Brown, youth to gallows, and his aborted insurrection. A few steps away on the same street one of the parks newest exhibits, Black Voices from Harpers Ferry, highlights a people's struggle for freedom and dignity.

For a breathtaking view of the rivers and surrounding Blue Ridge Mountains, follow the stone steps up the hill from High Street. Note the small stone Harper House, oldest surviving structure in the park (1775–1782), and **St. Peter's Catholic Church** built in the 1830s and still in use. Continue to Jefferson Rock and see the view that Jefferson claimed was worth "a voyage across the Atlantic." The path continues to Harper Cemetery and some very old gravestones, including that of Robert Harper. At the top of the hill is the former campus of **Storer College**, one of the first colleges for blacks in the country following the Civil War. Pack a picnic to enjoy along the way or back down by the river shore.

You can spend a full morning taking in the historic sites and peeking into the quaint shops on side streets. Time and weather permitting, hikers and bikers should get a feel for the countryside by exploring nearby trails. Options include a short walk to Virginus Island and more ambitious ventures along the **C&O Canal.** Walk across the Potomac footbridge to the Maryland side and pick up the path paralleling the Potomac. A highly recommended bike trip is the 11-mile stretch upriver to Shepherdstown. For another spectacular view, hike the Maryland Heights Trail to the top of the cliffs. Another choice is hiking a section of the Appalachian Trail, which crosses through the park. Maps are available in the Information Center.

Two special weekends are worth noting. The first is the Old Tyme Christmas weekend in early December sponsored by the Harpers Ferry Merchant Association when the whole town is candle-lit and garlanded in traditional greens. Merchants dress in colonial garb and organize caroling and music events. There is a live Nativity scene and a Lighting of the Yule ceremony. For more information call (800)848-TOUR. The second event, sponsored by the Park Service, is Election Day—1860, a living-history event that recaptures Lincoln's election, including political debates, speeches and rallies. Call (304)535-6298 for information about any park activities or write Harpers Ferry National Historical Park, Box 65, Harpers Ferry, WV 25425.

**Admission**: To the park: $5.00 per car. This fee allows admission for seven consecutive days. Any car with a passenger over 62 is admitted free. The fee for cyclists and walk-ins is $2.00 per person. School groups are free.

To the John Brown Wax Museum: Adults $2.50, seniors $2.00, students in junior high or high school $1.50 and in elementary school $.75. Special school rates available. Call (304)535-6342.

**Hours**: Park facilities: open daily year-round 8:00 A.M. to 5:00 P.M., and to 6:00 P.M. from Memorial Day to Labor Day. Closed Christmas Day. For information on walking tours call (304)535-6029. Tours can be arranged the rest of the year by reservation only (304)535-6298.

John Brown Wax Museum is open daily mid-March to December 9:00 A.M. to 5:00 P.M. Open weekends February and March 10:00 A.M. to 5:00 P.M.

**Directions**: The park is located approximately 20 miles southwest of Frederick, MD, via US 340. Signs along US 340 direct visitors to the Visitor Center.

# Martinsburg

Planned and laid out by General Adam Stephen, and named for a nephew of Lord Fairfax, Martinsburg was chartered on October 17, 1778. It prospered as an industrial center until the Civil War when, used as Stonewall Jackson's headquarters, it suffered from frequent change of hands.

## Blue Ridge Outlet Center

Although Martinsburg can boast its share of historic buildings, the city's single biggest tourist draw is the Blue Ridge Outlet Center, a converted four-story brick woolen mill built in the 1880s that houses over 60 discount retailers. Over a million shoppers a year from every state in the U.S. and most provinces of

Canada scour the shops for discount bargains. Savings of up to 70 percent on name brands in clothing, kitchen ware, jewelry, glass, books, brasswork and toys attract bargain hunters all year long. There are several pleasant restaurants within the huge building complex, so you don't have to break the momentum of your shopping spree to leave the complex for lunch.

Tip: Weekend traffic is very heavy. Come early to find nearby parking.

Hours: Monday, Tuesday, Wednesday 10:00 A.M.–6:00 P.M.; Thursday, Friday, Saturday 10:00 A.M.–9:00 P.M.; Sunday 11:00 A.M.–6:00 P.M. Closed Easter Sunday, Thanksgiving Day and Christmas Day.

## Boarman House Art Center

After your shopping frenzy, and your money is gone, take advantage of a free cultural experience by seeing some of the historic properties of the city. An excellent walking tour map (limited supply) and brochures on local sites of interest are available at the Chamber of Commerce in the Boarman House Art Center. Noteworthy as one of the oldest brick buildings in Martinsburg (circa 1802), it serves as a civic arts center, sponsoring judged exhibits all year-long. With a special focus on promoting West Virginia artists, the gallery's shows range from traditional to contemporary art, representing various media—painting, pottery, quilting, sculpture, fiber arts and photography. The shop on the first level sells the work of more than 100 artisans, including lovely jewelry, carvings, glass and ceramics that make unusual gifts.

Hours: Chamber of Commerce: Monday through Friday 8:00 A.M. to 5:00 P.M. and the information lobby is open Saturday 10:00 A.M. to 5:00 P.M. Call (304)267-4841.

Boarman House Art Center shop and gallery open Tuesday through Saturday 10:00 A.M. to 5:00 P.M. Closed Sunday and Monday. Call (304)263-0224.

From the Boarman House follow the map along King, Queen and Martin streets. The courthouse at 100 King Street held the famous Civil War spy, Belle Boyd, after her arrest. At the very least, be sure to see the General Adam Stephen House and the Triple Brick Museum.

## General Adam Stephen House and Triple Brick Museum

General Adam Stephen, a Scottish-born doctor, completed his two-story native limestone home in 1789 after a distinguished career as a surgeon and soldier in the American Revolution. One of the first settlers in the area and a friend of George Washington,

General Adam Stephen built his house on a hill in Martinsburg, the town he laid out nearly 200 years ago.

he is credited as being the founder and planner of the town of Martinsburg. The wooden floors are original. The furnishings reflect the period of 1750–1830 and have been acquired from various sources. Of particular note are the 1785 pianoforte, Chippendale mirror and "necessaries" in each bedroom. Adams Stephen's Day is held on the property grounds in early June and is an all-day open house featuring arts and crafts, demonstrations, music and dancing.

Next door, the **Triple Brick Museum** (1874–76), so named because it was used as three apartment units, houses an eclectic collection of local history memorabilia: carved Indians, button and spoon collections, quilts, period clothing and an unusual wooden steam bath. Children are encouraged to touch and experiment with some exhibits like the musical instruments. The building is linked historically with the railroad out back as food was prepared here (before the days of dining cars) for passengers going through.

**Hours**: May through October on Saturday and Sunday from 2:00–5:00 P.M. To arrange a special tour at other times call (304)267-4434.

**Directions**: 309–313 East John St.

**Boydville,** a very historic building not within walking distance, is worth a drive by. The stately manor, run by the present owners as an inn, is not open for public tours. But for its historic value and grandeur, it's worth a peek as you drive past. Dating from 1812, the stone mansion survived the Civil War intact. Henry Clay and Stonewall Jackson were guests here, and one can well imagine them sitting on the gracious veranda enjoying a smoke and discussing politics and war strategy. Fortunately Boydville escaped being burned during the war, and its elegance and grace remind us of how much of our heritage was lost during those tragic days. Much of the interior wallpaper and woodwork is original, and it is beautifully furnished. Old boxwood and stately oaks grace the surrounding ten acres. The owner claims to have found coins from colonial times on the grounds.

**Directions**: 601 S. Queen St. For information on staying at the inn call (304)263-1448.

# Paw Paw
## *Paw Paw Tunnel*

One of the great engineering feats of constructing this part of the C&O Canal and the largest man-made structure on the canal, Paw Paw Tunnel runs through Sorrell Ridge and extends over 3,000 feet in length and 25 feet in height. German and Irish workers hand picked and shoveled through rocks and the thickets of papaw trees (thus the name) from 1836 to 1850 to complete this passageway. It does seem a pity their tedious labor did not accomplish George Washington's dream of linking the Potomac and Ohio rivers. Long ago drained of water, the tunnel is now open to hikers and bikers only. Be warned you may find bats inside. Don't disturb them.

**Tip**: Bring a flashlight. In winter a gate is put up at the entrance, but there is room to pass through.

**Directions**: From Berkeley Springs take Rt. 9 west to intersection of Rt. 29, bear right onto 29 to Paw Paw. After crossing bridge, Maryland Rt. 51 takes you ¼ mile to parking area for the tunnel.

# Romney
## *The Potomac Eagle*

If you're a laid-back bird watcher, keen to spot an American bald eagle in its natural habitat but reluctant to climb mountains or forge streams, consider keeping warm, sitting back in comfort and letting the train carry you through the "Trough" of the Potomac River Valley, one of West Virginia's nesting areas for this aristocratic predator. As the train chugs slowly along the unspoiled South Branch River, you will appreciate that the only other ways of getting through this narrow passage between the mountains is by canoe or on foot. The "Trough" is inaccessible by car, one reason eagles have taken up residence here after being designated as endangered in 1969. At least two active nests support a small community. Eagles do not build their own nests until they are about five years old, so the immature ones you spot (with mostly mottled, dark feathers) have not set up housekeeping yet. Sightings are not guaranteed, but in recent years eagles have been seen on over 90 percent of the excursions.

The 3½-hour trip from Romney follows the river to Sycamore Bridge near Moorefield before returning. Fall foliage and brilliant autumn sky set a dramatic backdrop for soaring birds. Warning: These rare, winged wonders are protected by law, and fines are severe for anyone caught near nesting areas.

The train moves slowly enough for you to observe other wildlife: hawks, deer, beaver or fish flashing in the river below. Choose from either standard coach accommodations or the luxury Classic Club Car where lunch is served.

**Admission**: May through September: Adults $15.00, children 4 to 12 $10.00, under 3 free; seniors $13.50. October and November: Adults $17.50, children $11.50, seniors $15.75, under 3 free. The Classic Club Car costs $35.00 in all seasons.

**Hours**: Departures late May through November 1, Saturdays 10:00 A.M. and 2:00 P.M., Sundays 12:30 P.M. During October, Sunday rides depart at 10:00 A.M. and 2:00 P.M. Special event trains in September (Civil War reenactments including an attack on the train), October (foliage and eagle watching), December (Santa Specials). Wine and cheese tasting and musical entertainment on other special event trains. Call for exact schedule (800)CALL-WV or (304)822-7464.

**Directions**: Departure is at station on Rt. 28 one mile north of Romney. For more information write: Potomac Eagle, PO Box 657, Romney, WV 26757.

# Shepherdstown

Settled in the early 1730s and incorporated in 1762, Shepherdstown claims to be the oldest town in West Virginia. The earliest European arrivals were Germans who set up business on the main street (now German Street) where today's artisans continue the tradition of hand-crafted excellence passed down from these first carpenters and clockmakers. Originally called Mechlenburg, the town became Shepherdstown after its founder Thomas Shepherd, who laid out the original plans and built an important gristmill that still stands.

During the American Revolution, the town sent more soldiers than any other town its size. Due to its strategic location on the wagon route and on the Potomac River, the town soon became a commercial center. With the completion of the C&O Canal in 1850, the town grew and prospered until the ravages and chaos of the Civil War. Unlike other towns in the area, like Harpers Ferry, Shepherdstown was spared burning, and most of the old homes survived the war intact. The two towns, however, did share the common curse of continual and devastating floods, and after the war neither ever fully regained the prominence of their earlier years.

**Shepherd College,** which continues to expand, has been here since 1871 and provides the stimulus to the town's cultural life. The history and charm of the pretty, tree-lined streets and handsome homes have attracted potters, painters and other artisans as well as an increasing number of tourists. Quaint shops filled with locally made crafts, book stores, historic inns and taverns entice visitors to poke leisurely from window to window.

What is designated as the Historic District on the walking tour map includes the old buildings on German, Princess and Mill streets. Start your visit at the **Visitor Information Center** at 102 N. King Street, open daily 10:00 A.M. to 2:00 P.M. or call (304)876-3325. Pick up the walking tour map (25¢) and various pamphlets about local sites. Depending on your time, you can follow the pamphlet route which starts at the library, or pick and choose from the brochure, but don't miss the following highlights.

**Directions**: From Frederick, MD, take Rt. 340 west past Harpers Ferry to Rt. 230. Take Rt. 230 north to Shepherdstown. Coming from Martinsburg, take Rt. 45 east.

## The Entler Hotel

Plan on doing the walk on a weekend when the museum at the Entler Hotel at the corner of German and Princess streets is open. Opened in 1786 as a hostelry by the Entlers and kept in the family for 126 years, the inn was an immediate success. Built in three stages (the last unit in 1809), the three-story brick structure has Flemish bond detail and a molded brick water table. It operated as a hotel, men's dormitory and a warehouse before being put on the National Register of Historic Places in 1973. In 1978 the state sold it to the town for $1.00. Today the Entler Hotel serves as the headquarters of the Historic Shepherdstown Commission as well as a museum chronicling Shepherdstown's colorful past.

On the first floor notice the lovely fan-shaped glass window dividing the parlor. The beautiful desks from the early 1800s with their secret compartments were crafted by German artisans as were the famous Joseph Craft grandfather clocks. The unusual half-table is so called because it could be split in two to appease covetous heirs.

On your way upstairs, look at the original, ruddy paint on the banister. Concocted from blood and milk during the early "make do" days, the paint cannot be removed by even the most earnest renovation efforts.

Upstairs, the Travelers Room, beautifully hand-stenciled around the doors, displays two rope beds, a foot warmer for long, chilly church services and various other antiques. Also on this level are a replicated Victorian Sitting Room and one of the first horse-drawn US Mail wagons, boldly painted "RFD" (Rural Free Delivery) on the side. Looking at the contents inside, one recalls that these first mailmen were valuable communication links between towns and often carried groceries and messages to isolated farmers. Other rooms display Civil War artifacts, Indian arrowheads and street scene photos of early Shepherdstown.

**Admission**: Free but a donation is encouraged.

**Hours**: Open April through October, Saturday 11:00 A.M. to 5:00 P.M. and Sunday 1:00 to 5:00 P.M.

**Directions**: On the corner of Princess and German streets downtown Shepherdstown. Call (304)876-0910.

**Tip**: Directly across Princess Street is the **Yellow Brick Bank**. In a modified Beaux Arts style, its whimsical, gaily embellished facade stands out from more traditional neighbors, like a bold upstart among aristocrats. Now a restaurant, it's a cheerful spot for lunch.

## The James Rumsey Monument

The James Rumsey Monument looms incongruously over the Potomac River from its perch on a quiet hill a few blocks from downtown. Commemorating the inventor's first public demonstration of his steamboat on December 3, 1787, the tall granite Ionic column supports a replica of the world, sleek and modern in appearance. Perhaps the contemporary style is appropriate since Rumsey was truly a visionary, foreseeing the need for mechanical propulsion to replace sails on river-going vessels and possessing the genius to design it. His contributions such as the water tube steam boiler and water-jet propulsion systems are still applied in today's technology.

The son of a Maryland blacksmith and farmer, Rumsey was born in 1743 and received most of his engineering know-how

In 1787, James Rumsey proved his steamboat could operate on the Potomac River at an amazing three knots per hour.

from his father. After moving to Bath (now Berkeley Springs) to start an inn, Rumsey and his competence for design and construction caught the eye of neighboring landowner George Washington, who later appointed him manager for construction of the new Potowmack Navigation Company to promote navigation on the Potomac and to open up the west through a canal system. After moving his workshop to Shepherdstown, he refined his steam-activated piston system, pumping water from an intake under the boat through the keel to produce jet action. There on the third of December 1787 he invited eight local ladies to join him on his new boat and publicly demonstrated that it could operate against the Potomac's current—at an amazing three knots per hour!

Even today Rumsey's success inspires admirers. An active Rumseian Society is dedicated to sharing the inventor's accomplishments with the public. This group planned and financed the construction of the half-scale replica of the *Rumseian Experiment*, which was successfully launched during Rumsey's bicentennial in 1987. The boat is kept at the Entler Hotel (open April to October). In summer, the society sponsors demonstration outings, appropriately one year at Mount Vernon. If you're "all steamed up" to see a demonstration, call the Rumseian Society for a schedule: (304)876-6907.

**Directions**: Follow Mill Street north until it dead-ends near the river.

## Thomas Shepherd Gristmill

Even though this picturesque mill is privately owned and open to the public only on special occasions, it's worthwhile strolling by to admire the remarkable cast-iron water wheel and fine stone work. Forty feet wide, it is the largest and oldest overshot water wheel in the world. Thomas Shepherd built this impressive structure on his original land grant of 222 acres before 1739, drawing clients who wanted their grain ground into flour from as far away as Maryland and Virginia. It is a tribute to its builder that this mill remains relatively intact while so many others that came much later, like those of the textile period, have long since disintegrated. All gears are intact and with minimal repairs could be put back into operation.

**Directions**: On the corner of Mill and High streets.

## O'Hurley's General Store

Just at the east edge of Shepherdstown near the railroad tracks on Rt. 230 is O'Hurley's General Store (not part of the downtown walking tour). You'll spot it as you round Toll House Turn, the flag flapping for attention and the front porch rockers luring travelers to slow down, stop and sample a bit of the past. Inside, owner Jay Hurley recreates a turn-of-the-century general store with merchandise authentic to that time and clerks attired in period dress. Country music, some of it Irish in keeping with the owner's heritage, provides background for exploring the staggering assortment of items, perhaps for discovering some hidden treasure in a dark corner.

The store is crammed with an overwhelming menagerie of intriguing "time tested" wares from over 100 suppliers: some handicrafts from local talent (candy, rugs, hand-painted porcelain thimbles); some from the handicapped; still others from self-help projects in the Third World. Cast iron pots, wooden toys, tin dishes (no plastic here) are stacked in, under and around rocking horses, baskets, hats, musical instruments, rush chairs, rope hammocks, harness bells, hats, campaign buttons, brass hardware and a collection of homesteading tools most browsers won't recognize: loom bobbins, a lard press, and a corn sheller. It's almost easier to list what's missing.

Compelling as the front rooms are, more captivating still is the **blacksmithing shop** out back. Here a young, gifted artist, Daniel Tokar, fills orders for anything in pewter, iron, copper, brass and silver. He can fashion a delicate spoon or forge canal sluice gates, taking on anything he's asked for, from "needles to ship an-

Jay Hurley and friend, Kate, greet visitors to O'Hurley's General Store and its time-tested treasures. Harriet Wise

chors." Effortlessly shaping an exquisite decorative leaf, he explains that "wrought iron" is a misnomer for the furniture and items turned out today. The tedious labor-intensive process of manufacturing wrought iron was last used by the Swedes in the 1960s. Now all "wrought iron" items are really made from mild steel. Today, real wrought iron is salvaged, saved and reworked for historic preservations. Even without customers, the store is cramped and the shop may be crackling with sparks, so large crowds coming to see a blacksmith demonstration cannot be accommodated easily.

Upstairs above the store, O'Hurley sleeps at night in the same room where he was born over a half century ago when the building was a gas station owned by his father. In addition to his shopkeeping, Jay is famed locally as the builder of a half-scale replica of the first steamboat, the *Rumseian Experiment* launched for the first time on the nearby Potomac River. The model is on display at the Entler Hotel downtown.

When you finally tear yourself away from these tempting treasures and prepare to leave the parking lot, notice the mail box nailed to the post outside—a clever transformation of an old pressure tank into a mail box.

**Tip**: This is a great place to find stocking stuffers for Christmas and unusual gifts for all occasions, if you can bear to part with them.

**Hours**: Tuesday through Saturday, 10:00 A.M. to 7:00 P.M., Sunday 12:00 to 6:00 P.M. Closed most Mondays.

**Directions**: Drive to 205 E. Washington St. (on Rt. 230), Shepherdstown, WV 25443, (304)876-6907.

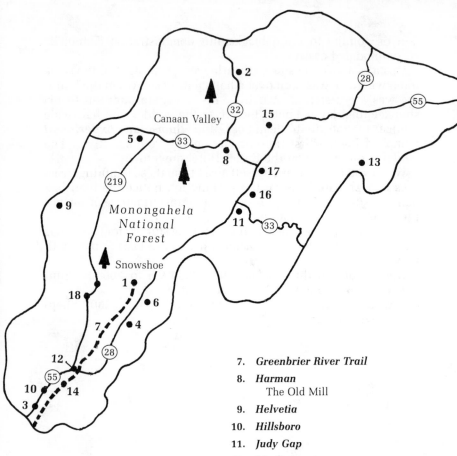

Canaan Valley

Monongahela
National
Forest

Snowshoe

## POTOMAC HIGHLANDS

1. *Cass*
   Scenic Railroad

2. *Davis*
   Blackwater Falls State Park
   Canaan Valley State Park

3. *Droop*
   Droop Mountain State Park
   Beartown State Park

4. *Dunmore*
   Seneca State Forest

5. *Elkins*
   Halliehurst

6. *Greenbank*
   National Radio Astronomy
   Observatory

7. *Greenbrier River Trail*

8. *Harman*
   The Old Mill

9. *Helvetia*

10. *Hillsboro*

11. *Judy Gap*

12. *Marlinton*
    Pocahontas County Historical
    Museum
    Watoga State Park

13. *Mathias*
    Lost River State Park

14. *Mill Point*
    Cranberry Glades Botanical Area

15. *Red Creek*
    Dolly Sods Wilderness Area

16. *Riverton*
    Seneca Caverns

17. *Seneca Rocks*
    Harpers General Store
    Smoke Hole Caverns

18. *Slatyfork*
    Sharps's Country Store

# Potomac Highlands

When you visit the Potomac Highlands it's not for art museums, shopping malls or symphony concerts. This masterpiece of nature is best appreciated by lovers of the great outdoors: those who prefer a warbler's trill to a Bach cantata, a folk fiddle to a Stradivarius.

Dividing eastern West Virginia into breathtaking valleys and ridges, the Appalachians rise to over 4,000 feet, then roll to hidden hollows, roaring rivers and waterfalls, and caverns of secret splendor. Over a million acres of park and forest—including the gigantean Monongehela National Forest that comprises much of the region—nurture large populations of deer, songbirds and other wildlife. Three unspoiled, protected wilderness areas support exotic fauna and flora rarely found elsewhere in this country. This is also the land of the bear and eagle, the snow hare and lady-slipper.

In summer, the Potomac's North Fork, the Greenbrier and Shaver's Fork rivers carry canoeists, rafters and tubers through gorge and gully, over rapids and around rocks, past hemlocks, hamlets and huge sandstone cliffs. In spring, these same waters are broken by casting fishermen who know trout stocking has begun. In fall, hunters carry home quail, turkey and venison from the vast woods. The magic of winter covers the mountains with enough snow to support several major ski resorts. Hundreds of miles of hiking trails double as cross-country ski routes, shared by fox, doe and owls.

History is here if you look for it (Cass Railroad and Pearl S. Buck Museum), a touch of the international (Helvetia) and food for thought (Davis and Elkins College). But it's that great pull of mountain air, clear running streams and verdant forest that brings you back again and again. Pack a lunch, grab your camera, hiking shoes and sense of adventure. Unless you plan to ski, you won't need much money. A day trip to Potomac Highlands reconfirms the old truism that the best things in life are free.

### A Word About Ramps

You shouldn't go cold into the Potomac Highlands—just following your nose—without being warned about the most popular item on the spring menu most anywhere in the region: ramps.

In early March temporarily deranged, driven devotees, grab sacks and diggers, abandon family and friends, and head for the hills to satisfy an annual craving for the first greens of the season. Scurrying up inclines, crawling on hands and knees on forest floor, ready to pounce on the first glimpse of a certain wild leek, these hunters are frenzied gatherers. The object of their lust is an innocuous looking member of the lily family: ramps. But, oh, can looks deceive!

Credited by some as tasting like sweet green onions and by others as something unique and indescribable, ramps leave the consumer with a breath (and, depending on how they are eaten, a body) smelling like something indescribable too. In fact those who do not share a passion for ramps say indulgers just plain "stink." Your only defense, they say, is to eat ramps too. Indeed, some people in movie theaters, churches, classrooms and other public close quarters have been driven to flee a roomful of ramp diners—so overpowering is the aftereffect. Yet, no name-calling or degree of social rejection deters a dedicated ramp lover. Indeed, there are few Highland counties that do not host a ramp festival, the most publicized being in Richwood. The self-proclaimed Ramp Capital of the World, Richwood has celebrated this controversial delicacy since 1937. Today townspeople gather to clean thousands of pounds of ramps for an annual community feast, usually in April. At the Elkins contest, a prize is given for the "most potent."

The cook-offs, usually supervised by the men of the community, are serious competitions, challenging the gastronomic imagination, and tolerance, of leek lovers. Ramps are pickled, fried, boiled, stuffed, stewed and eaten raw, turned into soups, souffles, salads, and sucked, chewed and chomped from hors d'oeuvres to the nut course. If you like garlic and onions, have an adventurous palate, or just want to defend yourself from fellow fanatics, don't miss one of these festivals honoring this succulent specialty. Colorful and odoriferous to say the very least, they offer a rare chance to experience, literally, the full flavor of Potomac Highlands.

For more information on visiting Potomac Highlands contact: Potomac Highlands Travel Council, PO Box 2758 (1404 Taylor Ave.), Elkins, WV 26241-2758, phone (304)636-8400 or 1(800)347-1453.

Randolph County Convention and Visitor Bureau, 200 Executive Plaza, Elkins, WV 26241, phone (304)636-2717 or 1(800)422-3304.

Tucker County Convention and Visitor Bureau, PO Box 565, Davis, WV 26260, phone (304)259-5315 or 1(800)782-2775.

Pendleton County Visitors Committee, Franklin, WV, 26807, phone (304)358-7573/7893.

Pocahontas County Tourist Committee, PO Box 275, Marlinton, WV 25954, phone (304)799-4636 or 1(800)336-7009.

# Cass

## *Cass Scenic Railroad State Park*

Just a few minutes from Snowshoe ski resort and one of the biggest crowd-drawing attractions in the state, the famous Cass Scenic Railroad is a must stop for train buffs of any age. In the first decade of this century, West Virginia had more miles of logging railroad line than any other state in the country, and Cass was a bustling, booming lumber town. All that remains today from that era are the 11 miles of restored tracks, a few restored buildings and the ruins that recall the town's heyday.

The 90-plus-ton locomotives, designed to carry enormous tonnage over and up steep mountain grades no longer haul logs. Instead, they transport passengers to another era at a leisurely pace of about 5 miles an hour—past remains of the saw mill, past a graveyard of old engines, past the water tower—still used to fill the engines' tanks—through forest growth, to two switchbacks, and up the mountain to fields of wildflowers and song birds—whistle screeching, smoke belching, clickety clacking and chug, chug chugging—a scene straight from the pages of *The Little Engine That Could.*

The open cars painted a cheerful green and red are converted from those used in logging service and powered by some of the last Shay and Heisler engines in the world. The trip is slow and noisy, but each car has adjustable speakers for the guide's narrative. Also, be aware of the wind direction. Soot and smoke from the engine can blow into faces and irritate eyes, so choose your seat carefully and warn children to turn away from the engine if smoke blows towards them. Brakemen in each car answer questions and demonstrate braking procedure.

Depending on your time and interest, you can choose from several Cass excursions. The shortest trip, 1½ hours, is to **Whittaker Station** about 4½ miles and back. A project is underway at Whittaker to preserve and display historic logging equipment (such as a diesel log loader, camp and log cars, and a steam skidder), and reconstruct a scene reminiscent of logging camps in the 1940s. The longest trip, 4½ hours and 22 miles round trip, is to **Bald Knob,** the second highest point in the state at over 4,800 feet. On a clear day you can see into Virginia from the observation deck and spot soaring eagles.

There are special rides to view the fall foliage during October and an extra-special Halloween trip children will not forget. On

The Cass Scenic Railroad carries passengers on a breathtaking trip up to Bald Knob, one of West Virginia's highest summits.

ELMER E. BURRUSS, JR.

selected summer Saturday evenings, dinner rides are scheduled featuring a barbecue and live music.

If you don't have time or are not inclined to ride the rails, you can experience the trip vicariously by watching the locomotive chug out of the station and by listening to the steam whistle blow. And you can visit the restored buildings near the station that offer displays on life in Cass present and past: the Cass Country Store, crammed with railroad memorabilia; the Wildlife Museum and its collection of marvelous stuffed birds and animals; the Historical Museum and the Cass Showcase, a miniature replication of the town in the 1900s with model trains demonstrating how timber was transported and processed.

**Restrictions**: No pets allowed on the trains.

**Admission**: To Whittaker Station, adults $9.00, children $5.00. To Bald Knob, adults $12.00, children $6.00. Children under 6 ride free.

**Hours**: To Whittaker Station: From Memorial Day through Labor Day, trains leave at 11:00 A.M., 1:00 and 3:00 P.M. daily, and during September and October, they run Thursday through Sunday only. The first two weeks in October trains may run every day. Call to check. To Bald Knob, the train leaves at NOON every day except Monday, Memorial Day through Labor Day, and

Thursday through Sunday in September and October. For information and reservations call 1(800)CALL-WVA or (304)456-4300.

**Directions**: Located about seven miles south of Greenbank National Radio Astronomy, on New Rt. 66, accessible from Highway 219 from the west and Highway 92/28 from the east.

# Davis
## Blackwater Falls State Park

Long before you see Blackwater Falls you hear its primordial echo. Just follow your ears—and other visitors. A spectacular backdrop for taking photos and easily accessible from a boardwalk, the falls draw tourists all year long. After making its dramatic 63-foot plunge, the Blackwater River tumbles and roars through a lovely wooded 8-mile gorge lined with rhododendron and hemlock. It is in fact the acids from downed, decaying hemlocks and red spruce needles that give the "black" appearance to the waters.

The park's second big attraction is the unusually heavy snowfall received in this region that covers the forest trails, providing marvelous cross-country skiing.

Summer brings other outdoor opportunities: tennis, hiking, fishing, golf, horseback riding and boating at minimal or no cost. Park sponsored programs include guided hikes, slide shows and craft workshops. More than a dozen trails wind through spruce, maple, beech and hemlock groves over rocky outcroppings, to smaller falls. Deer, birds and other wildlife abound. One trail connects with the Monongahela National Forest Trail system; another with Canaan Valley less than ten miles away. The easiest and most popular is the paved Gentle Trail, from the parking area near the trading post to a wheelchair-accessible observation deck. Special weekend programs like the Septemberfest Senior Fling, the astronomy weekend for beginning and advanced star gazers, and family walks and cookouts make this an attractive getaway for all ages.

Accommodating visitors on a year-round basis, a resort lodge and 25 deluxe cabins blend into their wooded settings. Guests dining at the lodge enjoy the sweeping view of the canyon below.

**Tip**: You should make lodge and cabin reservations a year in advance for peak seasons.

**Restrictions**: No pets are allowed in cabins or lodge rooms.

**Hours**: Office hours are 8:00 A.M. to 4:00 P.M. every day of the week year-round. Cabins and lodge open year-round. Sixty-five camping sites are available from the last Saturday in April through October 31. Park is open 6:00 A.M. to dark. Call

1(800)CALL-WVA or (304)259-5216 or write Blackwater Falls State Park, Drawer 490, Davis, WV 26260.

**Directions**: Coming from the south from Elkins take US 33 to Harman, then Rt. 32 north to the park. From the north, take Rt. 219 to Thomas, then Rt. 32 south to the park.

## Canaan Valley State Park

In the 1750s, one of the first Europeans to spot this gorgeous valley supposedly cried "Behold, the Land of Canaan." The name stuck. The unspoiled glory of its natural beauty—mountains, evergreen forests, rushing streams, meadows full of deer and songbirds, marshes and bogs rich in unusual plant life—is reason enough to justify comparison with the Promised Land. Today, if not a Biblical paradise, it truly is a Mecca for sports enthusiasts and naturalists year-round.

Sitting at 3,200 feet above sea level, the valley nestles in a bowl surrounded by Allegheny peaks as high as 4,200 feet that provide the altitude and incline for an extended snow season, sometimes into April, for both down-hill and cross-country skiing. To take advantage of an average annual snowfall of about 150 inches, a resort ski facility has been developed with chairlifts, snow-making equipment and ski rental and instruction, restaurants, a 250-room lodge and deluxe cabins: it is a major winter attraction, a favorite of out-of-state skiers as well as locals. In other seasons, 34 campsites, an 18-hole golf course, tennis courts, swimming pool and fishing/hiking opportunities—all tempt the day-tripper to consider an extended visit to this popular resort.

With over 6,700 acres of diverse natural beauty the area holds the second largest inland wetlands in the United States, an environment that attracts deer, black bear, Canada geese, fox, beaver, wild turkey and waterfowl. You may be lucky enough to spot a coyote intercepting a groundhog running for its burrow. These predators are commonly mistaken for wolves but have distinguishing features: a tan to grey coat, red legs and a long bushy tail tipped with black. The deer are so abundant and tame they are easily approached, but rangers ask you not to feed them or any other animal in the park. Bordering Canaan on the east is one of the great wild, undeveloped areas in the Mid-Atlantic, the **Dolly Sods Wilderness** (see section).

Eighteen miles of hiking trails criss-cross the park: the most ambitious is the Blackwater/Canaan Trail (marked with blue diamonds). About 8 miles one way, it connects Blackwater Falls and Canaan Valley State Parks, a dramatic contrast of high falls and valley scenery. A shorter walk is the boardwalk trail, which you can pick up at park headquarters. It leads from the small nature center to the lodge, past a beaver pond, over marsh and meadow.

Year-round the park sponsors many naturalist programs: craft lessons, nature lectures, walks and slide shows, hayrides, square dancing, star gazing, bird/butterfly watches, a ski weekend just for seniors, campfires and fishing expeditions. Bird watching here and at Dolly Sods is always rewarding and sometimes includes sightings of bald or golden eagles. Even in winter, a Christmas bird count can include over 38 species.

Canaan, with its resort facilities, is the only state park that is run by a private firm on a concession basis. Recreational opportunities are so diverse, whether on the ski slope, golf course or on a solitary wildflower trail, people want to return again and again to this pride of the Potomac Highlands.

**Tip**: To gain a spectacular view almost any time of year, take the chair lift up the mountain.

**Park Hours**: 6:00 A.M. to 10:00 P.M. year-round. Park office hours are Monday through Friday 8:00 A.M. to 4:00 P.M. To make overnight reservations, call 1(800)CALL-WVA or (304)866-4121 or write Canaan Valley State Park, Rt. 1, Box 39, Davis, WV 26260.

**Directions**: From Elkins take Rt. 33 east to Harman. Follow signs and bear onto Rt. 32 north. The park entrance is right on Rt. 32 about ten miles beyond Harman. The park office and a small nature center share a building. Stop here for brochures or continue on to lodge for more information.

# Droop

## *Droop Mountain Battlefield State Park*

Considered the oldest state park in West Virginia, Droop Mountain Battlefield State Park is a good picnic spot and can be easily combined in a day-trip with nearby Beartown. The ambitious early-riser could even include the Pearl Buck Birthplace, Cranberry Glades Botanical Area and/or Watoga Park (see entries), particularly if an overnight is planned in Watoga. The four parks are very different from each other and merit more than a quick visit.

Of particular interest to history buffs, this park honors the largest Civil War battle fought in West Virginia and the last important one, since, as a result of it, Confederate forces were driven out of the state for good. Fought on November 6, 1863, by nearly 7,000 men, the bloody battle claimed over 400 dead, some of whom may still be buried on park grounds.

Start at the small museum and the exhibits of bayonets, shells, revolvers and other artifacts, many of which were found on the grounds, including a gold and brass wedding ring discovered in 1986 that belonged to a fleeing Confederate soldier. For an authentic coverage of the battle, read the displayed *The New York Times* account dated November 21, 1863. If the ranger is there when you visit, he will explain the cannon outside and the adjacent graveyard. Ask him to tell the heart-breaking true story of two brothers who fought on opposite sides of this battle.

Criss-crossing the 287-acre park, 3½ miles of hiking trails, varying from very steep to nearly level, lead to war trenches, mountain springs, scenic overlooks, caves and a ravine that Union soldiers climbed to attack Confederates waiting above. Horse Heaven Trail traverses small cliffs to a rock from which dead horses were thrown after the battle.

Before leaving, drive or walk to the lookout tower and take in a panorama of Hillsboro, Monongahela National Forest, Watoga and Calvin Price parks. Picnic and play areas offer a good chance to rest and lunch before driving to other nearby attractions.

**Restrictions**: No camping.

**Hours**: 6:00 A.M. to 10:00 P.M. all year-round.

**Directions**: On Rt. 219, 15 miles south of Marlinton and 27 miles north of Lewisburg. For more information call the superintendent at (304)653-4254 or write Droop Mountain State Park, HC 64, Box 189, Hillsboro, WV 24946.

## Beartown State Park

Imagine a fairyland forest of giant cakes iced with green frosting. Now imagine how they might look if someone nibbled away at the bottom layer. Slowly, ever so slowly, the cake would tip, topple and eventually tumble over on itself, the icing flowing down the sides. This is similar to what is happening to the extraordinary sandstone formations that comprise Beartown State Park. Sitting precariously at the top of Droop Mountain (whose "drooping" profile resembles a melting lump), massive boulders, covered by ferns, mosses and lichen create a Disney World of crevices, cliffs, ravines, gullies and holes. In fact, the park is so named because caves here look like the perfect lair for any sensible bear. Growing from the sides, tops and among the rocks in delicate lacy patterns, hemlocks add their touch of magic—feathery-fine gossamer candles. One can well imagine the spell woven here at night under a full moon might be what Shakespeare had in mind when writing *A Midsummer-Night's Dream*—an enchanted venue for frolicking elves, sprites and wood nymphs.

The natural explanation for this bizarre and marvelous scene is less romantic but just as interesting. Ancient oceans, receding and returning over eons, laid down sandy surfaces, layer upon layer upon layer, their currents shaping, swirling, sculpturing each unique stratum. When the oceans withdrew for good, over 350 million years ago, the "cakes" remained, decorated with embedded shell fossils as proof of their origins. Over time, the

*A boardwalk leads through Beartown's fascinating forest of rock formations, caves, ferns and hemlocks.*                    LARRY BELCHER

forests claimed them, putting their verdant touch of vegetation on the scene. And what an awesome scene it is.

A ½-mile boardwalk takes you through part of the 107-acre wonderland. The ecology is extremely fragile and you are warned not to leave the walkway. Although these jolly green giants are breaking apart and away from each other at a rate of ½ inch every 200 years, you may see evidence of recent crumpling and fresh breaks, some caused by vandalism. Especially devastated by rock scramblers are the multi-colored lichen that bejewel their hosts like Tiffany trinkets. These symbionts of algae and fungae grow very slowly and provide the infant environment for other botanical beauties: the mosses, and later, small hemlocks. Like the bits in a chocolate-chip cake, irregular pits sprinkle the cliff surfaces, ranging in size from marbles to men. Ice sometimes remains in these holes until late summer.

If you don't believe that lightning can strike twice, look for the hemlock that defied this truism and is still alive. Another extraordinary survivor is the bi-truncated chestnut/oak, growing together like Siamese twins. At the extremis of the boardwalk, you will pass under a rocky outcropping with a tenuous cornerstone, further testimony to the ephemeral nature of these transit tortes.

**Tip**: The gate to the parking area is closed during the winter (November to March), but even when the gate is closed, you are welcome to walk in. When it's snowing you can see these cakes frosted vanilla. The superintendent will open the gate upon request. Call (304)653-4254.

**Restrictions**: No camping. Due to the delicate ecology, food and beverages are discouraged on the boardwalk.

**Hours**: 8:00 A.M. to dusk, April 1 through October 31.

**Directions**: On Rt. 219 about seven miles south of Hillsboro or 26 miles north of Lewisburg. For further information write Beartown State Park, HC-64, Box 189, Hillsboro, WV 24946.

# Dunmore

## Seneca State Forest

When you pull into headquarters here to register, you may very well find a staff member tending an abandoned infant fawn or an injured bird brought in by a camper. Named after the Indian tribe that once roamed these woods, Seneca Forest, the oldest state forest in West Virginia, contains nearly 12,000 acres of woodlands, much of which is laced by 23 miles of trails and the Greenbrier River. **Seneca Lake,** the focal point of the park, is a delightful, pristine spot, ringed with graceful conifers, rhododendrons and silent fishermen. The latter's quest is trout, but the visitor soon understands that it doesn't matter much if a fish is hooked or not: solitude, songbirds, a soft summer breeze and a glimpse of a browsing doe are reasons enough to be there. Farther into the park, fishermen cast into the river for bass, and canoeists, when waters run high in season, recreate an ancient scenario.

Of the seven rental cabins available, two are located beside the river and five around the lake. Use of a rowboat is included in the price. The most private, cabin number 4, is tucked into its own little cove with dock. All cabins feature stone fireplaces, fully-equipped kitchens with fridge and woodburning stove, gas lights, bed linens and towels. No running water, but hand pumps are conveniently located as are playground and picnic facilities. All cabin renters have free swimming privileges at nearby Watoga State Park. The more adventurous may choose to pitch a tent in the campground area; ten sites available on a first-come basis have access to toilet facilities, fireplaces and water. You don't have to spend the night to enjoy a family outing of rowing, hiking or picnicking in this pastoral, peaceful park.

**Restrictions**: No swimming in the lake; no pets allowed in cabins or cabin area.

**Admission**: Park is free. Weekly cabin rentals range from about $180.00 for a three-person to under $350.00 for an eight-person cabin; camping, $6.00 per site per night. Cabins are also available on a weekend or nightly basis. The season extends from the last week in April to the first week in December. For complete price list and reservations call 1(800)CALL-WVA or (304)799-6213, or write Seneca State Forest, Rt. 1, Box 140, Dunmore, WV 24934.

**Hours**: The park and its access to the lake is open from about 6:00 A.M. to 10:00 P.M. year-round; office hours are 8:30 A.M. to 4:30 P.M. weekdays and 10:00 A.M. to 2:00 P.M. on weekends in season. During winter, the office is closed on weekends.

**Directions**: Take Rt. 28 south from Dunmore for about four miles to forest entrance. From Marlinton, take Rt. 39 east to Rt. 28. Go north about 11 miles.

# Elkins

## Halliehurst

Due to the high price of riverside property along the Ohio, Wheeling millionaires built their Victorian mansions on long, narrow plots. Exteriors were misleadingly modest, fitting in with the utilitarian simplicity of nearby factories. In contrast, Halliehurst is a sprawling, magnificent estate on 220 acres of West Virginia countryside, a bold statement of wealth and power built with a coal and timber fortune. Its size (23,000 square feet) and bearing proclaimed the extent of the owner's holdings and position. Thanks to a brilliant restoration it is one of the grandest Victorian

Halliehurst Hall
Davis and Elkins College

Elkins, West Virginia

residences in the state—reportedly the largest shingled structure—and the pride of **Davis & Elkins College**.

Born in Ohio in 1841, lawyer-entrepreneur-politician Stephen Benton Elkins made his early money from land and mining investments in New Mexico. A Republican activist, he served as Secretary of War under President Harrison and later, after establishing himself in West Virginia, as a U.S. senator from that state from 1890 until his death in 1911. His personal wealth and political connections soared after forming a business partnership with Senator Henry G. Davis, whose daughter Hallie he married in 1875. Using their influence to bring the first railroad to the Potomac Highlands, the two men consequently acquired vast fortunes through coal and timber ventures. In 1889, Elkins chose the site for Halliehurst (named after his wife) close to a planned railroad terminus—near the booming town named after him.

New York architect Charles T. Mott designed the family summer house as a three-story model of a castle on the Rhine, with steep pitched slate roofs, wooden shingled siding, turrets, towers and enormous stone fireplaces. Remarkably modern for its time, the house boasted many bedrooms, six bathrooms and built-in closets. The cost of construction was around $300,000. Rambling porches added later softened the lines and added a flavor of gracious informality. In these kingly rooms some of the most powerful men of the era, including President Harrison, Grover

Cleveland and Andrew Carnegie, attended lavish parties and plotted political strategies that shaped history.

Perhaps the most enduring of Elkins's accomplishments was the founding, with his father-in-law and the Presbyterian Church, of Davis & Elkins College in 1904. Under the brilliant presidency of Dr. Dorothy MacConkey, this four-year, private, liberal arts college continues to expand and today has an enrollment of over 900 students. When Halliehurst was deeded by Hallie to the college in 1926, the estate became the nucleus of the campus. As the college grew over the following decades, the mansion served (and suffered) as the president's home, a dormitory, dining hall, offices and classrooms. Fortunately for all lovers of beautiful buildings, a massive fundraising effort in the 1980s lead to the extraordinary restoration we see today. It has been a National Historic Landmark since 1989.

In the interior, handsome wooden mantels and detailed trim testify to the glory of West Virginia wood—oak, bird's eye maple, cherry and slippery elm. Of particular interest downstairs are the enormous mantel frieze of dancing girls in the grand entrance hall, the banister spindles carved in harvest symbols, the baronial mantel in the library decorated with signs of the zodiac, an organ on which the West Virginia state anthem was composed and the Pullman Room, designed with arched ceiling to imitate a railroad coach. The window glass in the stairway landing is Tiffany.

Second-floor rooms include the gorgeous family parlor and a "swooning" room for ladies too tightly corseted. Although most rooms now function as college offices, they are exquisitely decorated. Antique furniture complements period reproductions of drapes, wallpaper and accessories, giving a warmth and cohesiveness to the overwhelming grandeur of the house.

Typical of Victorian architecture at this income level, the third floor is largely taken up by a grand ballroom—enjoyed by the four Elkins boys as a gym. It's on this level that the **H.M. Darby Collection** found a home after nearly 50 years of storage.

This extraordinary conglomeration of artifacts, weapons, pottery, bones, tools and "what-is-its?" is alone worth a trip to Halliehurst. It is the life's collecting of eccentric H.M. Darby, an Elkins builder, who spent many years scouring the country, haggling with dealers and innocents alike, for the exotic, the rare, the bizarre. Deeded to the college in 1942, the collection is so large and eclectic that only representative pieces can be exhibited at one time. Items are still being unwrapped, identified and tagged by dedicated volunteer curators, but some curiosities displayed now are a large fossilized mollusk related to the octopus that is at least 65 million years old, an Indian artifact used for curing madness, a narwhal whale tusk six feet long, baskets of all kinds, ceremonial pots, delicate glass, pre-Columbian spear points and miniature bellows once used to powder wigs. Disparate and fascinating, these marvelous one-of-a-kinds represent man's creativity from the Stone Age to the present.

Two outbuildings of interest remain from the original estate: the gate house and the ice house. The latter, now a coffee house and the social hub of college life, can be visited without reservations. You will pass the quaint gate house as you drive through the entrance on the park side of campus. The other Victorian mansion on the college grounds is **Graceland,** which belonged to Senator Davis. Also named to the National Register, it will probably be open to the public after extensive renovation is complete.

**Tip**: Ask about the rumored ghost and allow time to browse leisurely in the Darby Collection.

**Admission**: Exceptionally good tours of Halliehurst are conducted by volunteers on a pre-arranged basis and last about an hour, depending on the size and interest of the group. School groups are welcomed. No fixed admission is charged, but donations are very much appreciated—and deserved—as they are used for the restoration effort. Call the Office of the President (304)636-1900, ext. 243, Monday through Friday 8:30 A.M. to 4:30 P.M., or write Halliehurst, Davis & Elkins College, 100 Campus Circle, Elkins, WV 26241. The office is closed for two weeks during the Christmas-New Year's Holiday. Weekend tours can be arranged.

**Directions**: Halliehurst sits on the campus of Davis & Elkins College across from the Elkins community park. The entrance closest to the mansion is from Sycamore Street. Follow the one-way signs to the Office of the President.

# Greenbank
## National Radio Astronomy Observatory

How big is space? When and how were galaxies created? And what else is out there? The answers to such questions that have puzzled Man since he first looked heavenward are being discovered at the National Radio Astronomy Observatory (NRAO) in Green Bank. Depending on your interest in science and in the secrets of space, a visit here is one of the most fascinating exposures to what is happening on the frontier of extra-terrestrial research in the world. It certainly is one of the best bargains in the state: free admission.

The observatory is one of the world's major sites for receiving and analyzing radio waves to probe the mysteries of the universe. Every year hundreds of scientists from all over the globe come

The National Radio Astronomy Observatory, the state-of-the-art center for space exploration through the study of radio waves.

NRAO, OPERATED BY ASSD. UNIVS., INC..
UNDER CONTRACT WITH NSF

to study pulsars, black holes, galaxies, exploding stars and other objects billions of light years away. Six telescopes are currently in use, all with specialized functions. One measuring 140 feet is the world's largest equatorially mounted telescope, which means it rotates in all directions, giving it the versatility to measure both short and long radio lengths.

The *piece de resistance*, however, is the **state-of-the-art telescope** under construction, scheduled to begin operations 1995 at a cost of about $75 million. Standing higher than the Statue of Liberty, the giant will be the world's largest fully steerable radio scope with a reflecting surface larger than two football fields. Its enormous receiving capacity will assure Green Bank's position as the premier site for radio astronomy in the 21st century.

The drive to Green Bank through the Tygart Valley is beautiful, paralleling majestic Cheat Mountain Ridge. The observatory nestles on 2,600 acres of Deer Creek Valley—its white telescopes growing like monster mushrooms out of the flowered fields. Surrounding mountains act as a natural shield, protecting the area from radio interference. To assure its special status, the observatory mandates what radio waves are allowed to enter the "quiet zone" of 18,000 square miles—the world's only region where public and private radio wave transmissions are restricted.

Tours start in the center where displays demonstrate what radio waves are, how they are received and identified by their heat intensity, and what they can tell us about the objects and chemicals in space. A 12-minute slide show introduced by a staff member gives an excellent overview of the observatory and its operations. You will learn astounding facts about time and distance: the sun's radio waves reach earth in 8 minutes, the nearest star's in 4.3 years. Radio messages from the farthest galaxy take 10 billion years to reach earth: thus, waves received now record the explosion of stars millions of years ago and help document the history of creation. You will learn that pulsars, by virtue of the constancy of their pulses, are used by scientists as the most accurate measure of time. (Earthquakes disturb earth's rotation on its axis and interfere with exact time-telling on the planet.)

Following a question and answer session, a staff member leads the tour on a bus ride around the facility, pointing out specific scopes and explaining their special features. The setting and subject are so mesmerizing, you may be tempted to stay through the next tour as well. Do take time to absorb the photos and displays. Perhaps the most exciting model shows the future possibilities of radio astronomy promised by the radio astron project co-sponsored with the Russians to be launched in 1994. This satellite and the new telescope will penetrate the mysteries of space to its limit, beyond the last star, to the edge of time and the first explosion, to wonders we humans cannot imagine.

NRAO is operated by Associated University, Inc., with assistance of the National Science Foundation.

**Tip**: Bring a picnic lunch and absorb the "other worldness" of the setting, the songbirds and grazing deer. Cold drinks from the Coke machine are the cheapest around!

**Hours**: Tours are given every hour on the hour 9:00 A.M. to 4:00 P.M. every day from mid-June through Labor Day and on weekends only from Memorial Day weekend to mid-June and during the months of September and October. Cameras welcome.

**Directions**: On Rt. 92 about 35 miles northeast of Marlinton and 53 miles southeast of Elkins. Telephone: (304)456-2011 or write NRAO, PO Box 2, Green Bank, WV 24944.

## Greenbrier River Trail

Converted from the Chesapeake and Ohio Railroad bed once used for the timber industry, the 76-mile Greenbrier River Trail traverses some of the most scenic sites in West Virginia. Since the grade is nearly level (about ½ percent) and access is easy from a number of entry points, nature enthusiasts of all ages can find a manageable stretch to walk, jog, hike, bike or cross-country ski. Depending on time and endurance, explorers can spend an hour hiking or a week exploring small towns, fishing streams, tourist attractions, campgrounds, and state forests and parks (Greenbrier, Seneca, Watoga, Droop Mountain Battlefield and Cass). The trail crosses 35 bridges and passes through two tunnels: the 402-foot Droop Mountain Tunnel at mile post 30.9 and Sharpes Tunnel (511 feet) at mile post 65.7. Marlinton (mile post 56) is the largest town on the trail for food supplies, medical aid, overnight accommodations and tourist information. Stop at the Victorian train depot downtown, now restored as an information center, for maps and brochures.

The trail head is mile post 3, 1.3 miles north of US 60 at Caldwell on County Rt. 38 (Stonehouse Rd.). Mile post 80 is at Cass. One of the most beautiful sections of the trail—a favorite of the naturalist at Watoga State Park—is the stretch between Renick (24.5) and Horrock (29.6). Take Rt. 219 to Co. Rt. 11. At the bottom of the hill before crossing the bridge look for a parking lot and trail access. Spring is particularly lovely here when the redbud, trillium grandiflora, dame's rocket and Dutchman's-breeches are in full splendor. Head north and look where the river splits and forms islands for Canada geese, wood duck and other migrating waterfowl. Great horned owls have been spotted nesting along the rocky cliffs here. In spring, bird watchers have recorded 21 different kinds of warblers in two days. Around mile post 27, a swamp area is home to wild turkeys. Other wildlife you might surprise are deer, squirrels, black snakes, turtles and maybe black bear. Good specimens of beech, tulip poplar and river birch grow on the river islands and along the banks.

**Tips**: For biking the trail, north to south is the easier direction. Fat bike tires are recommended. Bring drinking water as stream and spring water are not potable. The gravel trail can be hot in summer, so mornings and evenings are best for hiking. For more information: Superintendent, Watoga State Park, Marlinton, WV 24954. Phone: (304)799-4087.

# Harman
## *The Old Mill*

This three-story, white frame gristmill is postcard-pretty, sitting right on Dry Fork River like a calendar scene. Two water-powered turbines still function, rotating the millstones (1,000 lbs.) that grind grain into flour. Most of the 1877 structure, on the National Register of Historic Places, and its machinery are still in working condition, but you must arrange ahead to see a demonstration. The mill is primarily used as a museum and retail artisan shop. Antique engines, spinning wheels, period artifacts are displayed along with homemade preserves, woven rugs, iron and wood-work, glassware and pottery representative of traditional West Virginian mountain crafts. You may be lucky enough to walk in during a weaving demonstration on one of the old looms. Consider combining an outing here with a visit to the federal fish hatchery in nearby Bowden—kids will enjoy both spots.

**Admission**: Suggested donation $.50.

**Hours**: Memorial Day to June 15 and August 15 to Labor Day: 1:00–5:00 P.M. Saturdays and holidays only. From June 15 to August 15, Monday through Saturday 1:00 to 5:00 P.M. Closed Sunday.

**Directions**: Located one mile north of Harman on Rt. 32. For further information call (304)227-4466.

# Helvetia

Want a total escape for the day to a romantic Old World fairy-tale town? Consider the Swiss version of Brigadoon, wrapped up in a mountain mist: Helvetia. This tiny hamlet of only 25 inhabitants, tucked in a remote niche of the Potomac Highlands, was settled in 1869 by a group of Swiss immigrants who really ended up here by accident and later became the center of a substantial farming community. At its peak, the town supported 500 people. Although today's residents don't speak German as their forebears did just a few generations ago, they do continue to celebrate their unique heritage of Alpine and Appalachia in colorful fashion.

Called Helvetia after the original Latin name for Switzerland, the entire town of about 10 buildings is on the National Register of Historic Places, a tribute to those proud citizens who have so carefully preserved the church, library, beekeepers hut (now an inn) and one-room schoolhouse. The museum, an original settler's cabin, displays Helvetian artifacts, including the original Swiss flag the first pioneers brought with them. If guests are not occupying the inn, you may ask to see the collection of Swiss memorabilia from the early settlement days: cooking utensils, farm implements, clothing, books, musical instruments.

There are two good times to visit: when you want a quiet retreat—a place to paint, think, hike, dine on country cuisine and just browse around absorbing charm. Park at the **Hutte** restaurant, cross the gurgling stream to the common, inhale that clean, cool air, stop and peek in the store and post office. The other good time to come is when the town, hosting one of its annual festivals, explodes into music and dance; revelers fill the streets, and the delicious aroma of local dishes will make you very hungry indeed. One of these festivals, Fasnacht (the Saturday before Ash Wednesday), celebrates spring. Helvetians and visitors alike don masks and costumes, set their feet a-tapping to Appalachian music, and have a ball to scare Old Man Winter away. Another event, the Helvetia Fair on the second weekend in September, honors fall produce with a parade of farm animals, wagons and floats.

Getting here is half the fun. Whether you're coming from Elkins or Buckhannon, the road is curvy and scenic, passing through lovely forest, which harbors a variety of wildlife. Deer, bear, owls are not uncommon fellow travelers, so drive slowly and allow extra time to get there.

**Tip**: Plan to have lunch in the quaint Hutte Restaurant. Among the homemade specialties: Helvetian sausage, cheese, sauerbraten, sauerkraut and a hearty Stout Soup. Special Sunday brunch. Just beyond the restaurant is a stable with goats. Kids (the human kind) are welcome to pat and feed the animals.

**Admission**: Entrance to all buildings is free.

**Hours**: Church is open all day, museum open on Sundays from May to October, NOON to 4:00 P.M. For restaurant information or to see the inn call (304)924-6435.

**Directions**: Coming from Buckhannon, take Rt. 20 to French Creek and then Rt. 46 to Helvetia. Coming from Elkins, take Rt. 250 South, turn right at Mill Creek onto Rt. 46 to Helvetia. For more information write: Eleanor Mailloux, Swiss Village of Helvetia, Helvetia, WV 26224.

# Hillsboro

## *Pearl S. Buck Museum*

The only American woman to receive both the Nobel Prize for Literature and the Pulitzer Prize (the latter for *The Good Earth*), Pearl Buck is one of West Virginia's most famous daughters. That her birthplace is a farm in the stunning setting of Hillsboro is a surprise to many readers who associate this author with China, where she spent 40 years of her life. Her missionary parents, having lost earlier children to sickness in China, returned to the United States for Pearl's birth in 1892 and stayed until she was a few months old before resuming their vocation in the Orient.

Now a house museum, the handsome two-story columned wooden manor was built between 1860 and 1880 by Buck's maternal grandparents—a replica of the house they left behind in Holland. The interior, furnished with period pieces, is grand and bright for a farm house of that period, evidence of the family's relative wealth and the carpentry skills of her grandfather. The walnut cabinets in the two rooms flanking the entrance hold memorabilia—fans, boxes, clothing—reflecting the rich blend of East and West that shaped the author's long and productive life. Copies of her 107 novels and 200 short stories, many of which have been translated into over 50 languages, line the bookshelves. A costumed guide explains the tiny shoe and ancient, grotesque (to contemporary minds) tradition of binding feet practiced by Chinese nobility. Much of the original furniture, including the eight-day clock, and rope bed, and his dresser were hand crafted by Buck's grandfather. You will learn the origin of the expressions "sleep tight" and "pop goes the weasel." Ask about the secret hiding place in the attic steps. The tour ends in the downstairs kitchen with a view of the back hills so bewitching one marvels at the strength of a religious vocation that called the owners to relinquish such a beautiful heritage.

**Tip**: Consider combining a visit here with a hike in the Watoga State Park, bear watching in the Cranberry Glades, or admiring the rock formations at Beartown State Park (see separate entries).

**Admission**: Adults $3.00, children $1.00.

**Hours**: Guided tours from May 1 to November 1, Monday through Saturday 9:00 A.M. to 5:00 P.M. and Sunday, 1:00 to 5:00 P.M. Open holidays except Thanksgiving, Christmas, New Year's Day. Phone: (304)653-4430 or write Pearl S. Buck Museum, P.O. Box 126, Hillsboro, WV 24946.

**Directions**: On Rt. 219, about ten miles south of Marlinton.

# Judy Gap
## *Spruce Knob*

A drive to the top of Spruce Knob in the Monongahela National Forest—and, at 4,861 feet high, the top of West Virginia—is an easy trip that can be made fairly quickly, but going at a leisurely pace, you can turn it into an all-day adventure or longer. There are camping sites throughout the area and over 60 miles of hiking trails.

A scenic, but indirect route to take, approaching Spruce Knob from Rt. 33 (20 miles west of Harman) is up Rich Mountain Road and along pretty Gandy Creek that gurgles and sings its way over rock formations. There are many stopping sites to fish, picnic or just admire the red spruce, stands of hemlocks and cascading falls. In season, wildflowers bloom prolifically. If you prefer lake-side angling, plan a stop at 25-acre **Spruce Knob Lake,** which now has a pier accessible to the handicapped. The trout limit is posted at four a day, but if you don't fill it, bring camping equipment and spend the night: adequate facilities nearby. Since there is no lifeguard, swimming is not allowed, but canoes and row-boats open up opportunities to explore the shoreline. For the less ambitious, it's a quiet, serene spot for just reading a book and listening to the birds.

Continuing up the mountain, you'll see the vegetation change from beech, birch and other hardwoods to mountain ash and other alpine flora that can withstand wind and severe cold. The whispering one-sided spruces at the top are testimony to the strong prevailing westerly winds that shape limbs to stick out on only one side. Climb the small observation tower and take in the view: west to the Monongahela National Forest and Middle Mountain range; north to the Alleghenies and east to the Shenandoahs. If you're lucky, you might spot an eagle riding the air currents, taking advantage of these heights to survey the landscape for prey. Take the half-mile **Whispering Spruce Trail** from the parking area. Over 40 inches of rain annually encourage a variety of flora. Look for lady slippers in June, pink mountain laurel and rhododendron in July, huckleberries and blueberries later. You are welcome to pick for your own consumption, but be warned that you must share your berry patches with the local bear population. Also watch out for snakes like copperheads and rattlers, which naturally like rocky areas.

**Tip**: Weather conditions at this altitude are unpredictable and can change quickly. Bring a sweater even in summer. Watch out for sudden patches of fog in moist weather. Frost can occur any-time of the year. Winter travel is not advised.

**Directions**: If you're in a hurry and want to drive to the top quickly without meandering, take one of these routes: From the east, take Briery Gap Road (Country Road 33/4 at Gateway General Store), 2 miles south of Riverton off US 33, for 2.5 miles to Forest Road 112 and follow the signs to Spruce Knob; From the south, turn left off US 33 south of Cherry Grove onto 28/10 and follow for 11 miles to the lake, then follow signs to summit; From north, take Whitmer Road (County Road 29) south from US 33 to Whitmer for 8.3 miles. From Whitmer, continue south on Whitmer Road for 10.3 miles and turn left on Forest Road 1 for 2.5 miles to the lake.

For further information call the Seneca Rocks Visitor Center at (304)567-2827 or the Potomac Ranger Station (304)257-4488, HC 59, Box 240, Petersburg, WV 26847.

# Marlinton

## *Pocahontas County Historical Museum*

Banker Frank Hunter built his square two-story wood frame house facing the Greenbrier River for his bride, Anna, in 1904. Placed on the National Register of Historic Places in 1976, it is now owned and operated as a museum by the Pocahontas County Historical Society. If you are passing through Marlinton in summer months, the museum is worth seeing.

Displays in the entrance room include Indian artifacts and historical photographs. Other first floor rooms house Civil War stamps, swords and medals, items that recall the logging and railroad history of the area, a stuffed black bear and a Bible printed in 1690, thought to be the first Bible in Greenbrier Valley. The Pearl S. Buck Library contains a collection of books signed by the Nobel prize winning author, who was present at the dedication of the museum in 1963. Look in the sunporch for the unusual "cooling board," used for preparing corpses for burial.

Upstair rooms store the Society's collection of farm implements, craftsmen's tools, doctors' instruments, weaving and spinning implements and early washing machines.

The two-acre grounds extend to the river, and you are welcome to explore and use the picnic tables. An authentic log cabin, dating from about 1840, gives an idea of how early settlers lived. The cemetery nearby reportedly holds the remains of Confederate soldier Woodsy Price. Reports of his ghost creaking through the museum at night have lead to local lore.

**Admission**: Adults $1.00 ages 12–18, $.50, under 12 free.

**Hours**: Open June 13 through Labor Day, 11:00 A.M.–5:00 P.M. on weekdays; 1:00–5:00 P.M. on Sundays.

**Directions**: About ¼ mile south of Marlinton on Rt. 219.

# Watoga State Park

Because the lovely Greenbrier River forms several miles of its boundary, this park received its unusual name from "Watauga," the Cherokee word for "river of many islands." With over 10,000 acres of lake, trails, woodland, mountainous terrain, recreation and camping areas, Watoga is the largest and one of the most popular of the state parks. It is impossible to explore all there is to do here in one day, but it's sure fun trying.

If you are a naturalist, this park will tempt you to stay a week. A resident staff member operates a strong nature program that keeps you busy from early morn to well into the night. For starters, get up early and join a bird hike around the 11-acre Killbuck Lake. Then join a stream stomp to the Greenbrier River and collect aquatic insects and fish and learn about stream ecology. Next, hike some of the dozen miles of trails, identifying the diverse flora and fauna. You may see a bear, and you get your money back if you don't spot a deer. After the fishing contest, take an evening stroll along the Greenbrier River Trail and count wildflowers. Just before sunset, sneak over to the beaver dam for a "backyard beaver watch" and observe these furry woodchoppers at work. After dinner, test your nocturnal sensory skills with a night hike at the T.M. Cheek Overlook. (All these activities, directed by a knowledgeable, enthusiastic guide are free, even if you are not staying in the park.)

In between activities, try to fit in a horseback ride, a tennis, croquet or volleyball game, a swim in the pool, a row on the lake, a movie or marshmallow roast. Or stop in at the nature museum, examine a beaver skull up close and compare animal/bird sightings.

If you are too tired to drive home, spend the night and start all over again the next day. The accommodations range from camping to luxury, heated wood-paneled log cabins with handicapped access. The cabins all have electric lighting, modern bathroom and kitchen and are fully equipped for housekeeping. Most were built years ago by the CCC and retain their individuality and quaint charm: stone fireplaces, porches, decks, wooded seclusion. In case your fish wasn't big enough to feed the family, a restaurant and commissary are in the rustic administration building. They stay open well into the late fall.

**Tip**: Campers: For privacy go to Beaver Creek; for fishing and swimming, reserve at Riverside. For primitive accommodations, ask about Laurel Run. Cabins: number 8 is a favorite, with loft; number 19 is a luxury, four-bedroom, the only one with special features for the handicapped.

**Restrictions**: Do not feed animals in park. Pets are not allowed in or near the cabins.

**Admission**: Free. Minimal cost for boat rental, game courts, horseback riding.

**Hours**: Park is open all year from dawn to dark; park office open 8:00 A.M. to 8:00 P.M. from Memorial Day to Labor Day; 8:30 A.M. to 4:30 P.M. weekdays, 9:00 A.M. to 5:00 P.M. weekends the rest of the year.

**Cabins**: Deluxe are open all year long; standard from April 15 to the fourth Monday in October.

**Camping**: Beaver Creek grounds are open from the Thursday before Memorial Day to November 1. Riverside grounds open April 1 and close immediately after the deer rifle season in early December. For more information call (304)799-4087 or write Watoga State Park, Star Route 1, Box 252, Marlinton, WV 24954.

**Directions**: Look for the sign directing you to the park on Rt. 219, just north of Hillsboro. Follow the road two miles to the west park entrance. Another option is to turn south from Rt. 39 at Huntersville and go nine miles to north entrance of the park.

# Mathias

## *Lost River State Park*

Another jewel in the state park system and one of the oldest, Lost River State Park is ideal for either hanging out with the kids for a week, a quick weekend retreat away from children or a day's fling anytime of the year. The name denotes the pretty river nearby that disappears under a mountain and reappears, in its journey north, as the Cacapon River.

The park's fully-furnished 24 cabins (9 deluxe, 15 standard) are spaced among the trees for optimum privacy, allowing kids to run wild, scream, explore the woods, race to the swimming pool and athletic courts. At the same time, there's plenty of space and peace for reading and rocking on the porch. In addition to a stone wood-burning fireplace, cabins have fully-equipped kitchens, cooking utensils, appliances, tableware and baths with showers. Towels, blankets and bed linens are provided. The deluxe cabins are heated for winter use. A small commissary on site provides basic food supplies. Feeling lazy and reluctant to cook? Treat the family to modestly priced home cooking three times a day at the rustic park restaurant near the main office.

Miles of horse and hiking trails wind through the 3,712 acres of park woods, one leading to the Cranny Crow Overlook, at 3,200 feet above sea level. Browsers soon discover the **Lee Museum,** a simple white cabin "Light Horse Harry" Lee built in 1800 as a retreat from a smallpox outbreak. Later used as a summer house for his family and now a modest museum, the two-story structure is on the National Register of Historic Places.

The recreation area on a hill near the pool challenges the visitor to try it all: tennis, badminton, horseshoes, croquet, basketball, archery and volleyball. Playground equipment, swings and see-saws scattered throughout the park entertain the younger crowd. The stables are open 9:00 A.M. to 5:00 P.M. Tuesday through Sunday: Cost $8.00 for ½ hour of riding and $12.00 for a full hour. During summer months, park staff organize special activities such as history and wildflower walks, scavenger hunts, slide programs, movies and children's nature activities and games. A recreation hall has shuffleboard, Ping-Pong, pool table, video and board games. Because the facilities for families are so good, the price so affordable, and the location so close to Washington (2½ hours), these cabins are booked months—sometimes a year—in advance. The fall is a particularly popular time to enjoy the serenity of the woods. Plan 8—12 months in advance, but don't hesitate to inquire at the last minute about possible cancellations.

**Restrictions**: No pets allowed in cabins or cabin area. No camping.

**Admission**: Weekly rentals range from about $300.00–$600.00 depending on the cabins and number of guests. Nightly and weekend rentals are available only from Labor Day to the second week in June. The deluxe cabins are heated and open year-round. Standard cabins open the last weekend in April and close the fourth Monday in October.

**Hours**: The park is open year-round from 6:00 A.M. to 10:00 P.M. Office hours are 8:30 A.M. to 4:30 P.M. Monday through Friday and 10:00 A.M. to 6:00 P.M. weekends and holidays year-round.

**Directions**: From the town of Mathias, turn west off of Rt. 259 and follow the secondary road for four miles to the park entrance. For information call 1(800)CALL-WVA or (304)897-5372 or write Lost River State Park, Rt. 2, Box 24, Mathias, WV 26812.

Nearby sites of interest: The **John Mathias Homestead**, some of which dates from 1797, located at junction of Lost River State Park Road and Rt. 259, represents the state's earliest architecture. **Lost River General Store**, 7 miles south of Baker on Rt. 259, claims to be "older than the State of West Virginia." The structure now houses a crafts cooperative attracting talent and tourists: lovely selection of quilts, home preserves, pottery, wine, jewelry, woven cloth, pressed-flower stationery, toys, honey, baskets, candles and Christmas trim. Open seven days a week, Memorial Day through Columbus Day weekends, 10:00 A.M. to 5:00 P.M. For more information call (304)897-6169 or 5847.

# Mill Point
## *Cranberry Wilderness Area*

Protected by the Forest Service to allow woodlands to return after turn-of-the-century logging, the 36,000-acre Cranberry Wilderness together with the 50-acre **Cranberry Botanical Area** is considered the most significant biological environment in the Allegheny Mountains and a unique opportunity to study the reemergence of the forest. Left undisturbed by man for nature to reclaim, the bogs, locally called "glades," are being taken over by such species as beech, hickory, maple, hemlock, yellow birch and red spruce. Of particular note is a venerable grand-daddy yellow birch, estimated to be nearly 300 years old.

The wilderness is home to many songbirds, deer, small mammals and to the largest, most stable breeding population of black bear in the state. Recent rumors of panthers stem from reported tracks and marks found on deer carcasses.

The area contains bogs (acidic wetlands) whose peat conditions shelter plant life left from northern glacial retreat—found elsewhere in this continent primarily in Canada. Four of the most accessible and representative of the bogs are in **Cranberry Glades,** a natural "bowl" at 3,400 feet elevation that is kept cooler than similar climes at this height due to surrounding mountains. Here rare plants from the ice age come from seeds left 10,000 years ago. Snake-mouth orchids, Indian pipe, cinnamon fern, monkshood, jack-in-the-pulpit, skunk cabbage, trillium, wild sarsaparilla, trout lily, jewelweed, mountain laurel and elderberry are only a few of dozens found here among the spongy mosses. You can spot many of them from the ½-mile-long Cranberry Glades boardwalk constructed through two bogs to view nature with minimal impact from man. Look carefully for the tiny sundew, a carnivorous plant, whose leaves are smaller than a fingernail, the pitcher plant and the elephant-ear shaped leaf of the skunk cabbage. Despite its odor (which explains its name), bear love this plant, apparently for digestive purposes, and in summer you'll find the area strewn with broken stalks from their munchings. Walk quietly and watch for harmless snakes, frogs and mice that live here. Bird watchers should find warblers, finches, woodpeckers, owls and thrushes. The beebalm attracts hummingbirds.

In late summer, the temptation of new cranberries draw bear and deer into the open: reason enough for leaving your dog in the car. The wheelchair-accessible boardwalk is open 24 hours a day, early morning hours being best for observing animals and birds and communing privately in this pristine sanctuary. Forest Service staff give guided tours at 2:00 P.M. on Saturdays and Sundays in season.

Any visit to this area should begin at the **Cranberry Mountain Visitor Center** located at the junction of Rt. 150 and Rt. 39/55. Orientation exhibits demonstrate how resident animals adapt to seasons and each other, Indian and early pioneer activity, the coming of the railroad and logging camps, and the felling of ancient forests for crops that changed life here forever. Slide shows explain the origin of the glades, native snakes, and backpacking and fishing opportunities. Pick up a map of the boardwalk and the 60 miles of wilderness hiking trails, and pamphlets on camping options and other nearby points of interests. Open from Memorial Day to Labor Day and on weekends the rest of the year (except for December holidays) from 9:00 A.M. to 5:00 P.M. Phone: (304)653-4826.

**Directions**: Take Rt. 219 south from Marlinton for about 8 miles to Mill Point. Take Rt. 39/55 about 6 miles to Visitor Center. The entrance to the Cranberry Glades Boardwalk is 6/10 mile beyond the center on Rt. 39/55.

**Restrictions**: Removal of plants and animals and use of motorized vehicles, bicycles and other mechanical transport is prohibited in the wilderness. Backpacking is permitted, but the trails are primitive and are not recommended for beginners. Ask at the Visitor Center for a trail map.

# Red Creek
## *Dolly Sods Wilderness Area*

More than 10,000 acres of the Monongahela National Forest on Allegheny Mountain is designated as the Dolly Sods Wilderness and Scenic Area. Ranging from 2,600 to over 4,000 feet high, this high plateau is rugged, wind-swept terrain—the reign of the hawk—shaped by glacial activity to the north that explains the distinctive flora and fauna more similar to Canada than the surrounding environment. Bogs, rocky plains, beaver ponds, waterfalls, hardwood and spruce forests, streams and over 40 miles of hiking trails combine to make this a naturalist's paradise.

This is the refuge of the elusive bobcat, the threatened Cheat Mountain salamander and the endangered northern flying squirrel. The snowshoe hare, here in their most southern range, have large, hairy feet, like snowshoes, that allow them to traverse the snow without sinking. Reported sightings of mountain lions persist. Even skeptics concur that this is country so wild and isolated, so populated with deer and other game, that big cats could survive here undetected. Other mammals thriving here are weasel, mole, shrew, mice, raccoon, skunk, woodchuck, fox, deer and bear.

The scenic area to the east and north end of the wilderness is easily accessible by car for a day-trip and offers sweeping vistas, interpretive trails, berry picking, camping and picnicking. Many of the large boulders scattered throughout the area were once covered by a red spruce-hemlock forest, logged and burned during the 1880s to create grazing land or "sods." Now stripped of a humus layer, the ground has difficulty supporting trees, which struggle to take root and mature. But many kinds of flora thrive in this diverse habitat: ferns, mosses, berries, grasses, wildflowers, conifers and hardwoods. You are allowed to pick the wild blueberries for your own consumption, so plentiful and delicious in late summer. Be aware that bear are very fond of blueberries, and you may have to share the area with them. In June and July the Sods are ablaze with rhododendron, mountain laurel and azalea.

For an unforgettable mountain experience get up early and spend a morning with trained volunteers from the Brooks Bird Club who band migrating birds during the late summer and fall. For 35 years, bird banding has taken place at the **Allegheny Front Migration Observatory,** a fancy term for the simple shelter and netting operation set up against the side of a mountain. The action starts at the first crack of dawn. Some of the dedicated bird lovers have camped for weeks near the banding station to be sure they are up and ready to monitor nets early. They are experts at deftly and quickly removing the trapped birds from the fine nets, strung up to catch the unsuspecting flyers heading south. Within a few minutes, the birds—some quite tiny—have been examined, their sex, age, species and general health carefully chronicled, their delicate legs banded before being released to continue their voyage. The volunteers are so gentle that the birds suffer no ill effects despite their frantically beating hearts. This is a rare chance to examine these winged beauties so closely. Mostly songbirds, their colors dazzle in the morning sun: sapphire indigo buntings, emerald warblers, ruby rose-breasted grosbeak, topaz yellow goldfinches and golden-crowned kinglets and multi-jeweled hummingbirds. There are also thrushes, vireos, robins, catbirds, nuthatches, sparrows, juncos, finches, many kinds of warblers, even a stray hawk, owl and woodpecker.

The volunteers blow gently on the little scalps to determine the thickness of the skull (and thus determine the age) and on the birds's breasts to see how much fat has been stored during the summer. In some cases, the sex can be determined by wing length or feather coloration. Notes are made of "repeats"—those birds already banded from a previous year. In one recent season over 8,200 birds, representing 89 species, were banded in less than 3 months (with the volume peaking in September). While some volunteers band and document their findings, others collect important data by counting monarch butterflies and other travelers: an astounding 17,000 blue jays were counted in less than three months.

While performing their ministrations, these carefully trained volunteers patiently explain why this banding process is so important: to learn how birds age, where they go when migrating, what their social structure is and what scientists can learn about environments, like the rapidly disappearing rain forests where birds winter.

To get a good overview of the Sods, stop at the Scenic Overlook and take the short, marked trail. The trees and flowers here are representative of the area. A longer trail about ⅓ mile is the Northland Loop Trail, just before the Red Creek Camp Ground. Trees here are typical of growth at the higher elevations. The trail leads to a bog and boardwalk. Look for cranberries, dewberries and the unusual insect-eating sundew among the mats of spongy mosses. You'll notice how shrubs and red spruce are gradually claiming bog area.

**Tip**: The winters can be brutally cold, with weather conditions changing rapidly. Because the roads are not plowed, travel in the Sods is not recommended during the winter. Be prepared for fog, wind and rain any time of year. Bring your own drinking water. Be aware of flash flooding during heavy rains and seek high ground.

**Hours**: Volunteers band from dawn to late morning every day of the week from mid-August to mid-October, or until it's too cold for birds or volunteers.

**Directions**: The banding station is in the scenic area. From Harman take Route 33/32 north towards Canaan Valley. Turn right onto Dry Fork Rd. and follow, turning right when the road runs into Lanesville Rd. The road become gravel. Continue about 10 miles, bearing left onto Forest Rd. 75, to the Red Creek Campground and park in the parking area across the road. From here follow the trail a short distance to the bird banding station.

Looking for hawks and eagles? Continue on Forest Rd. 75. Just before the road starts going back down the mountain, you'll see a large outcropping of rocks (popularly called Bear Rocks). Your view of the skies and its denizens is best from here, and you may be lucky enough to see a migrating golden or bald eagle.

Access to Dolly Sods from Petersburg: Follow Rt. 28/55 south about 10 miles to Jordan Run Rd. Turn right and go one mile to Forest Rd. 19. This meets Forest Rd. 75 at Bear Rocks. Wilderness access points are on your left and the scenic area ahead six miles.

For more information stop at the Seneca Rocks Visitor Center on Rt. 33, (304)567-2827, or write Potomac Ranger Station, HC 59, Box 240, Petersburg, WV 26847 (304)257-4488.

**Restrictions**: Because of its protected status, there are restrictions on camping and motorized vehicles. No saddle/pack animals allowed.

# Riverton

## *Seneca Caverns*

Two caverns, Seneca and Smoke Hole (see entry), developed for tourism are within 12 miles, in opposite directions, of Seneca Rocks. Each has its own "awesome" ambience and splendid variety of limestone formations. Neither tour has facilities of any kind for the handicapped. Because of the slippery steps and dark passageways, children should be monitored carefully.

The largest of West Virginia's commercial underground caves, Seneca Caverns is 3.4 miles long and, at its deepest point, extends 165 feet below the earth's surface. Even during extreme hot or cold temperatures at ground level, inside remains a constant 54 degrees F, which explains why Seneca Indians sought shelter here during the winter for many years before Europeans stumbled on the caves in 1790. Arrowheads and other artifacts found deep within the caves support this theory, though one questions how well man functioned in the absence of natural light. Carved hundreds of millions of years ago by an underground river, these limestone caves were thrust above water level during the ice age, perhaps the result of an ancient earthquake. Over the next 50 million years, ground seepage slowly formed, drop by drop, the stalactites you see today. New shapes are constantly evolving and growing, at the rate of one cubic inch every 125–175 years.

The guided tour, about 35 minutes, snakes up and down through a number of rooms and passageways lined with dripping formations resembling animals, waterfalls, fruit and human figures, among other recognizable shapes. Legend says that Princess Snowbird, an Indian maiden, was married in the largest of the caverns, the Grand Ballroom 70 feet in height. Among the names given the individual caverns, children's favorites are Candy Mountain and Fairyland, a Disney-like fantasy whose effect is heightened by clever lighting. As the name implies, Mirror Lake reflects the stalactites hanging above it—magical, mystical, mysterious. Although the guide will tell you that dogs are allowed if you carry them, DO NOT DO THIS! You need both hands to hold onto the rails. As in most caverns, the passageways are dimly lit, wet and sometimes slippery, so wear shoes with a good grip. Watch your head going under low-ceilinged areas, and don't allow children to run.

Seneca Caverns is located in the lovely German Valley farm area, well worth the scenic drive getting there. The rustic setting and lack of obtrusive signs support management's claim that theirs is a less commercialized venture than other caverns, its trade, less of an impact on nature.

**Admission**: Adults $6.50, seniors $5.85; children 6–11 $3.25, under age 6 free. Group rates available.

**Hours**: Guided tours from April 1 to Labor Day, from 8:00 A.M. to 7:00 P.M. Special arrangements can be made from November 1 to March 31.

**Directions**: About 40 miles southeast of Elkins and 12 miles from Seneca Rocks. Take Rt. 33 south from Seneca Rocks through Riverton. Follow signs to entrance. For more information call (304)567-2671.

# Seneca Rocks
## *Harper's Old Country Store*

Since 1902 members of the Harper family have been selling to locals and tourists alike knickknacks, clothing, bait, souvenirs, beer and food items at Harper's Old Country Store. Sitting like a set for a Western movie, right at the intersection of Rts. 33 and 55 at Seneca Rocks, it's a hard place to miss. Bold lettering on the facade states a proud identity. The wooden porch begs and beckons passersby to stop for an ice cream sandwich, stretch legs and poke through the crammed aisles, purchase a hunting or fishing license or carry-out pizza from the attached restaurant. The stuffed golden eagle and its shelf mate, a coyote, have been peering down at visitors for 75 years. A fairly recent addition is the mounted black bear holding a sign that states: "Shot by Joe Harper May 17, 1983. Reason: killing sheep."

In addition to essentials like gasoline and beer, browsers find raccoon-skin hats, rawhide jump ropes, sheepskins, sassafras roots, Indian headdresses and candlesticks locally made from fence posts. The current proprietor is the great-great grandson of the Joe Harper who originally founded the store. The front porch is one of the best vantage points for getting a vicarious thrill watching climbers pull themselves up treacherous Seneca Cliffs, just across the way.

**Hours**: Open year-round from 7:15 A.M. to 8:30 P.M. and on Sundays from 8:00 A.M. to 8:00 P.M.

**Directions**: Located at the junction of Rts. 33 and 28 in Pendleton County, across from Seneca Rocks. Phone:(304)567-2586.

# Seneca Rocks

Driving south along Rt. 55 from Petersburg, there is no way you can miss one of the great landmarks of the state—Seneca Rocks. Like surrealistic dinosaur teeth, they literally lunge 900 feet out of the North Fork River bank—huge gray mammoths reaching into the sky, often crowned by a soaring hawk. These Tuscarora quartzite giants date from the Silurian Period, about 400 million years ago when an ancient ocean covered the area. As the waters receded, underlying rock was pushed up forming jagged cliffs of exceptional hardness. Indians celebrated their majestic beauty in folklore, and the site has been on maps since the first European settlers arrived.

Undoubtedly, Indians had scaled these cliffs before the initials "D.B. Sept. 16, 1908" were carved by the first documented climber, probably a surveyor. Because of the spine-chilling difficulty of the climb, the U.S. Army trained troops here during the forties for scaling European peaks. Today it is considered by many as the most challenging climb in the East.

Unfortunately, the **Seneca Rocks Visitors Center** lost its collection of historical photographs when it burned to the ground in the spring of 1992. However, old postcards show the unusual 30-foot, 2,000-ton pinnacle that rested between the large humps at the top of the cliffs until it toppled in October of 1987—testimony to the mercurial whims of nature.

**Tip**: These difficult rocks are for experienced or supervised climbers only. Bring a picnic and watch an expert maneuver the cracks and crevices in an ant-like ascent. Or hike the West Side Trail 1.5 miles—steep but safe—to gain a valley view from the observation deck 40 feet below the top of the ridge line. Interpretive signs explain geologic points of interest. There are benches for resting rest along the way.

Because these cliffs offer some of the best climbing challenges in the East, two outfitters give instruction here April through October. The Seneca Rocks Mountain Guides offers professional climbing instruction for beginners, leaders or private tours. For information call (304)567-2115 or write to them at Box 223, Seneca Rocks, WV 26884.

Seneca Rocks Climbing School has been operating for twenty years and offers two, three and four-day courses for beginners and advanced climbers. Call (304)567-2600 or write Box 53, Seneca Rocks, WV 26884.

**Hours**: The Visitor Center, in a temporary structure until the new building is completed, is open April 1 to October 31 daily from 9:00 A.M. to 5:30 P.M. and from November 1 to March 31 on weekends only, from 9:00 A.M. to 4:30 P.M. The center offers an

11-minute video of Spruce Knob-Seneca Rocks National Recreation Area.

**Directions**: Located near the junction of Rts. 33 and 55 in Pendleton County.

## Smoke Hole Caverns

A more commercialized venture than Seneca Caverns and right on Rt. 28/55, Smoke Hole Caverns boasts the "World's Longest Ribbon Stalactite," a spectacular limestone formation of overlapping ribbons weighing 2½ tons, measuring 13' x 16' and estimated to be between five to six million years old. Formed nearly 225 million years ago, these caverns have a long history of human usage. Legend claims that during frigid winters Seneca Indians used the caverns to cure meat. Smoke venting from the ceiling gave the place its name, "Smoke Hole." Civil War soldiers hid ammunition here, and later, local settlers eased the winter chill by brewing moonshine where the eyes of the law could not find them. In 1942 the caves and their magnificent contents opened to the public.

Guided tours—about 45 minutes—lead through the Room of a Million Stalactites (some resembling delicate straws), over Crystal Cave Coral Pool stocked with shimmering trout, past formations called Rainbow Falls and Alaskan Glacier, a bubbling artisan fountain and glistening columns formed when stalactites and stalagmites "marry." The turnaround point is the Queen's Room and Bath adorned with a canopy of dripping golden stalactites. Rippled flowstones along the walls grow at the painful rate of one cubic inch every 125 years.

One room dramatically demonstrates the fact that West Virginia lies on a fault: What was once the ceiling is now the wall, and the wall, the floor as a result of quake activity that rotated the formation 190 degrees.

This is an easier, shorter walk than the tour at Seneca Caverns but usually more crowded. Passageways are wet but well lit. Still, watch your step on the stairs, use the hand rails and keep your head down passing from one room to another. One spot is named Tall Man's Ache for a good reason.

**Tip**: Dress appropriately. Whatever the weather outside, the interior temperature is a constant 56 degrees F. As in most caverns, small children may be intimidated by dark, underground passageways.

**Admission**: Adults $7.00, children 5 to 13 $3.50, under 5 free.

**Hours**: Open year-round with tours about every 30–45 minutes; Memorial Day to October 31 hours are 8:30 A.M. to 7:30 P.M.; November 1 to Memorial Day, 8:30 A.M. to 5:00 P.M.

*The world's longest ribbon stalactite, over five million years old, grows one cubic inch every 125 years in Smoke Hole Caverns.*

**Directions**: On Rts. 28 and 55, about 13 miles north of Seneca Rocks and 8 miles south of Petersburg. Motel and cabin facilities on site. For more information call 1(800)828-8478 or (304)257-4442 or write Smoke Hole Caverns, HC 59, Box 39, Seneca Rocks, WV 26884.

# Slatyfork

## *Sharp's Country Store*

Resoled Depression shoes, the first phone in Pocahontas County, a stuffed golden eagle shot in 1909, maple syrup, fresh bait, horseshoe nails, T-shirts, bear traps, an Edison gramophone, Indian weapons, Civil War relics—just a sampling of what's for sale and on display at Sharp's Country Store in Slatyfork. Now in the third generation of Sharp family ownership, the store was built in its present site in 1927 and has served as a gathering place for locals to exchange news and advice ever since. It is also a great stopping place for the road weary. Fill up the gas tank, choose your flavor of hand-dipped ice cream and browse through the collection near the door of clippings and photos that document local history. Owners Linda (granddaughter of store founder L.D Sharp, first Slatyfork postmaster, 1901) and husband Benny are willing to share stories of the memorabilia, antiques and stuffed animals stacked round the cereal and soap boxes. Ask about the log cabin out back where General Lee took supper.

In your pokings around, you may uncover a flea-market treasure. At the very least, you'll experience the warmth, smell and security of the general store most towns lost years ago. Before leaving, admire the huge red oak directly across the street that is reputedly hundreds of years old, perhaps predating the American Revolution.

**Hours**: Open all week 7:00 A.M. to 9:00 P.M.

**Directions**: Located on Rt. 219, four miles south of Snowshoe Ski Resort.

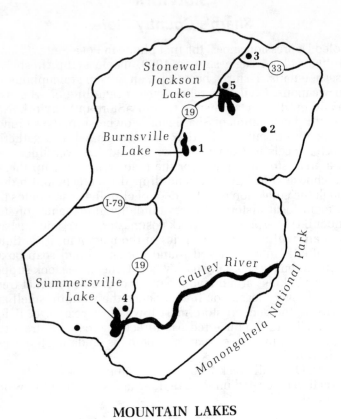

## MOUNTAIN LAKES

1. ***Burnsville***
   Bulltown Historic District and Burnsville Lake
2. ***French Creek***
   West Virginia State Wildlife Center
3. ***Jane Lew***
   The Glass Swan
4. ***Summersville***
   Carnifex Ferry Battlefield State Park
   Summersville Lake and Dam
5. ***Weston***
   Jackson's Mill Historic Area
   Stonewall Jackson State Park and Dam

# Mountain Lakes

Smack dab in the middle of the state a chain of lakes, rivers and reservoirs shimmer green and blue under the mountain sky—a playground for anglers, water skiers, scuba divers and boaters. In fall, the waters of Summersville Lake—so serene in summer for family frolics—are unleashed into the Gauley River, spawning some of the most exhilarating white-water rafting in the East. The new Stonewall Jackson Lake is already widely regarded as one of the best spots in the state for muskie, walleye and trout. For those wanting an early morning's start on outsmarting the bass and crappie in Burnsville Lake, there is an attractive campground conveniently located right on the shore.

For history buffs, reenactments at Carnifex Ferry Battlefield recall the horror of the Civil War, and Jackson's Mill and Bulltown historic areas offer fascinating living-history presentations of frontier and colonial life when West Virginia was still part of the Virginian wilderness. To appreciate the "wild" aspect of life even more, a visit to the West Virginia State Wildlife Center in French Creek brings the traveler nose to nose with animals, large and small, fierce and friendly, that are native to the state.

If it's town life you must have, stroll the streets of Weston for a lesson in Victorian eclectic architecture or join the throngs of revelers at Buckhannon's famed Strawberry Festival in May. But it's the seductive serenity of the waters and the chance to find privacy, peace and pleasure far from the roaring crowd that lure the adventurer and angler alike to the Mountain Lakes: a great place to get "caught" up on the natural blessings of West Virginia.

For more information on visiting the Mountain Lakes contact: Lewis County Convention and Vistor Bureau, P.O. Box 379, Weston 26452, phone (304)269-7328.

## Burnsville

### Bulltown Historic District and Burnsville Lake

**Bulltown Historic District** is the fortunate result of the damming of the Little Kanawha River to create Burnsville Lake. To help preserve historic log structures that were endangered during the damming process, the U.S. Army Corps of Engineers disassembled, moved and reconstructed them at their present location near the front gate of the Bulltown Campgrounds. The picture-book pretty complex is representative of different kinds of structures and lifestyles in Central West Virginia from 1815 to 1870. The site is also notable for being the battleground for the Battle of Bulltown, a 12-hour skirmish between Union and Confederate forces on October 13, 1863. Living-history demonstrations reenact such typical 19th-century scenes as quilting, wash day, apple-butter and soap making, gardening, weaving and other chores.

Start at the interpretive center and see the six-minute slide show on Burnsville Lake and its facilities. Note the enormous salt box used for curing meat, historic exhibits of Civil War artifacts and turn of the century memorabilia. If you can plan to be there at 2:00 P.M., you can join a guided tour of the houses, church and battlefield. At other times, follow the one-mile interpretive trail.

**The Cunningham Farmhouse**, built about 1815, was seized by Union forces during the war, evidenced by the bullet hole you can see in the wall. It is typical Southern "dogtrot" style in which passage is not possible between the two pens without going outside. The nearby granary is the oldest outbuilding on the farm. The Cunningham House is an example of a log home that was subsequently covered with boards and painted white.

Further along the walk is a good example of a cat and clay chimney, made of boards and mud rather than stone. This structure, the **Johnson House**, was built around 1883 by a freedman.

The trail will take you along the site of the Weston and Gauley Bridge Turnpike used by both sides of the war to transport troops and supplies. Up on the hill, **St. Michael's,** one of the earliest Catholic churches in this part of the state, looks over the hills to the battle site. It is elegant in its white wood simplicity. The straight austere pews segregated men and women during Sunday worship. At 11:00 A.M. every Sunday in season, a special tour is given focusing on the development of religion in Appalachia with an explanation of bell tolling and the significance of the servis berry and tree. In the adjoining meadow a reenactment of the Battle of Bulltown takes place the second week of July. Children who miss being in school during the summer can take advantage of an unusual program. For three hours kids can go to a subscription school, experiencing the education process in rural Appalachia in the mid-1800s, with lessons, games and homework from authentic period textbooks. Most of the children attending are from the adjacent Bulltown Campgrounds on **Burnsville Lake**. The 968-acre lake and surrounding wildlife area attract many families who like to swim, water ski, fish, boat and explore the finger creeks and hiking trails. Anglers cast for largemouth bass, walleye, crappie and catfish. The muskellunge fishing is reportedly some of the best in the state.

The supervisor of the Historic District, whose family has deep roots in the area, is particularly knowledgeable about the history, local lore and traditions of this part of Appalachia and is proud to share his heritage with visitors. After your tour, he may offer you this traditional West Virginia farewell. "Come on back. We'll treat you ten different ways; you're bound to like one of them."

**Hours**: Interpretive Center: May 1 to September 1, 10:00 A.M. to 6:00 P.M.; September 1 to October 15, 10:00 A.M. to 4:00 P.M. Closed October 15 to May 1. Large groups should call to prearrange tours: (304)452-8170.

**Directions**: From Buckhannon, take Rt. 33 west to I-79 south to Rt. 19 south. Follow Rt. 19 about 15 miles south of Ireland to Bulltown entrance. Or, exit I-79 at Flatwoods turning left on US 19 north traveling for approximately 10 miles.

Camping sites (240), operated by the U.S. Corps of Engineers, are available at Burnsville Lake from the first week in April to December 1. For reservations and information: (304)452-8006 or (304)853-2371 or 2398 (fishing report); or write Bulltown Campground, Napier, WV 26631.

# French Creek
## West Virginia State Wildlife Center

Warning: This state-of-the art facility, only seven years old, is definitely not a petting zoo! The animals are so at home in their surroundings it's easy for the visitor to forget that these beguiling creatures are captive—and wild—guests.

By displaying indigenous wildlife in a natural setting, the center's intent is to educate people about West Virginia wildlife and heighten preservation and environmental consciousness. Because animals have the space to roam, romp and rest in a secure yet natural setting, visitors don't feel sorry for the imprisoned beasts. Spreading over 300 acres of woods, open meadow and rocks, the habitat environments are so inviting, spacious and clean that on occasion a bear or a deer from the wild try to join their captive friends. Case in point is the two-year old cub that tried to crawl into an enclosure holding Jack, a 20-year-old black bear who, due to a misspent youth of popcorn and soft drinks, now tips the scales at an impressive 600 pounds.

The majestic elk and bison have acres of grass to graze on. A loop walk of 1.25 miles leads through hardwoods sheltering gray wolf, deer, wild boar, coyote, eagles and owls. Charlie, a playful mountain lion, is a star attraction. Among the most reclusive of

*A common sight throughout the state, white-tail deer add silent grace to the West Virginia landscape.* STEPHEN J. SHALUTA, JR.

felines, these lovely cats with aristocratic faces and enormous paws are no longer found in West Virginia forests. In keeping with the natural environment theme, the center "recycles" deer killed by cars by feeding them to the large cats.

The center is justifiably proud of its new otter exhibit. River otters were nearly eliminated in the state at the turn of the century, but under the aegis of the Division of Natural Resources some have been returned successfully to certain locales. The display and its pool allow visitors to watch these inexhaustible, hyper-active swimmers from above and below water and marvel at their energy, grace and *joie de vivre*.

The minimal entrance fee is a bargain for all you see and will help finance planned expansions such as a nocturnal animal exhibit, reptile display, aquarium and auditorium.

**Tip**: The walk is handicapped accessible. There is a large picnic area with grills and tables, a good spot for families to barbecue dinner after visiting the animals, particularly during summer months when the sun sets late. Take your time and stroll leisurely. You'll see and hear more if you let nature come to you.

**Admission**: Adults 16 and over $2.00; children 3 to 15 $1.00; children under 3 free.

**Hours**: Year-round from 9:00 A.M. to dusk.

**Restrictions**: Bringing in pets and feeding the animals are prohibited.

**Directions**: 12 miles south of Buckhannon on Rt. 20. From north take Exit 99 from I-79 and follow Rt. 33 east to Rt. 20. From south, take Exit 67 off I-79 and follow Rts. 19 and 4 about 3 miles to Rock Cave and Rt. 20. For more information write Box 38, French Creek, WV 26218. Phone: (304)924-6211.

# Jane Lew
## *The Glass Swan*

If you ever wanted to see how those Venetian glass blowers produced their one-of-a-kind treasures but you lacked the cash to fly to Italy, there's a satisfying substitute free of charge in a visit to the Glass Swan Studio in Jane Lew. At one time there were nearly 100 operating glass factories in the state; now the number is down to less than a dozen. The Glass Swan is a small but interesting operation, and the retail store nearby carries lovely items at reasonable prices, including little birds, ice cubes and glass candy kisses that make good souvenirs. The owner, who built his studio from parts of other studios that have closed, along with his helpers demonstrate a variety of glass ware, and what procedures you'll see depends on what order they are filling that day: hand blowing, glass cutting, decorating among others.

One specialty is cobalt blue tableware. You'll see that it takes six people, each performing a specific skilled task, to make one wine glass—in about one minute. Another specialty here are the hand-formed **marbles** made with special wooden tools. There are over 30,000 marble collectors in the U.S., and some of the marbles made here are sent to Japan, an enthusiastic marble market. Among the most popular designs are the leopard's eye, clam broth (cobalt blue with orange lines), end-of-day (swirls inside crystal) and a new design, cobalt strawberry, with layers of gold overlay. It all seems so easy but requires years to develop

85

the confidence, speed, skill and judgment to turn out these little gems so effortlessly.

**Hours**: Exhibitions are given daily Monday through Saturday, but it's best to call ahead to be sure of the hour (304)884-8014. During the summer May through August the studio is open 9:00 A.M. to 2:00 P.M.; winter hours, September through April, 9:00 A.M. to 3:00 P.M. The retail store is open 9:00 A.M. to 5:00 P.M. Monday through Saturday.

**Directions**: For factory, from I-79 take Exit 105 to Rt. 119 north. Go two blocks and turn left onto Depot Street. The studio is one block down on corner on right. The retail store is a few blocks away, on Rt. 119 as you enter Jane Lew. Write: The Glass Swan, Box 736, Weston, WV 26452.

# Summersville
## *Carnifex Ferry Battlefield State Park*

Carnifex Ferry Battlefield State Park with only 156 acres is primarily a commemoration to a significant Civil War battle, but in the fall, during the height of rafting activity on the Gauley, many visitors come to watch the white-water excitement from the park overlooks, one of the best views anywhere of the river.

Every year in mid-September, a weekend-long **reenactment** with about 300 participants relives the Battle of Carnifex Ferry that took place here on September 10, 1861. On that date General William S. Rosecrans and his Federal troops engaged Confederate forces under General John B. Floyd, forcing them to retreat across the ferry to the south side of the Gauley River. This battle was claimed a decisive victory for the Union as it secured the control of the Kanawha Valley and determined its role in the statehood movement. Had the Confederates won, this part of West Virginia (then called Western Virginia) might have remained in Virginia territory after statehood had been established. However, the Federals paid a terrible price for the victory, suffering the most serious casualties when two of their own units mistakenly fired upon one another in the dark. The tragedy contributed to a loss of 27 dead and 103 wounded; the Confederates suffered only 9 wounded and no fatalities.

The clothing worn by reenactors, the weapons they carry and the camp site they create are authentic reproductions. Although for safety's sake there are no bullets fired nor bayonets used, you will learn how the men loaded their muskets, a complicated, awkward process of biting off the end of a paper cartridge, pouring gunpowder from it down the barrel, setting the bullet on top of the power with a ramrod, and priming the piece with a cap

Hundreds of participants take part in the annual reenactment at Carnifex Ferry Battlefield State Park.    CLAUDE LEVET

before firing. An experienced soldier could perform these steps and fire his weapon three times a minute.

A small museum (Patteson House) with displays and battle artifacts is open during the summer. Year-round you can follow the self-guided signs along the battle site and use the picnic area.

**Hours**: Park open from dawn to dusk year-round. Museum open every day from Memorial Day to Labor Day from 11:00 A.M. to 6:00 P.M.

**Directions**: Located on the Gauley River via Rt. 129. From Rt. 19 south of Summersville take Rt. 129 west to Carnifex Ferry Rd. For more information call (304)872-3773 or write Carnifex Ferry Battlefield State Park, Rt. 2, Box 435, Summersville, WV 26651.

## Summersville Lake and Dam

Built by the U.S. Corps of Engineers to control flooding of the Kanawha and Gauley rivers, the Summersville Lake project has resulted in an aqua playground for fisherman, scuba divers, water skiers, boaters, white-water rafters and kayakers. With 60 miles of shoreline fingering into surrounding hills, the lake is also a splendid sightseeing destination for those who just want to gawk at the pretty scenery and dare-devil rafters (see also Whitewater Rafting section).

The dam, constructed at a cost of about $48 million, is 390 feet high (about the size of a building 40 stories high) and 2,280 feet long and is the second largest dam of this type in the eastern U.S. In summer the lake is raised 1,652 feet above sea level for water recreation and is stocked with trout, bass, walleye, bluegill and catfish. Picnic, boat launching and camping facilities and a wildlife management area with nature trails accommodate both day trippers and overnight guests.

Between Labor Day and Columbus Day lake water is released at the rate of 2,600 cubic feet per second, creating some of the best white-water conditions in the East. Stop at the visitor center to get brochures and maps and see the movie *The Oldest New River* and videos on various aspects of water safety. Group tours can be arranged to see how the outlet release operates by calling (304)872-3412.

**Hours**: Visitor center open from 7:15 A.M. to 4:00 P.M. Monday through Friday.

**Directions**: From Beckley take Rt. 19 north to Rt. 129 west to the dam site. Turn left after the dam to reach the visitor center. Follow signs. For more information write Resource Manager, Summersville Lake, U.S. Corps of Engineers, RR #2, Box 470, Summersville, WV 26651-9802.

## Weston

Sitting in the middle of north central West Virginia on Rt. 33, Weston is a bustling town with a past. Civil War history and turn-of-the-century architecture make for an interesting combination of styles. Combine a brief stop here with a vist to one of the glass factories in Jane Lew or with a trip to Jackson's Mill Museum (see entries).

Coming into Weston on Rt. 33/119 look for the **Farmer's Market** on the right where a good selection of local produce is for sale in season. Downtown Weston is sprinkled with charming gingerbread-trimmed houses and Victorian mansions. The best example of the latter is the **Jonathan-Louis Bennett House**, now serving as the only public library in Lewis County. Built in 1875 in the High Victorian Italianate style, the facade has retained the original bracketed cornices, latticework and roof tower. Its good condition can be attributed in part to the fact that it was deeded to the townspeople on the condition that the exterior never be changed. Most of the seventeen rooms inside the three-story brick mansion hold stacks of books, office space or are closed off to the public. But during library hours visitors are welcome to step inside, peruse a few original pieces such as the roll-top desk and chandelier in the entrance, look at the photos of the prominent Bennett family and gawk at the grandeur that-was. Tours can be pre-arranged. That a happy family once lived here is documented by the saying on the wall that "Go East, Go West, Home Is Best."

**Hours**: Open Monday through Friday 10:00 A.M. to 6:00 P.M. and Saturday 10:00 A.M. to 2:00 P.M. For prearranged tours call (304)269-5151 or write Louis Bennett Library, Box 740, Weston, WV 26452.

**Directions**: In downtown Weston at 148 Court Ave.

Worth seeing briefly while passing through town and just a few blocks from the library are the **Citizen Bank** at 201 Main St., and, across the Tygart River, the hand-cut stone hospital, the state's oldest institution (1864). The bank, considered the finest example of art deco architecture in West Virginia, is noteworthy not only for the handsome detail in its original structure but for the ingenious way in which its new addition was designed to match. The ornamental iron work was made by the same company for the addition in 1980 that supplied iron for the original bank in 1927 and for the National Cathedral in Washington, D.C. Inside, the ceiling is 45 feet high and embellished with the state seal in 24-karat gold leaf. Note the carving around the lobby entrance door and majestic American walnut paneling. On the upper level over the safe deposit vault is the board room where directors convene around a handsome conference table of walnut, tiger wood and bird's-eye maple. The bank staff is rightly proud of their work surroundings and encourage visitors to look around and say hello during business hours, Monday through Thursday 9:00 A.M. to 3:00 P.M. and until 6:00 P.M. on Fridays.

## Jackson's Mill Historic Area

Can you guess what a straw flattener was used for? Or a sipper jug? These and other quaint tools and artifacts displayed at the **Jackson's Mill Museum** chronicle life on the Virginia frontier and recall the debt we owe our forebears for their imagination and indefatigable industry. The site also gives a glimpse of the early life of one of America's military geniuses.

Considered by many as the greatest commander of the Civil War, Thomas J. "Stonewall" Jackson spent most of his youth on his grandparents' farm after being orphaned at the age of six. Growing up in pretty West Fork River Valley, Jackson played on the prosperous land and later worked at the family sawmill until he left for West Point at the age of 18. The mill was a thriving business, the first one in the region, and provided timber for many of the buildings in the vicinity, including those in nearby Weston.

On the National Register of Historic Places, the gristmill/museum that stands today dates from 1841 and is made from lumber produced at the original sawmill. The 2½-story wooden structure has a stone foundation and is the result of many years of careful restoration.

You will be greeted by a charming hostess in period dress who explains the history of the historic area before showing an excellent 30-minute movie on the life of Stonewall Jackson. You are then free to roam around and admire such unusual relics from the last century as a McCormick reaper, storage bins hand hewn from a gum tree (1895), a corn grinder from an old log, an apple butter kettle that holds 75 gallons, a chicken watering jug and old plows. Upstairs holds more exotica: flax hetchels and brake, straw flattener (for making straw hats), broom clamps, a Sabo varmit trap and a cheese press. Looking at the old wooden washing machines, you'll recognize what drudgery wash day entailed before the days of dry cleaners and spin cycles.

Two other structures on the grounds merit attention. **Blaker Mill and McWhorter Cabin.** Disassembled stone by stone, the mill was transported from its original location and rebuilt on these premises as a gift from a Blaker descendant from Delaware. In the process of restoration, it will eventually be used to demonstrate grain grinding. The McWhorter Cabin, also relocated to this property, is 200 years old. The inside chimney reminds us that the inhabitants had to worry about Indian attacks (an outside chimney was more vulnerable). The builder, Henry McWhorter, who as a boy had served in New York in the Revolutionary War before coming south, lived with his family in this 18 x 24-foot hand-hewn log structure for 37 years. The tiny cabin served multi-purposes as a post office, church and meeting house. In summer, with bright flowers blooming in the kitchen garden, it is "cute" and inviting, but those cracks in the door must surely make for a cold dwelling when winter winds blow. It is an authentic and convincing reminder that the old days were very tough indeed.

**Admission**: To Jackson's Mill Historic Area: Adults $2.00; children under 12 $1.00.

**Hours**: Memorial Day through Labor day, 12:00 to 5:00 P.M. Closed Mondays.

**Directions**: From Weston, take Rt. 19 north about 2 miles and turn left onto Jackson Mill Rd. Follow signs to Jackson Mill 4-H Conference Center. For further information call (304)269-5100 or write Jackson's Mill Historic Area, PO Box 670, Weston, WV 26452.

## Stonewall Jackson State Park and Dam

One of the newest parks in the state system, with 3,800 acres, Stonewall Jackson is very popular, primarily for its boating and

*Year-round, fishermen and boaters explore the 82 miles of shoreline around Stonewall Jackson Lake in one of the newest state parks.*  <small>COURTESY U.S. CORPS OF ENGINEERS</small>

fishing opportunities. One of the largest in West Virginia and the result of damming West Fork River under the supervision of the U.S. Corps of Engineers, the manmade lake has 82 miles of shoreline extending 26 miles into the surrounding hills: 2,650 surface acres of water in all. Unlike other dammed lakes, this one isn't drawn down and is accessible for boating year-round. A modern marina provides docking for boaters and slips for 374 boats. A sternwheeler also docks here that takes visitors out on excursions and dinner cruises. Anglers come for the bass, crappie, bluegill, catfish and walleye.

Resort facilities are still being developed but a golf course, cabins and lodge are scheduled for completion during the next few years. There are 34 camping sites on or near the water. You should start your visit at the Corps visitor center in the administration building where displays and artifacts explain the building of the dam. In season, tours of the dam and its inside operations are conducted, and plans are for a video presentation on various aspects of the dam. There is a state park visitor center as well (near the marina) where the ranger will give you information on hunting, fishing and wildlife. On the nature trails and water, bird watchers may see various songbirds, redtail hawks, eagles and osprey that are attracted by the lake's abundant fish-life.

**Admission**: Stonewall Jackson is the only state park charging admission: $1.00 per vehicle.

**Hours**: Visitor center at the dam site open every day from 8:00 A.M. to 4:00 P.M. all year. Group tours are given on request by calling (304)269-4588 and on Sundays from 1:00 to 4:00 P.M. from Memorial Day to Labor Day. Campgrounds are closed from December 15 to April 1. The park's visitor center is open Monday through Friday 8:00 A.M. to 4:00 P.M. For more information call 1(800)CALL-WVA or (304)269-0523.

**Directions**: About 13 miles south of Weston. From I-79 take Exit 91 (Roanoke) then follow Rt. 9 south for 2½ miles to park entrance. For dam site, take Exit 96, turn left and go ½ mile to visitor center. For more information write Stonewall Jackson Lake, Rt. 3, Box 370, Brownsville Rd., Weston, WV 26452. For tape on recreation information call (304)269-7463.

Summer berry pickers and honey gatherers must share nature's bounty with black bear, West Virginia's official state animal.

STEPHEN J. SHALUTA, JR.

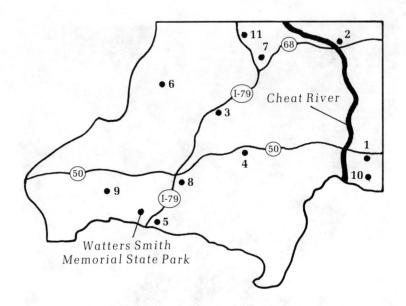

## MOUNTAINEER COUNTRY

1. **Aurora**
   Cathedral State Park

2. **Bruceton Mills**
   Coopers Rock State Park

3. **Fairmont**
   Marion County Historical Society Museum
   Pricketts Fort State Park

4. **Grafton**
   International Mother's Day Shrine
   Tygart Lake State Park and Dam

5. **Lost Creek**

6. **Mannington**
   Mannington Round Barn and West Augusta
      Historical Society Museum

7. **Morgantown**
   West Virginia University

8. **Quiet Dell**
   West Virginia Mountain Products Co-op

9. **Salem**
   Fort New Salem

10. **Silver Lake**
    Our Lady of the Pines

11. **Star City**

# ═Mountaineer Country═

Taking its name from the WVU's famed football team, Mountaineer Country is an exciting blend of the sophisticated and the simple, of bustling urban areas and pristine parks and forests.

Dynamic Morgantown, with its university, theaters, museums and vibrant student population, dominates the intellectual life of the region, and no where else in the state is the spirited pride of being a West Virginian expressed more passionately than at Mountaineers Field on a fall Saturday afternoon. Those seeking a quieter escape—history buffs, sportsmen and nature lovers—find plenty of attractions within a short drive of the city. Two reconstructed forts, through their superb living-history demonstrations, carry the day-tripper back to the settlements of 18th- and 19th-century Virginia frontier. The gorgeous Cheat and Tygart rivers, perfect in places for white-water rafting, are both dammed, in part for lake recreation. Fishing, water skiing, swimming and boating options make these waters favorite destinations for family outings. Of particular appeal to families is the site designated as the first place Mother's Day was celebrated.

For a view of what the natural past was like, spend an hour or so in Cathedral State Park, a forest of virgin hemlock reaching heavenward, one of the few to survive the great logging era. Nearby, the tiny Our Lady of the Pines is a unique, and complementary, spiritual experience.

Thirsty after a day's fishing? Stop at a local winery and pick up a dry white to go with your trout or a hearty red to do justice to that famous Italian pasta made in Clarksburg. Whatever you choose to put on your plate, or itinerary, from Mountaineer Country is sure to satisfy an appetite for good living.

For more information on visiting Mountaineer Country contact:

Northern West Virginia Convention and Visitors Bureau, 709 Beechurst Ave., Morgantown, WV 26505, phone 1(800)458-7373 or (304)292-5081.

Barbour County Convention and Visitors Bureau, Rt. 2, Box 205, Philippi, WV 26416, phone (304)457-4956.

Bridgeport–Clarksburg Convention and Visitors Bureau, 132 W. Main St., Bridgeport, WV 26330, phone 1(800)368-4324 or (304)842-7272.

Grafton–Taylor Co. Convention and Visitors Bureau, 220 W. Main St., Grafton, WV 26354, phone (304)265-3938.

Marion County Convention and Visitors Bureau, PO Box 1258, Fairmont, WV 26554, phone 1(800)834-7365 or (304)363-7037.

Preston County Convention and Visitors Bureau, 200 1/2 W. Main Street, Kingwood, WV 26537, phone (304)329-0576.

# Aurora
## Cathedral State Park

At Cathedral State Park diffused light filtering through spreading branches recalls the stained-glass windows of Chartes or Notre Dame. Like the vaulted arches of Romanesque masterpieces, majestic limbs span vast space and join to form lacy patterns. Dignified as church columns, even fallen trunks, left untouched to complete nature's course, seem to bring a spiritual message: the inevitability of life's circle and a promise of rebirth. In the hushed stillness one waits in awe, like a privileged guest invited to witness a miracle.

This 133-acre sanctuary holds the only stand of mixed virgin timber left in the state, but its crowning glory is the spectacular hemlock, inviolate and pure. Many of these giants are several hundred years old, predating the earliest European explorers. One specimen called the **Centennial** is considered the largest of its kind east of the Mississippi, with a circumference of 21 feet, a height of 121 feet, and a spread of 68 feet. Some estimates place this ancient evergreen at older than 500 years.

Seven miles of trails lead over bridges and brooks, around and through clusters of hemlock rising 90 feet high. Some primordial instinct draws the eye up, way up, to seize the ceiling of needled limbs, reaching, touching, embracing in a mosaic of shadow and light, mysterious and mystic. The forest floor is so shaded by the canopy of branches that little ground cover grows. Mosses, ferns and wildflowers compete with the multi-colored mushrooms and fungi rooting on rotten stumps. Because this is not the vegetation animals usually feed on, the silence is seldom broken by bird song or the snap of browsing deer.

Reaching for the sun among their venerable peers are yellow birch, red oak, black cherry, maple, chestnut, beech and other hardwoods, stately and gracious in their own right.

These woods were saved during the years of heaviest logging by being on private property (the centerpiece of Brookside Inn and Resort). Later the property was sold to the state for a park with the proviso that it "never be touched with ax or saw." In 1966 the park entered the National Registry for Natural History

Landmarks as an "area that possesses exceptional value in illustrating the natural history of the United States."

Leaving the ancient forest primeval, one is grateful for this rare chance to see how much of North America looked before Columbus, yet is moved by the sense of an irreparable loss.

**Restrictions**: Absolutely no camping, hunting or fishing.

**Tip**: Be prepared to unwind, absorb, reflect and walk the trails at a leisurely pace. Free trail maps available in the parking area. If you want to increase the experience of solitude in the woods, consider visiting in the snow.

**Directions**: From Grafton take Rt. 50 east about 25 miles to Aurora. The park is about a mile east of Aurora, within a few miles of the Maryland State line.

**Hours**: 6:00 A.M. to 10:00 P.M. every day of the year. Restrooms are closed from the first frost to April 1. The resident caretaker gives a guided tour every Wednesday at 1:00 P.M. Memorial Day to Labor Day. To arrange special tours at other times, call (304)735-3771 or write Caretaker, Cathedral State Park, Rt. 1, Box 370, Aurora, WV 26705.

# Bruceton Mills

## *Coopers Rock State Forest*

The view from the overlook at Coopers Rock State Forest—of the Cheat Lake and River 1,200 feet below and the forests spreading into Pennsylvania and Maryland—is one of the most breathtaking in the state. More than 400,000 people a year walk out on the sandstone overhang to absorb the beauty of river, gorge, sky and mountain. The gorge is lined with cliffs and massive boulders that add their statement of beauty and power, tempting rock climbers and enchanting hikers who follow miles of trails through forest valleys and ridges. Most beautiful in early summer when the rhododendron flower, the trails are also appealing in winter for cross country skiing. Anytime of year, visitors will spot wildlife: songbirds, fox, deer, raccoon, chipmunks, squirrels, hawks, wild turkeys, and even an occasional bobcat weighing up to 30 pounds. Be cautioned that rattlesnakes like rocky areas and are not uncommon here in summer months.

Several trails in the forest pass by the **Henry Clay Iron Furnace,** which in the early 1800s supported a community of more than 1,000 people. This area along the Cheat was once one of the major iron centers in the country (1798–1862), due to the availability of iron ore, limestone, hardwood trees for an energy source, and the proximity to a transportation route, via the river. Another industry, timber, was prominent during the early 20th century, and by the time the land was purchased for a state forest (1936) most of the woods had been logged and burned. During the Depression the CCC (Civilian Conservation Corps) put up numerous rustic structures, some of which still stand and are on the National Register of Historic Places. One of these is the large stone and wood picnic shelter near the overlook. Coopers Rock was named for a man who hid from the law in these woods and made a living by selling his barrels to locals, thus "coopers" rock.

This, the largest of the state forests, encompasses nearly 13,000 acres, land now recovered from industry with lovely second-growth woods. Criss-crossing its boundaries are creeks and fishing spots. Glade Run is stocked with trout weighing up to four pounds. Campgrounds are available in several areas, but day trippers will come for the view, a picnic, and a hike on some of the 50 miles of trails. Three of the most popular are: The Virgin Hemlock Trail (2.4 miles round-trip) to a hemlock grove over 300 years old; Raven Rock Trail, (4 miles round-trip) which ends at an overlook with a spectacular view of the river; and Rock City Trail (2 miles round-trip), a flat and easy walk.

**Tip**: Hunting is allowed, so wear bright-colored clothing (preferably orange) during the season (October through February). Concession stand on grounds.

**Hours**: Trails are open during daylight hours all year. The campgrounds and roads (except for cross country skiing) are closed from the first Sunday in December to April 1.

**Restrictions**: No rock climbing allowed on the scenic vistas, including the overlook.

**Directions**: From Morgantown take I-68 east about 10 miles to Exit 15. For more information call (304)594-1561 or write Coopers Rock State Forest, Route 1, Box 270, Bruceton Mills, WV 26525.

# Fairmont

## Marion County Historical Society Museum

Built in 1911 as the sheriff's residence, this sandstone house is conveniently tucked between the court house and the jail. The sheriff could check on his incarcerated charges without going outside by just walking through the runway from the second floor to the jail, which, as you'll see from its barred windows, still securely holds law offenders. A gift to the Marion County Historical Society from the county commissioners, the house offers three floors of donated memorabilia and antiques, arranged for the most part around the life and times during different wars in U.S history.

If you want to see the rooms in their chronological order, start on the third level with the Colonial Room. Here artifacts recall the bloody years of nearby Pricketts Fort and the French and Indian Wars. Cabin furnishings such as the pewter dishes, pine furniture and hand-loomed bed coverings reflect the simple life of early settlers. Styles during and after the Revolutionary War are pictured in the Constitution Room and the Philadelphia Parlor where tea is about to be poured. The delightful Children's Room is filled with period toys, miniature dolls, colorful blankets (probably made by a loving granny) and pets. The happy scene is truly a tribute to the joys and innocence of childhood.

On the second floor, the rooms representing the Civil War, span the years 1820–90, also a period of revolutionary inventions that changed the world: the telephone, telegraph, electric lights, the reaper, sewing machine and railroad. The latter is commemorated in the fascinating models set up in the Train Room.

The wealth, verve and exhilaration of the early part of the 20th century are depicted in the Twenties Room. (As the result of the coal boom and related industries, Fairmont, in 1920, was rated as having more millionaires per capita than any town in the country.) The liberation of women from traditional stereotypes is suggested by the flapper dress, the satin robe flung with abandon on the bed, and the motorized sewing machine under its carved cabinet. The dining room downstairs represents the years leading to WWI: a time of prosperity, large dining tables and multi-course meals.

As you enter (or leave) the museum, note the framed headline from the *New York Herald*, April 15, 1865, announcing the death of President Lincoln and the search for his assassin, John Wilkes Booth. From war weapons to ladies' fashions and Victorian toys, this is a museum the entire family can enjoy together.

**Tip**: Take a good look at the impressive white dome of the court house next door. The neo-classical details, pediments and four clocks are topped by the figure of blind Justice holding up scales.

**Admission** : Free but donations appreciated.

**Hours**: 11:00 A.M. to 2:00 P.M., Monday through Friday, and Saturday 10:00 A.M. to NOON.

**Directions**: From I-79 south take Exit 37 (Downtown), bear left at McDonalds onto Rt. 310, go through three lights and turn right over the old bridge, then left onto Adams St. The court house sits on the corner and the museum is next door.

## Pricketts Fort State Park

"Living in old times was hard. Women and children cried a great deal and the men and boys cussed a lot. And everybody prayed enough, in church, in the fields, in the woods, wherever and

*Living history interpreters at Pricketts Fort State Park demonstrate weaving, gunmaking and other 18th-century skills.*

*when ever they had the feeling for it. . . . We put up with a lot of trouble but we stayed brave, and God was by us every minute. . . .*" Keziah Batten Shearer (1776-1872)

These poignant words express the confidence early settlers had in their beliefs and their need for constant divine protection. Displayed in an exhibit in the **Pricketts Fort Visitors Center,** this excerpt sets the scene for a most convincing living-history presentation. Here begins your journey to the days of refuge forts, Indian attacks and life on the frontier of Colonial Virginia. Park at the Visitors Center where you'll need to buy tickets to the fort (reconstructed in 1976) and Job Prickett House. In the exhibit area a review of maps, 18th- and 19th-century artifacts and weapons gives you a good general sense of those perilous days when the first Europeans came to stay.

Arriving before 1759, Jacob Prickett, Sr., his wife and family of ten children were among the earliest settlers to this part of western Virginia—a mountainous land of huge hardwood trees, rivers, rich soil and abundant wildlife including bison, fish and fowl. Despite their initial tolerance of the intruders, the Indians saw increasing numbers of foul-smelling white foreigners burn forests and kill some wildlife to the point of extinction. They declared war on the White Man in 1774. For their own protection the settlers built a refuge fort to which they could flee when their homes were under siege or when they were caught in the fields unprepared. During these devastating, unpredictable assaults Indians destroyed everything they could, carrying off only blankets and horses. For 20 of the 25 years it stood (1774–99), the fort was in continuous use, harboring the lucky ones who had time to grab children and whatever essentials they could. Between 80 to 100 families (due to the large family size, about 1,000 people) waited out a reign of terror that could last from a few hours to as long as seven weeks.

The fort was built on Prickett's land because it offered a high vantage point for defense and was near a creek and a major transportation route. (The nearby Monongahela River connected to the Ohio and Mississippi.) Originally, a 150-yard stockade fence was in place to discourage Indians from attacking the fort itself.

From early spring through late fall, Indians attacked homes and individuals at any time with no warning. Jacob Prickett's 16-year-old son, Isaiah, was murdered and scalped within sight of the fort, his companion, Susan Ox, abducted and never found. As you will learn from the costumed interpreters, scalping was not a Native American practice but a bounty ritual the Indians learned from French trappers. Victims of this mutilation did not necessarily die, but the wound—around the hairline to the bone—took about two years to heal over. Hair did not grow back.

In the **Meeting House** at the large fireplace you may watch preparation of simple meals. The interpreters stress the isolation of settlers and their need for self-sufficiency. You may see a weaver demonstrate the old looms and tell how flax, the common man's cotton, was grown and turned into clothing. Thread and buttons had to be made as well as the cloth. A simple petticoat represented two years of processing, spinning and weaving.

As you investigate the fort, you will probably hear a blacksmith pounding out his ware. During the summer months, he is one of the 18th-century specialists who demonstrate period skills. Another is the gunsmith. His public demonstration of 18th-century firearm manufacture is unique in the state.

It is interesting to compare the spartan starkness of the fort to the comparative luxury of the **Job Prickett House,** just a few yards away. Job Prickett, Jacob's great grandson, built this handsome two-story home with bricks handmade on site, just 60 years after the fort was dismantled. The glass windows, high ceilings, well equipped kitchen, built-in cupboards and Victorian furnishings represent how quickly "civilization" accelerated in this area. This is a warm, spacious, affluent home in which 18 children were raised. Although it took about three hours to cook a meal over the fire, this generation of Pricketts lived in a style their grandfather could not have imagined, free from the daily fear of the tomahawk.

During the year, the fort sponsors several special events. Spring offerings include a music weekend with dulcimers, banjos and fiddles playing traditional Appalachian music. In summer, encampment demonstrations show various lifestyles and cultures of eastern settlers between 1700–1799. In fall, the smell of cider and fresh apples herald the annual Apple Butter Weekend, and in December, an 18th Century Christmas Market is an opportunity to admire and purchase a variety of crafts and gifts by candlelight. Hot wassail and cookies are served and period entertainments shared.

**Tip**: Allow a minimum of two hours here. The setting along the water is lovely, a good picnic spot. The Museum Shop at the Visitor Center has a variety of unusual, high quality handmade toys, musical instruments, candles, cards, crafts and other gift items:good stocking stuffers for Christmas.

**Hours**: Mid-April to the end of October, Monday through Saturday 10:00 A.M. to 5:00 P.M. and Sunday 12:00 to 5:00 P.M. Special tours can be arranged in advance.

**Admission**: Adults $4.00, seniors $3.50, children 6–12 $2.50, children under 6 free. Last admission ticket sold at 4:30 P.M.

**Directions**: From I-79 take Exit 139, north of Fairmont. Then follow signs to fort, about two miles. Watch out for the narrow bridge that accommodates only one car at a time. For more information call 1(800)CALL-WVA or (304)363-3030 or write Pricketts Fort Memorial Foundation, Rt. 3, Fairmont, WV 26554.

# Grafton
## *International Mother's Day Shrine*

*"I believe there never was a man both good and great. . . that did not owe it to his mother."* Alexander Campbell

Did you ever wonder how and when our celebration of Mother's Day began? Although we take this holiday for granted as having always been on our calendar, we have only been celebrating an official day for mothers since 1908. It was the second Sunday in May of that year that the first Mother's Day service was held in **Andrews Methodist Episcopal Church** in Grafton, WV, the brainchild of Anna M. Jarvis.

Born in 1864—one of twelve children—Anna Jarvis was a teacher in Grafton public schools for a number of years. Her mother, Anna Reeves Jarvis, was a community activist who organized women's groups to improve sanitation and health conditions and to care for injured soldiers from both sides of the

Civil War. On the second anniversary of her mother's death, the second Sunday in May 1907, Anna Jarvis held a small private service honoring her mother with friends and announced her intentions of promoting a national Mother's Day. Through her efforts, the first Mother's Day service was held on May 10, 1908, in the same church where her mother had taught Sunday School for 20 years.

The sermon to a congregation of 407 included Christ's words from the Cross to Mary, "Woman, behold thy son" and to John, his beloved disciple, "Behold, thy Mother." Miss Jarvis sent 500 white carnations to be given to each son, daughter and mother attending. In 1914, President Wilson approved a congressional resolution proclaiming the second Sunday in May (the anniversary of Anna Reeves Jarvis's death) as Mother's Day. His proclamation ordered the flag to be displayed on all government buildings. Within a short time the day was adopted internationally and is now celebrated all over the world. According to Hallmark, more cards are sold for Mother's Day than for any holiday except Christmas.

Historic Andrews Church became the International Mother's Day Shrine when it was incorporated on May 15, 1962. Built in 1873, the church is a handsome two-story brick building right on Main Street. Guided tours are available for drop-ins, but large groups should call ahead to secure a guide. Of particular note upstairs are paintings by a local artist, the original handsome wooden pews and altar and stained-glass windows. On the entrance level, look for the photographs of both Annas—elegant, striking ladies—and the miniature doll replica of Anna Jarvis. On the wall hangs this quaint poem written by an appreciative offspring:

Whose love can equal the love of a Mother;
Whose the devotion so loyal and true!
Who suffers so much with such joy for another,
Who works with such pleasure as Mother for you!
You hail with delight the friendship of others,
You revel in love of the sweetheart you've won,
Yet, where do you find a friendship like Mother's,
Unbroken 'til death calls, and life's work is done.

**Tip**: Parking is limited on Main Street. There is ample space in back of the church.

Four miles south of Grafton on Rt. 119 you pass through the town of Webster. Look for the birthplace of Anna Jarvis, a two-story white wooden house that is being restored by the DAR.

**Admission**: Free but donations appreciated. Open April 15 to October 31, Monday through Friday 9:30 A.M. to 3:30 P.M. A special Mother's Day service is held each year at 2:30 P.M. For group tours phone (304)265-1589 or 1177.

**Directions**: 11 E. Main Street, Grafton, one mile south of the junction of US Rts. 50 and 119. Mailing address: PO Box 457, Grafton, WV 26354.

## Tygart Lake State Park and Dam

If you want to rough it here, you can find campgrounds, but this park is really a luxury locale, offering resort-quality overnight accommodations at the wood paneled lodge or at one of the fully-equipped modern cabins. The lodge sits on a landscaped hill with a spectacular spanning view of gorgeous deep-blue **Tygart Lake**. A steep, wooded shoreline rings its 13 miles of liquid sapphire like a crown. If you prefer to stay dry, it is almost as much fun watching the action on the water and at the marina from the dining room window as it is to be out there yourself.

Particularly clean and warm, the lakes attracts scuba divers as well as fishermen, swimmers, boaters and water skiers. For small children a beach offers calm waters and the security of lifeguards. The water quality is so high that stocking is not necessary to maintain the fish population. Anglers come for the muskie, crappie, perch, walleye and some of the best bass fishing in the state. Those seeking quiet waters explore the backwater inlets in canoes. Trails around the shoreline and through the park draw hikers and naturalists. Volleyball and horseshoe courts, a nearby championship golf course, picnic tables, playgrounds, launching areas—there is something here for nearly everyone. Pick up a map and brochures at the park office at the third picnic area (in summer) or at the lodge (in winter).

During the summer season, the park naturalist schedules movies and slide programs, bird walks, fishing rodeos, guided hikes and other nature programs.

**Hours**: Mid-April to October 31, 8:30 A.M. to 10:00 P.M. seven days a week. Winter hours are 8:30 A.M. to 4:30 P.M. Monday through Friday. All facilities except the office at the lodge are closed November 1 to mid-April, but the park is open daily from dawn to dusk.

**Directions**: Take north/south US 119 or east/west US 50 to Grafton and follow signs to the park entrance, about 4 miles. For lodge reservations call (303)265-2320, for cabins, (304)265-3383 or write Rt. 1, Box 260, Grafton, WV 26354. For additional park information call 1(800)CALL-WVA.

Before settling down to park athletics, orient yourself to the how and why of wondrous **Tygart Dam** by stopping at the U.S. Army Corps of Engineers visitor information center, near the dam site. Like Burnsville and Stonewall Jackson lakes, Tygart Lake is a Corps project. Completed in 1938, the lake is the result of damming this part of Tygart River for flood control, low flow augmentation and water supply purposes. A serendipitous bonus, of course, is a recreation area of unusual beauty. A ten-minute video explains the history and construction of the dam. If you can plan to be here on a summer Wednesday, you'll get a first-class tour by the Corps park ranger of the dam itself, inside and under the works. At any time during park hours, you can stroll out onto the walkway and get a feeling of the enormous power operating around you, the lake on one side and the rushing waters (a minimum of 240 million gallons per day) flowing back into the Tygart River on the other. Nearly 2,000 feet long and 230 feet high, the dam is one of the oldest and largest concrete dams east of the Mississippi. Before leaving the information center, look at the fish tanks holding representative specimens that live in the lake. Then rent a boat or launch your own, picnic, hike, explore or just go jump in the lake!

**Hours**: Information center open 7:30 A.M. to 4:00 P.M. every day of the year; tours of the dam every Wednesday at 12:45 P.M. during June, July and August; hours may vary from year to year, so call to verify (304)265-1760). For more information, write Area Resource Manager, Tygart Lake, Rt. 1, Box 257, Grafton, WV 26354.

# Lost Creek
## *Watters Smith Memorial State Park*

This 532-acre park is worth visiting on a hot summer's day because you can combine an educational excursion to an historical site with a refreshing swim in the pool and a relaxing picnic. The buildings in the historic area honor Watters Smith and his descendants, who worked the surrounding farm for four generations, spanning the years from 1796 to the early 1900s.

The simple, weathered hand-hewn structures underscore the rigors of the early settlers' lives. A small log cabin represents the first dwelling, and the Smith Residence, built in 1876, now furnished with period antiques, stands as a typical example of a 19th-century farmhouse, with rambling additions tacked on as family and fortune grew. Before exploring, stop at the visitor center, a museum displaying old farm, household equipment and period pieces such as a bull fiddle used as a noisemaker to serenade newlyweds. Pick up a brochure explaining the self-guided tour of the grounds: a barn, hog pen, mill room, corn crib, smokehouse, blacksmith and woodworking shops. In season docents in both the museum and Smith Residence explain the history of the site and the occasional hearthside cooking and craft demonstrations. Nearby picnic shelters have play equipment and are popular for family reunions.

**Admission**: Donations welcome. Rental fee for picnic shelters.

**Hours**: The swimming pool is open and docent tours conducted from 11:00 A.M. to 7:00 P.M. every day of the week from Memorial Day weekend to Labor Day. Tours other times by reservation.

**Directions**: From I-79 south from Clarksburg take Exit 110 bearing right to Lost Creek. Follow signs to park, about 7 miles.

# Mannington

## *Mannington Round Barn and West Augusta Historical Society Museum*

Round barns, not uncommon in Pennsylvania-Dutch country but rare in West Virginia, are interesting structures and challenging to build. This one (now owned, along with the school museum, by the West Augusta Historical Society) is the only restored round barn in the state. Each roof shingle had to be hand tailored to accommodate the curves and slope of the graduated covering. The cupola, intended as a vent for stored hay, adds an aesthetically graceful, finishing touch and a marvelous 360-degree view of the surrounding countryside.

In addition to sheltering cows and storing feed, this 1912 barn was also the farmer's home and the center of a 400-acre farm. Your tour will probably start in the kitchen where photos show the original builder, Amos C. Hamilton, and his family. Strong characters they were, especially his grandmother, who peers boldly from her frame while inhaling her snuff. The floor and roof are original, as are the rib-like rafters, which heighten the effect of being inside a whale. Three levels of artifacts and equipment chronicle early 20th-century farm life: harnesses, buckets, curry combs, a surrey, a wooden mouse trap, a bee smoker, fruit dryers, butter churns, water separators, milk coolers, lard presses, copper clothes boilers, horse memorabilia, corn shellers, an enormous horse-drawn potato picker, and an 1891 fire truck. Children are particularly fascinated with the wooden homemade bobsled that could carry at least a dozen people, a life-size fiberglass horse in his stall and the broom machine.

Benjamin Franklin is said to be the founder of the broom industry in this country. He learned to grow seeds from English broom corn and cultivate the crop for domestic use, thus making a clean sweep of British imports.

You'll learn about the ingenious spring-fed watering system, which the cows learned to turn on and off and the natural gas deposits on the property that heated the barn.

The 1912 Round Barn in Mannington now houses antique farm equipment and artifacts instead of cows. STEPHEN J. SHALUTA, JR.

After the kids have a chance to explore the nooks (no crannies here), take them to the **West Augusta Historical Society Museum** downtown, a school they will not mind attending. If you are "of a certain age," you may feel a pang of nostalgia when you enter this 1912 brick school, now a museum. The wide wooden stairs have not groaned under the tread of Buster Brown shoes for many years, but you can almost hear the bell ringing, doors banging open and the giggles and shouts of kids on their way to recess. Photos of past students, some from the earliest years here, old-fashioned desks and Prom Night decorations keep the feeling of the building's original purpose. But it's the "little bit of every-thing," donated to the historical society and displayed in the spacious, bright classrooms and corridors, that fascinate: a surrey that converts into a sleigh, antique musical instruments and an 1886 Swiss music box that plays out a waltz with the clarity of a live performance, land deeds from 1790, a treasure chest of Indian flints, a priceless tin handpainted portable pantry that was carried on wagon trains, an elegant hand pumper (the fore-runner of the vacuum cleaner) and a working model of an oil well. It's difficult to choose a favorite among these one-of-a-kinds, but don't miss these: the brass ox horn covers, samples of paper money (1770s and earlier) issued by the colonies before independence (one wonders why the denominations were $7½ and $9) and a foot-operated chair-saw that afforded aerobic exercise while preparing fuel for the fire.

Children particularly enjoy reading the rules for teachers' conduct (for a change) prescribed by the 1912 school board. "You will not marry during the school term; you will not wear a dress shorter than two inches above the ankle; you must wear at least two petticoats; you may not loiter downtown in the ice cream store. . .or keep company with men; you may not smoke cigarettes. . .or dress in bright colors."

In the school yard a colorful 1912 caboose housing a miniature railroad museum and a tiny log cabin, built in 1870 and open for visitors, top off a most unusual playground.

**Admission**: Separate requested donation for each site: adults $2.00, children 4 to 12, $.50.

**Hours**: Open Sunday, May through September 1:30 to 4:00 P.M. or anytime for a group of six or more by special appointment. Call (304)986-2636 or 986-1089 or write West Augusta Historical Society, PO Box 414, Mannington, WV 26595.

**Directions**: To the barn, take Rt. 250 North from Fairmont about 12 miles. Just before entering Mannington, take a left (past shopping mall) onto Flaggy Meadow Rd. and follow signs. To the museum, continue into Mannington on Rt. 250; the brick school is on your right.

# Morgantown

The Indians greeted the first European settler to this wooded, scenic area on the Monagahela River by murdering him. Ten years later, in 1768, Zackquill Morgan had better luck and settled a permanent community. By the end of the 18th century the town was an industrial center with a mill, tanneries, stores, churches, a wagon factory and boat yard. For most of the 19th century, Morgantown grew slowly, prospering as a typical American riverside town, with small businesses clustered among private homes in or near the main street (High Street). With the coming of the railroad and the oil and gas industries, the town awakened to an economic boom in the 1890s, a decade that saw its population double. As residential areas spread to new suburbs, downtown Morgantown became increasingly commercial.

A single architect, Elmer F. Jacobs, gets credit for giving the city a complete facelift to fit its new role as an industrial, prosperous center. He designed over 400 structures, replacing the simple homes of quieter days with imposing Romanesque and Queen Anne revival-style banks, post offices and office buildings. Many of these, some on the National Register of Historic Places, are on High Street, which still retains a sprinkling of modest Victorian homes—an eclectic mix. Day trippers interested in history and architecture should follow the walking tour brochure of historic downtown Morgantown, free from the Northern West Virgina Convention and Visitors Bureau.

Today, downtown buzzes with another kind of industry: youth. It's the vibrancy of college students, roughly a third of the city's population, that the visitor feels on the streets, in shops and restaurants. And no day tripper should come without visiting at least one of the three university campuses. Before exploring academia, pick up all the information you will need at the Northern West Virginia Convention and Visitors Bureau, one of the best run and equipped visitor centers in the state. You'll want to see the building that houses the Bureau in any case, the **Seneca Center**, a clever, stunning renovation of a turn-of-the-century glass factory. Handsomely renovated to accommodate up-scale shops, the 1898 brick building reflects its original purpose in the red water tower and 100-foot glass furnace chimney. In the entrance level, a gallery-like display of how glass was made here warms up the open spaces with sophisticated flair. Fine examples of colorful glassware—one pattern made here was chosen by Jacqueline Kennedy for the White House–highlight the small exhibit of tools, photos, and explanatory murals.

**Hours**: Seneca Center: Monday through Friday 8:30 A.M. to 6:00 P.M., Saturday 10:00 A.M. to 5:00 P.M. Convention and Visitors Bureau (on second level of Seneca Center): Monday through Friday 8:30 A.M. to 5:00 P.M. Call 1(800)458-7373.

**Directions**: From I-79, take exit 155 (Star City) and go 2 1/2 miles on Route 19 South (turns into Beechurst Ave.) From I-68, take Exit 1 (S. University Ave.) and go 4 miles on Routes 119 and 19 North. Seneca Center is at 709 Beechurst Avenue, Morgantown, WV 26505. For more information on center call 304-291-3181. Visitors Bureau: 1-800-458-7373.

## West Virginia University

If Morgantown can be called the heart of Mountaineer Country, then the 22,000-student West Virginia University is the beat–the dynamic that propels the life pulse in and around the city. Whether you're looking for theatrical performances, rock concerts, art exhibits, sport events, museums, academics or just a ride on one the most exciting and efficient public transportation systems in the world today—you'll find it somewhere on campus.

By far the largest university in the state, WVU spawns a particularly spirited and loyal student body whose fidelity to their alma mater endures long after graduation, as evident in the large number of gray-haired fans who pack the 65,000-seat stadium to cheer the Mountaineers' nationally ranked football team. Adding to the fall pageantry is the famous "Pride of West Virginia" marching band that struts its blue and gold during half time—a marvelous show. As some indication of the crowd attendance, note that with the exception of those in China and Russia, the McDonalds near the stadium on a home game Saturday is the busiest McDonalds in the world! So remember, a Saturday in autumn is not a good time to visit Morgantown unless you are going to the game.

### *The University Tour*

The best way to get an overview of all the facilities of the three sprawling but easily accessible campuses is by taking the bus/walking tour offered by the **University Visitors Center.** The tour of all three campuses—Downtown, Health Science and Evansdale–lasts about two hours, starting at the center with a 15-minute movie orientation that tells about the 175 different degree programs offered by 15 colleges and about the social and academic campus routines. You then board the bus for an enthusiastically student-led tour that passes important buildings on the Evansdale and Health Science campuses before going downtown. In addition to the impressive football stadium and Mountaineer Field, highlights are:

The Coliseum that seats 14,000 for track, swimming, basketball and other sport events as well as concerts.

The Creative Arts Center with rotating art exhibits and the Lakeview Theater that stages hundreds of performances a year ranging from Shakespeare to opera. For a more in-depth tour arrange an appointment by calling (304)293-4841.

The Core Arboretum where seven trails lead through a habitat of West Virginia trees, flowers and plants. You're welcome to return and hike at leisure. For more information call the Biology Department (304)293-5201.

The bus then takes you to the downtown campus, the hub of which is the **Mountainlair**, ranked among the top student unions in the country. Every day thousands of students pass through to take advantage of the concerts, lecture series, dinner theater, art exhibits, the recreation center and a food court that is the envy of mall-hoppers. Near the union are the three handsome brick and stone buildings, one with a double clock tower, that form the core of the original school, the **Woodburn Circle** dating from 1909. From this bus tour you'll know which buildings hold particular interest and where you can get tickets to on-going activities. Two small museums on the Evansdale campus are well worth calling about because you need to make arrangements in advance: Cook-Hayman and COMER museums (see entries).

110

**Tip**: When you're ready for lunch, try this campus favorite found on most menus: "Fries and Blue," French fries with bleu cheese dressing. Delicious.

**Admission**: The bus tour is free, but you must make reservations.

**Hours**: The Visitors Center is open Monday through Friday, 9:00 A.M. to 6:00 P.M., Saturday 9:00 A.M. to 4:00 P.M. and Sunday 12:00 to 4:00 P.M. Tours are at 11:00 A.M. and 2:30 P.M. Monday through Friday and Saturday at 10:00 A.M. Call 1(800)344-WVU1 or (304)293-3489 to arrange a tour. To learn of WVU activities and events open to the public call (304)293-6692 (24 hour service).

**Directions**: From I-79 take Star City (Exit 155) follow campus signs, going about 1 mile (past Holiday Inn). Stay in left lane and turn left onto Patteson Dr. The Visitors Center is about 200 yards on the right in a low grey building at 120 Patteson. For further information write the WVU Evansdale Campus Visitor Center, 120 Communications Building, P.O. Box 6690, Morgantown 26506-6690.

## Personal Rapid Transit (PRT)

On your bus tour around town, you will notice little white cars resembling amusement park rides traveling on their own tracks (or guideways), discharging passengers at several locations. These mini-cars are part of the most modern transit system in the world, one that connects the university campuses quickly, safely, comfortably and, for students, free of charge. Holding a maximum of 15 people at a time (eight seated and 12 standing), the computerized vehicles whiz passengers to class at a top speed of 30 miles per hour. Because the availability of cars is timed to handle class schedules and peak hours, there is always a car available in less than five minutes. When classes are in session, the PRT transports 16,000 riders a day, leaving no student an excuse to be late for class. The longest ride on the five-stop trip (about 3.5 miles) takes only 11½ minutes. With a short wait, the round-trip takes less than 30 minutes. For Morgantown visitors the PRT is bargain entertainment and service at only $.50 a ride. This ingenious system also alleviates parking problems and traffic congestion during rush hours.

Another unique feature is that a passenger can take a car to the desired destination without stopping at any intervening station—thus, the "personal" transit system. The system operates on a flexible schedule determined by the computer coordination of all 73 cars.

This state-of-the-art concept was a joint project co-sponsored by the WV Department of Transportation and the university at a cost of about $120 million. As an experiment it has vastly

The Personal Rapid Transit, one of the most efficient transportation systems in the world, carries 16,000 riders a day to classes on WVU's three campuses. Stacey Vavrek

succeeded in meeting its purpose of moving a large number of people safely and quickly. The vehicles, heated and air-conditioned, are driven by electricity so that a malfunction will close down the entire system, eliminating the chance of collision or derailment. The PRT is justly proud of the fact that since its inception in 1975, over 40 million people have ridden over 11 million miles on the 73 cars without a single accident to date.

The PRT is environmentally sensitive. Because it is electrically run there is no air pollution, and the noise is almost nil because the cars run on rubber-tired wheels. Made of Cor-Ten steel, the guideways rust on the outside, providing a durable protective shield for the interior. Maintenance is therefore minimal. Since the cars are automated, no operators are needed inside, but each station is watched by cameras connected to a central monitoring point, which discourages vandalism and protects waiting passengers from molestation. Freshmen and other newcomers to the system soon learn from a chastising voice, broadcast through nearly invisible speakers, that inappropriate behavior is observed and violators caught.

As a demonstration project, the PRT has served as a model for large cities with major transportation problems and stands as an example of how they may better cope with population and environmental demands in the next century. Don't leave Morgantown without at least one ride on this "funtastic", futuristic flight, a one-of-a kind experience kids of all ages enjoy.

**Tip**: You must have the exact change in quarters.

**Admission**: $.50 each way, $1.00 round-trip. Students ride free with a student card included in tuition costs.

**Hours**: Monday through Friday from 6:30 A.M. to 10:15 P.M., Saturday 9:30 A.M. to 5:00 P.M. Closed Sundays and university holidays and vacations.

**Directions**: Stops are Walnut Street, Beechurst Avenue, Engineering (near Patteson Drive and Monogahela Blvd.), Towers (near Towers Dr. and University Blvd.) and Medical Center (at WVU hospital). For more information write Personal Rapid Transit, 99 8th Street, West Virginia University, PO Box 6565, Morgantown, WV 26506-6565, or call (304)293-5011.

### COMER Museum

Although the College of Mineral and Energy Resources (COMER) had collected for many years memorabilia and artifacts from the coal, oil and gas industries, proper space for display was not available until the college moved into the new COMER building in 1990. Now housed in a 600-square-foot museum, the collection includes mine lamps, hand tools, oil and mineral samples, working models, fossils, miners' caps, reference material and thousands of photographs, some dating from the early 1900s. You'll learn that miners' "scrip" was not legal tender but used to purchase goods from company stores and that canaries were used to test for carbon monoxide in the mines because they were sensitive to the gas and could be revived and used again after collapsing.

In line with its purpose of "preserving the social, cultural and technological history of West Virginia," the museum has hosted an innovative Coal Mining Cultural Heritage Day. Intended to improve the negative image of the coal industry, activities emphasized the culture and heritage of mining communities through dramatic presentations, music and oral and written history. This celebration may be repeated in the future along with other cultural events commemorating these industries that shaped the economic and cultural ethos of the state.

**Tip**: Free samples of bituminous coal available for stuffing Christmas stockings.

**Hours**: Hours vary each semester depending on availability of work-study students, but it's usually open three afternoons a week and on weekends for special occasions. To make arrangements for a tour call (304)293-4211.

**Admission**: Free but donations are welcome.

**Directions**: On the ground floor of the COMER Building (off the Hurst Atrium) on the Evansdale Campus. Parking is available at the Coliseum. A shuttle bus, which stops at the museum, leaves the main gate of the Coliseum every 15 minutes starting on the hour. If you're arriving via the PRT, get off at the Engineering stop. For more information write The COMER Museum, PO Box 6070, Morgantown, WV 26506-6070.

### Cook-Hayman Pharmacy Museum

Doesn't everyone like The Pharmacist? With his generous common sense, free advice and patient, sympathetic ear, it's no surprise that in this age of computer prescriptions, when the human element is often replaced by machines, that the number one profession in the "trust" polls is The Pharmacist. Often it is he (and in increasing numbers, she) who personally dispenses the remedy, communicating contraindications and dosages with parental concern. It is The Pharmacist to whom many, confused by modern terminology, turn for clarification and confidence. To get an understanding of the history of this important vocation and its fascinating evolution in the past 100 years you can do no better than to arrange a visit to the Cook-Hayman Pharmacy Museum in the WVU School of Pharmacy.

This little museum, with its shelves of glass bottles, each labeled with an impossibly unpronounceable Latin name, is more than a replica of a 19th-century pharmacy. It is an adventure into the mysterious world of potions and pills before the days of drug companies when pharmacists made their own mixtures and even molded suppositories by hand. Herbs of all kinds, bark, roots and plants that were ground, moistened and taken internally or applied to wounds directly, are on display in hundreds of intriguing jars. One wonders what purpose they might have served and how the pharmacist could keep their properties and applications straight. Mixing exactly the right ingredients was the challenge of these early wizards, many of whom in emergencies played the role of the doctor, administering directly to the sick. You'll see a 19th-century travel kit for physicians who made house calls on horseback, leaving the patients with little glass vials of curatives. You'll learn that some ingredients, like sweeteners, were added just to make the mixture palatable; others for aesthetic appeal.

Turn-of-the-century mirrors, apothecary cabinets with their stained-glass doors and antique oak furniture recreate the aura of these potent chemists and their inscrutable ministrations. Even the show globes, elegantly-shaped bottles of colored liquid that traditionally symbolized the pharmacy, recall Merlin's magic powers. Books, scales, instruments, a curious prescription filing system that apparently worked, pill molds, porcelain bed pans, thermometers, a stunning collection of pestles and mortars (one dating from 1648), a percolator for extracting juices from plant material—sit among early samples of Pepto Bismol, a tonic for curing grey hair, and a bottle of bright green beetles (Spanish flies) which, as every fan of Victorian romance already knows, were sometimes used as an aphrodisiac, but more often for the raising of very unromantic but therapeutic blisters.

Behind a counter the rows and rows of colored bottles and ceramic jars invite conjecture. Each orange, blue, or green glass was chosen for a good reason. Dark glass controlled the light entering the bottle: exposure to sun could adversely affect the stability of a liquid.

You'll see a display that explains how a chemical extracted from a fungus could be standardized into correct doses by feeding it to a rooster. As the rooster ingested different strengths of the ergot, the color of his comb changed, turning blue when the fowl was overdosed. If the comb became a deep red, the pharmacist knew the mixture was the right strength for humans.

A Charleston poster advertises James H. Rogers, "Druggist and dealer in medicines, chemicals, paints, oils, dyes, window glass, putty and varnishes."

For all the seemingly mysterious procedures involved in 19th-century medicine making, the hand-made excelsiors caused surprisingly few fatalities. Indeed, many of the "recipes" were based on time-tested Indian or folk remedies. Aloe, for instance, has been applied to burns from time immemorial. One exception, however, was the prescribed use of morphine during the Civil War that lead to unrecognized addiction.

The process of filling a prescription has come a long way from those days, yet the friendly, reassuring smile of The Pharmacist continues to allay fears. He still has time to share a joke, as though confirming the well-recognized adage that laughter is still the best medicine of all.

**Admission**: There is a set-up charge for demonstration lectures for large tour groups. Individuals, free.

**Hours**: Open weekdays during school hours. You must call the School of Pharmacy to make arrangements for a tour: (304)293-5101.

**Directions**: The museum is in the Health Sciences Center near the hospital on the Evansdale campus and accessible by PRT. For more information write the Cook-Hayman Pharmacy Museum, WVU School of Pharmacy, WVU Health Sciences Center, PO Box 9520, Morgantown, WV 26506-9520.

## Eastern Roller Mill

In the last century the mill was the economic center of the community in many rural areas, providing bread for the table as well as a place to exchange news and gossip. Today's supermarket has replaced these purposes in part, but who can chat for long in those crowded aisles? And where is the white bread?

The Easton Roller Mill, near the Morgantown airport, is special because it is one of the few remaining steam-driven mills in the Mid-Atlantic and, despite being inoperative since 1930, it remains in excellent condition. Initially operating as a gristmill, it later ground corn, wheat, flax and rye, producing up to 120 ground bushels a day.

Built between 1864-67 of hand-hewn oak timbers, the 3½ story mill boasts a particularly impressive brick chimney, the spine of the structure. For a functional building, the detail and decorative touches are exceptionally fine, testimony to the skill and pride of the craftsmen who worked on it.

Inside you'll see the equipment for two milling techniques: the steam engine, originally generated by coal, and part of the old millstone system and the newer roller mills. The corn sheller and crusher show that the mill was also important for processing animal feed. On the second floor you'll see the large storage bins and sieves. Here grain was purified and dressed to become flour, the whiter and finer the better. Dark flour was not relished, its healthful nutrients unrecognized by 19th-century consumers. On the top floor, note the elevator heads that controlled the transportation of grain through the mill.

Owned by the Monongalia Historical Society, the mill is lovingly cared for by proud members who care about preserving and sharing their heritage, particularly with youngsters who think bread always grew in supermarkets.

**Hours**: Open the first and third Sundays from May 1 to October 30 from 12:30 to 4:30 P.M. School tours by appointment any time of year.

**Admission**: Free but donations appreciated.

**Directions**: From I-68 take Exit 7 towards Morgantown. Go one mile, turn left onto Route 119 South and turn left onto the first blacktop road. The mill stands about ¼ mile on right.

For a special tour call (304)599-0833. For further information write Monongalia Historical Society, PO Box 127, Morgantown, WV 26505.

## Forks of Cheat Winery

West Virginia wine? Why not? And some of it is very good indeed. This small, family-run winery six miles north of Morgantown looks like a page from a guidebook to vineyards of the Pyrenees.

The scenery getting here is dramatically pretty, recalling the mountains of Spain and France and the little inns along the way that cater to the pleasures of the palate. Cows and horses grazing on hillsides along Stewartstown Road add their own touch of Old World ambience.

In operation for only three years, Forks of Cheat has grown from a production of 500 to 2,200 gallons a year, and this from only four acres cultivated with French hybrid and American grapes. Their four white wines range from a fruity Niagara to a dry, crisp Villard. The Delaware blush is light and dry. Most of the reds are from French hybrids: Foch, Leon Millot and Dechaunac.

On the production end, two people run the relatively simple operation of winemaking, an ancient, miraculous process of transforming the juice of a grape into "nectar of the gods." All grapes are picked by hand, then pressed, crushed and left to ferment, with sugar added, in large, air-tight containers. Before being bottled, the wine is filtered about six times. With the proper equipment, two people can bottle and cork about 22 cases of wine an hour.

Your tour will cover the entire process from vine to wine. Leave time for testing and tasting afterwards in the sampling area.

**Tip**: White wine devotees should try the Seyval.

**Hours**: Tours and tasting Monday through Saturday from 10:00 A.M. to 6:00 P.M. and Sunday 1:00 to 6:00 P.M.

**Directions**: From Morgantown take I-68 East to Exit 7 (Pierpont Rd). Turn left onto Route 119 North and go about 3½ miles before turning right onto Stewartstown Road (second paved road on right). Continue 1.9 miles on Stewartstown to winery on your left.

## Morgan Shirt Factory and Outlet

Here's a switch of a stitch. Morgan Shirt Factory actually exports their shirts to markets in the Far East and Asia!

If you've ever complained about the cost of a Brooks Brothers shirt, you need to take a tour of this factory to appreciate the skilled hand work, the time, and precisely coordinated multi-steps performed by a dozen people to make a first-quality long-sleeved dress or sport shirt.

First of all, the patterns are all cut by hand. You'll see the cutters marking out the shirt piece by piece, several at a time, according to the neck and sleeve-length size. Vivid plaids, distinguished stripes, prints, dizzying checks, and classic blue and white broadcloth—all smelling of warm, brand-new freshness—lie in heaps on tables from where, one by one, they are positioned, pinned and snipped and passed on with incredible speed to another pile, this one for seamstresses.

Working with the determination, concentration and confidence of the Shoemakers' Elves, seamstresses then match pieces, backs to fronts, and mate them on machines with such alacrity and force one cringes. How do they work so fast without making a mistake? Without sewing a finger or two into the fabric? One reason work proceeds quickly is that salary is determined by the number of shirts produced; there is a minimum of talking or distraction. Secondly, the noise level is so high, verbal exchange is almost impossible.

After the sleeves are inserted, pockets and flaps attached, buttons are matched to button holes by another group of deft experts and the shirt sent on for the trickiest part: aligning and securing the collar exactly straight.

No machine pressing in this factory. After inspection, each shirt is ironed by hand, folded by hand, pinned and boxed by hand. About 150 dozen shirts leave this factory every day, some for foreign markets, others to retail stores in the U.S., including the attached outlet. All bear famous-name labels: Ralph Lauren, Joseph Abboud, Brooks Brothers, Polo, and Barry Bricken among them.

After seeing the operation in its entirety, you're equipped to tackle the bargains in the factory outlet store and to appreciate the step-by-step precision that went into that "simple" shirt.

**Hours**: Tours can be arranged by calling (304)292-8451; best hours are between 9:00 A.M. and 2:00 P.M. Monday through Friday. Outlet hours are Friday 4:30 to 8:30 P.M. and Saturday 10:00 A.M. to 2:00 P.M.

**Directions**: The factory and outlet store are located in Marilla Park, Morgantown, WV 26505. Heading towards Morgantown on I-79 take I-68 East to Exit 4, Sabreton exit. Turn right off the exit and go towards Morgantown. You will be on Rt. 7. Go through 2 lights and turn left onto Old Rt. 7. Continue about 500 yards, turn right onto bridge and right again after bridge; follow creek to factory.

## The Old Stone House

This quaint house squeezed between modern commercial buildings sits so close to the street it stands out as a charming relic from another time—a time when such proximity might have had a useful purpose. Did vendors pass fresh bread and produce straight through the window? Even among the hustle bustle of downtown Morgantown, the stone house looks like an illustration for a Grimm's fairy tale.

Built in 1795 by Jacob Nuze after he'd been held captive by Indians for three years, it is the oldest stone dwelling in Monongalia County and has been on the National Register of Historic Sites since 1972. The two-story structure has enjoyed a colorful past as a tavern, pottery, tannery, tailor shop, church and residence. Its present incarnation is as a craft/gift shop owned and run by a civic non-profit organization, the Service League of Morgantown, specializing in promoting West Virginian artisans. Most of the Christmas decorations, aprons, ceramics, glassware, wreaths, wood and art work sold here are hand crafted by locals. A small second-hand resale operation supplements proceeds from the gift items to support community projects like school libraries and children's theater. So, if you plan any shopping, come here first. You'll be helping a worthwhile cause and encouraging local talent as well as taking home something authentically West Virginian. Special teas arranged by appointment.

**Hours**: Monday through Saturday 10:00 A.M. to 2:00 P.M.

**Directions**: At 313 Chestnut Street, the house is easily accessible by PRT (½ block from Walnut Street stop). For further information call (304)296-7825.


# Quiet Dell

## *West Virginia Mountain Products Co-op*

There is always something lively going on at this craft co-op to watch or participate in. Spinning demonstrations, folk singing, dulcimer playing, weaving classes and enthusiastic conversations continue on as shoppers pick through the maze of high quality hand-crafted ware of all kinds. Even the caged bunny at the entrance, who will donate his Angora fur for a scarf, looks busy.

The activity is a conscious goal to educate the public as well as to support artists through the sale of their products. Owned and operated by volunteer members, the co-op encourages West Virginia heritage arts, and what a variety you'll choose from. Christmas decorations, sparkling stained-glass sun catchers and lamps, musical instruments, hand-blown glass, rocking chairs and chests, iron utensils, hooked rugs, quilts, stuffed animals, yarn toys, porcelain dolls, wreaths, flowers, paintings in many media, baskets, ceramics, jewelry, knitted and crocheted sweaters and scarves, woven tableware, cross-stitched and creweled pillows, wall hangings. It's easier to list what's not here. About 80 artisans contribute their time and resources to keeping the co-op a dynamic, thriving venture.

Associated with the shop is the Running Horse Yarn weaving/spinning school run by two fiber artists who raise their own merino sheep—for the softest wool in the world—and Angora goats and rabbits. They produce and sell luxurious yarns, hand-woven fabric and finished garments from these natural animal sources.

Demonstrations for schools and organizations may be arranged upon request. Bus groups welcomed.

**Hours**: Monday through Saturday 10:00 A.M. to 6:30 P.M., Sunday NOON to 6:30 P.M.

**Directions**: Located in Quiet Dell. From I-79 take Exit 115 to Route 20 South. Turn left off the exit, and immediately look for the shop on a hill on your right (in back of gas station). For further information call 304-622-3304 or write West Virginia Mountain Products, Inc., Route 1, Box 215-B, Mt. Clare, WV 26408.

# Salem

## *Fort New Salem*

Over two hundred years ago, in the spring of 1792, a group of Seventh Day Baptist families at Fort New Salem, Virginia, gathered to offer Thanks for the end of their 2½-year Odyssey. These hardy travelers from New Jersey founded a community now known as Salem, West Virginia. Their descendants inherited— and continue to contribute to—a culture rich in tradition and spirit. Fort New Salem with its collection of relocated log structures represent the history and ethos of these mountain people from 1792 to 1901.

Under the auspices of Salem-Teikyo University, the fort serves as an educational center as well as an outdoor living-history museum. A Masters of Arts in Education, with an emphasis in Appalachian folk life, as well as public workshops are offered by the university, located less than a mile from the replicated frontier settlement. Many of the fort buildings double as classrooms for teaching traditional crafts and folk ways. Depending on when you time your visit, you'll witness on-going demonstrations and workshops such as printing, blacksmithing, tinsmithing, carpentry, needlework, weaving, quilting and hearth cooking.

Start your visit at **"The Sign of the 3 Barrels"** visitor center and store. Some of the handsome tin, ironware and wood work hand crafted on the premises are for sale here. Moving counterclockwise, you'll pass a reconstructed Blockhouse and the Meeting House—center of the original community's spiritual life and also used for trials and schooling. Men and women entered through separate doors and sat in segregated pews for their Saturday (Sabbath) worship. Delila's House is representative of slave quarters around 1815.

Log structures at Fort New Salem represent the history of West Virginia's mountain people from 1792–1901.

At the **Old Kitchen** you can pick up such tips as how to kill lice on chickens (Rub chickens with lard, the older the better) or how to revive a poisoned dinner guest (Put flame of candle to corpse's finger or toe. If wet blister rises, "life is not extinct"). No 19th-century community could stay healthy without an **Apothecary.** The one here with its bundles of drying herbs shows how dependent rural communities were on the wide and creative use of herbs for all kinds of medicinal purposes, from birth to the grave. Caterpillars were driven off with a sprinkling of bay leaves; catnip stimulated the appetite; basil discouraged flies; thyme repelled snakes and lavender cured colds. Even today, aloe is applied to burns and jewelweed to poison ivy rash.

The farmhouse is typical of the earliest rural lifestyles, but many like it have survived well into this century, reverence for independence, self-reliance and simplicity passing on from one generation of strong mountain Christians to the next.

The print shop demonstrates the nearly lost arts of printing, including paper and ink making, book binding and marbling.

Accounts of happenings outside an isolated area were brought by travelers who stayed at taverns; thus the **Green Tree Tavern** and others like it became the communication center where news, gossip, advice and nourishment were dispensed with good cheer.

Throughout the year, special festivals honor Appalachian seasonal and folk traditions. (Changing seasons were opportunities for community gatherings and celebrations.) Every December the fort hosts an old-fashioned Christmas celebration that reflects Appalachia's rich ethnic heritage. Real candles light up trees, choral groups fill the frosty air with English and Appalachian carols, dulcimers accompany dancers and revelers accompany the "Belsnickle," a German practice that evolved into Halloween trick-or-treating.

**Tip**: The staff is particularly knowledgeable and patient in explaining on-going demonstrations to children. This is a mini-scale Williamsburg experience without the congestion, confusion and cost.

**Admission**: Adult $3.00, children 6 to 12, $1.50; under 6 free.

**Hours**: Open April 24 (for Folk Fair) and from April 26 through May 21, Monday through Friday, 10:A.M. to 5:00 P.M.; Memorial Day through October 31, Wednesday through Sunday, hours are weekdays 10:00 A.M. to 5:00 P.M., and Saturday and Sunday 1:00 to 5:00 P.M.

**Directions**: From Clarksburg take Rt. 50 west about 12 miles to the exit at Rt. 23. Follow signs. For further information call (304)782-5245 or write Fort New Salem, WV 26426.

# Silver Lake
## *Our Lady of the Pines*

Our Lady of the Pines claims to be the smallest church in 48 states. Hidden from road sight by pine trees in the village of Silver Lake, the tiny stone church measures 24' × 12' outside and 16' × 11' inside, just enough space for an altar and six pews seating a total of 12 worshippers. The white wooden cupola and cross atop the entrance give a grace and spirituality that define the purpose of the structure. To fit the proportions of their surroundings, the essential fixtures were handmade: the altar crosses and linen, the Stations of the Cross, the tabernacle and candle holders. A painting on wood of the Last Supper hangs from the altar. Six stained-glass windows bring warmth and color, setting a scene for reflection and prayer.

Flowers are carefully cultivated on the grounds during the months the church is open to the public, from spring to fall. Also on the premises are the wishing well and "the smallest mailing office," a miniature post office of the same stone and style as the church.

Built by Mr. and Mrs. P.L. Milkint in 1957–58 in memory of their parents, Our Lady of the Pines is visited by thousands of visitors every year who stop to peek, pray and pitch pennies into the wishing well. All visitors are welcome.

**Tip**: For a different yet comparable spiritual experience combine this stop with a visit to the hemlock heavens at Cathedral State Park, a few miles north on Rt. 50.

**Hours**: Open during the day, spring to fall.

**Directions**: On Rt. 219 in Silver Lake, about 8 miles north of Thomas. Look for signs.

# Star City

## *Gentile Glass Co., Inc.*

This remarkable family business has been in operation since 1947 and its founder, Mr. Gentile, is still on the premises, usually in the outlet store, to tell you all about it. His wife, Gertrude, is considered the First Lady of Glass Paperweights and she'll gladly talk to you too. Some member of the family has been making paperweights since the early 1900s and a fourth generation is carrying on the tradition.

Downstairs in the production area, you'll see a highly skilled glass artisan use an ancient "off hand" process to create a paperweight from scratch, adding all those mysterious colors, swirls, curls and curlicues that make each one unique. Best of all is seeing how he blows in the bubbles and controls the shapes with various tools in a seemingly effortless dance of fluid movements. Depending on the complexity and size of the paperweight, this artist can turn out a finished product in 3½ to 7 minutes. The small staff, mostly family still, is particularly welcoming and willing to explain each step as it is demonstrated.

The factory also makes hand-cut crystal ware. It produced the famous design, the Morgantown Rose Pattern, or as they call it more colorfully, the "Wild, Wonderful West Virginia Rose." Custom-monogrammed crystal glassware is another specialty. But it's their paperweights that dazzle and enchant the most. Choose your favorite upstairs in the showroom outlet: a large variety of gift selections at reasonable prices.

**Hours**: Tours Monday through Friday, 8:00 A.M. to 11:00 A.M. and 12:30 to 2:00 P.M. Outlet Hours: Monday through Friday 8:00 A.M. to 4:00 P.M. and Saturday 8:00 A.M. to NOON.

**Directions**: Located in Star City about three miles north of Morgantown. Take Exit 155 from I-79 to Rt. 7 East and then Rt. 19 South over bridge. Turn left at first stop light, go one block to University Avenue, then go left down the hill one block and turn right onto Industrial Avenue. Go half a block to 425. For further information call (304)599-2750.

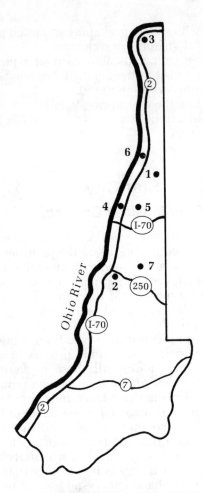

# NORTHERN PANHANDLE

1. *Historic Bethany*

2. *Moundsville*
   Grave Creek Mound State Park

3. *Newell*
   Homer Laughlin China Company

4. *Wheeling*
   Independence Hall
   Valley Voyager
   Victorian Wheeling House Tours

5. *Oglebay Complex*

6. *Wellsburg*
   Brooke Glass

7. *New Vrindaban*
   Palace of Gold

# Northern Panhandle

The Northern Panhandle sticks up like a birthday candle on the West Virginia map. It is so narrow in places that many residents can shop, work, dine out and go to the movies in different states in one day.

Defining the shape and life of the region, the Ohio River is the panhandle's spine, the vital nerve center supplying stimulus for the industry, transportation and recreation that have centered along its shores since French explorers stumbled onto them 250 years ago. Spanning these waters and connecting the state to Ohio, is the famous Wheeling suspension bridge. It is the oldest in the U.S. and when completed in 1847, it was the longest of its kind in the world (over 1,000 feet).

Called the Gateway to the West from its days as a jumping-off point to the frontier and the first capital of the new state of West Virginia, Wheeling remains a hub of activity. Although no longer the grand dame of prosperous Victorian days, the city attracts tourists year-round to several theme festivals, the most renowned being the Winter Festival of Lights—when that candle on the map sparkles in a big way. From November through February, over a million visitors come to gaze at hundreds of thousands of lights in downtown Wheeling. Strung along the bridge and a ten-mile drive of displays, lights dazzle like diamonds, transforming the skyline into a Disney fantasy.

To the north, where the state lines narrow to a few miles wide, the traveler can visit one of the world's largest manufacturers of dinnerware. To the south, Grave Creek Mound State Park documents man's ancient history in the area. No trip to the Northern Panhandle is complete without a visit to the Palace of Gold, truly one of the great manmade wonders in the country, set in a natural beauty only God could create.

For more information on the Northern Panhandle call or write The Wheeling Convention and Visitors Bureau, 1000 Boury Center, Wheeling, WV 26003. Phone 1(800)828-3097 or (304)233-7709.

# Bethany

## *Historic Bethany*

About a half hour's drive north from Wheeling, Bethany is a pretty, old-fashioned Norman Rockwell scene with tree-lined streets, a small general store and enough historic buildings to put the entire village on the National Register of Historic Places. The peace and tranquility of the countryside provide an appropriate ambience for reflection and scholarly pursuit. Alexander Campbell—debater, educator, businessman, statesman, editor, philosopher and a leading influence in one of America's largest indigenous religious movements—must have thought so too in 1840 when he chose to put the state's first degree-granting college here. He believed passionately in the importance of education and its inextricable link to freedom. His words, written nearly 150 years ago, seem remarkably applicable in today's global community: "Intelligence and freedom are but two words for the same thing. An intelligent community will always be free; an ignorant one, never. As we advance in education, as we promote universal intelligence, we promote universal freedom."

Named by *U.S. News and World Report* as one of the top liberal arts institutions in the country and by *Barrons* as one of the best buys in college education, **Bethany College** thrives today with an enrollment of around 800 students.

Campbell lived and worked for half a century in a "gentleman farmer's house" (the Campbell Mansion) and donated the land for the first church at Bethany, where he often preached. Surviving his first wife and their eight children, he reared another family of six and lived to be nearly eighty. His long distinguished life and visionary writings left a unique heritage that marks Bethany's history and charm today.

Start your visit by going to the **Historic Bethany Information Center** (Delta Tau Delta Founder's House) to arrange a tour of the mansion and Meeting House (fee charges) and/or to get information on the historic Campbell sites and maps for your own self-guided walking/driving tour. Group tours must be arranged in advance. Drop-in visitors will find a guide at the mansion during open hours, April through October. Walking-tour brochures are also available at the College Information Center on the main campus (near entrance), open from 9:00 A.M. to 5.00 P.M. Located a block from campus, the Historic Bethany Information Center, housed in the first building restored in Bethany, dates from the 1850s and was made from bricks fired in one of the town's early kilns. From here you can walk to the Meeting House and Old Main before driving to the Campbell Mansion.

**Hours**: Center is open 9:00 A.M. to 5:00 P.M. Tuesday through Friday.

Old Main at Bethany College, one of the best examples of Collegiate Gothic architecture in the country.  COURTESY BETHANY COLLEGE

**Directions**: From Wheeling take Rt. 88 north to Rt. 67 east (right turn) to Bethany, less than a mile from the junction. Phone (304)829-7285. For further information write Historic Bethany, Bethany College, Bethany, WV 26032.

The architectural showpiece on the Bethany College campus is the grand **Old Main** building. Begun before the Civil War, it suffered fire, alterations and long delays before arriving at its present appearance in 1911. During the 1980s, the college spent $4 million dollars to restore it, inside and out. Often compared to the similar, arched design of the University of Virginia buildings, the Old Main is considered among the earliest and best of collegiate Gothic architecture in the country. Over 400 feet long, the brick and stone facade is broken by five arched entrances and climaxed by a splendid clock tower rising more than 140 feet high. While retaining its Gothic majesty on the outside, Old Main's renovated interior accommodates contemporary classroom requirements such as computer facilities. In the Academic Parlor on the second level, (which can be seen by appointment only), five handsome oil paintings by Edward Troye grace the walls. From campus, walk east on Rt. 67 to the Meeting House.

On the edge of the village, the brick **Old Bethany Meeting House** (1850) sits on the original site—and retains some of the stonework—of the first church at Bethany (1835). The present building, which served the community until 1915, has large double-hung windows leading to the pulpit from where Campbell preached. Straight-backed pews separated the sexes during services. Entrances on either side of the pulpit discouraged latecomers. Open for guided tours by appointment. From here drive east on Rt. 67 about a mile to the Campbell Mansion.

The oldest section of the **Alexander Campbell Mansion** dates from the 1790s when his father-in-law, a cabinet maker, used hand-hewn oak timbers to construct the three-story structure with real window glass, a "mansion" according to frontier standards. The parlor is walnut paneled and boasts hand-tooled molding and carved cornices. Campbell and Margaret Brown were married in this room in 1811 and purchased the home shortly afterwards from her father. As Campbell's family and public stature grew, he added several additions for guests, family and students: a school room, dormitory, dining room, porch and the elegant "Strangers Hall," in which he entertained such dignitaries as James A. Garfield, Henry Clay and Jefferson Davis. Note the original hand-painted French wallpaper.

A property of the college, the mansion was re-opened in 1990 to the public after extensive restoration. Rooms are furnished mostly with Campbell family pieces. The fieldstone basement held the original kitchen and fireplace. Partly to escape the distractions of domestic activity, Campbell built a little hexagonal brick structure with cupola a few yards from the main house for his study. Here, starting at daybreak, he wrote sermons and debates. Glass-enclosed bookcases still line the walls. Many of his 59 volumes were composed in this sanctuary. From here too he directed his business enterprises: printing, farming, sheep raising. Two other outbuildings survive from his farm: the spring/ smokehouse and a one-room schoolhouse.

On a hillside down the road a few steps is "God's Acre," the **Campbell Cemetery**, burial grounds for Alexander, 13 of his 14 children, many of his descendants, former presidents of Bethany College and other leaders of his religious movement (today known as The Disciples of Christ, Churches of Christ and Christian Churches). The grounds are encircled by a wall, and stone steps lead to the entrance. A monument of Italian marble signals Campbell's grave site.

**Admission**: Adults $3.00, students $1.50.

**Hours**: The mansion is open from 10:00 A.M. to NOON and from 1:00 P.M. to 4:00 P.M. April through October, Tuesday through Saturday and Sunday 1:00 to 4:00 P.M. Last tour begins at 3:00 P.M. By appointment only November through March.

# Moundsville
## Grave Creek Mound State Park

Traders, hunters and fishermen in a widespread area along the Ohio Valley from about 1,000 B.C.–200 A.D., the Adena were the first of an important group of prehistoric people from the Woodland Period called "mound builders." They took great pains to bury their deceased under large conical earthen mounds, ranging from 20 to 300 feet in diameter. The mound at Grave Creek State Park was their largest and required the removal of 60,000 tons of dirt—without the use of the wheel or horses! Originally encircled by a moat 40 feet wide and five feet deep, the mound measures 69 feet high and 295 feet at the base and probably took at least 100 years to complete (250–150 B.C.).

In 1838, excavators penetrated two chambers and found skeletons, shells, ornaments and a flat sandstone tablet inscribed with markings whose meaning still baffles experts. Later drilling produced stone tools and flints. Some authorities believe a mound of this size was reserved for the elite because most people then were cremated.

Today the burial site and the adjacent Delf Norona Museum compose the nucleus of the seven-acre Grave Creek Mound State Park. An easy five-minute climb takes the visitor to the top of the landscaped mound. Inmates at the state penitentiary across the street take a special interest in their view because it is they who maintain the park grounds.

The museum, contemporary and bright, houses a collection of Adena artifacts, tools, pipes, pottery and ornaments. Display models show how an Adena community lived and built their mounds. This is the size and kind of museum that inspires children–limited but fascinating subject matter that can be covered in less than an hour.

**Tip**: Have lunch in the museum's acclaimed West Virginia Dining Room, open Tuesday through Friday, 11:00 A.M. to 2:00 P.M. Reservations needed for group lunches.

**Hours**: The park and museum are open year-round, Monday through Saturday, 10:00 A.M. to 4:30 P.M.; Sunday 1:00 P.M. to 5:00 P.M. Closed on major holidays. Access to the mound closes at 4:00 P.M.

**Admission**: $1.50 for adults; $.75 for children.

**Directions**: From Wheeling, take Rt. 2 south to Moundsville. The park is at 801 Jefferson Avenue, directly across the street from the penitentiary and one block east of Rt. 2, between 8th and 10th streets. Phone (304)843-1410 or write Grave Creek State Park, Box 527, Moundsville, WV 26041.

# Newell

## *Homer Laughlin China Company*

Newell sits on the Ohio River almost at the very top of the state's bizarrely-shaped Northern Panhandle. At its narrowest point, this skinny finger of land is just a few miles wide, allowing residents to shop, work, dine and play in Ohio or Pennsylvania as easily as in their native state.

After the East Liverpool Company launched its successful and enduring ceramic business here in 1871, other companies followed and prospered, making Newell famous as "The Pottery Capital." In their heyday, Laughlin China employed 60 workers who produced 500 dozen pieces of dinnerware a day. They were the first to produce whiteware, winning a prestigious award at the Centennial Exposition in Philadelphia in 1876. In 1936 the company introduced a new line, **Fiesta**, which became an overnight rage.

Originally glazed in just five vivid colors—red, yellow, green, ivory and blue—the line has since been tempered to softer, pastel shades. But it is the bright bold, riotous rainbow of dishes, mixed and stacked that many of us remember from Grandmother's kitchen—alas, now broken, thrown out or replaced by less breakable, oven-proof and far less exciting contemporary ware. But today, recognizing Fiesta's value, serious collectors haunt flea markets and plunder attics for any "virgin stock." Their passion approaches cult proportions, and competition for early pieces is stiff. Even a small pitcher in good condition is a bargain at $20.00. A full set in mint condition sells for thousands. In 1941 one dinner plate sold for well under a dollar, a teacup for $.30.

You'll not find an overlooked, original Fiesta saucer on your visit here, but you may find a bargain at the retail store, which discounts many of the company's current patterns in the display area. Your 45-minute tour demonstrates how clay is mixed with water to make slip. The slip is machine- or hand-pressed into molds, dried, smoothed out, glazed, decorated, fired, inspected and packed. You'll see two different kinds of kilns and a variety of decorating procedures: silk-screening, hand and machine lining and decal application. Handles are attached and defects corrected by hand before the drying stage. Be prepared to walk the ½-mile tour route.

**Hours**: Tours start at 10:30 A.M. and 1:00 P.M., Monday through Friday; groups of more than 10 by appointment only. Retail factory outlet open 9:30 A.M. to 5:00 P.M., Monday through Saturday; NOON to 5:00 P.M. on Sunday.

**Directions**: From Wheeling, the fastest route is to cross into Ohio and follow Rt. 7 north until you cross into WV on Newell Bridge. It's the East Liverpool Exit. Follow Rt. 2 one mile south to the outlet at 6th and Harrison. Another option is to take Rt. 2 north into Newell. Allow an hour from Wheeling. For further information write the Homer Laughlin China Co., Newell, WV 26050 or call (304)387-1300.

# New Vrindaban
## Prabhupada's Palace of Gold

Called "America's Taj Mahal," this shrine is spectacular evidence of what man accomplishes when divinely inspired. And what a surprise it is! Following signs from Rt. 250, up three miles of steep farmland, past simple rural dwellings, cows and mobile homes, the visitor is completely unprepared for what waits at the end of the dusty road. Only a few remnants of the sixties' culture—a tie-dyed skirt fluttering on a clothes line or graffiti scrawled on a shuttered shack—reassure the voyager he is not lost. Suddenly, around a curve the green hills roll back and a fantasy of pink, black and gold turrets looms from the earth. Chanting voices beckon the visitor through the gate in the wall. The aroma of a thousand roses suffuses the crisp mountain air, and bubbling fountains reflect an endless sky, unblemished but

*Rising from the mountains like a mirage, the gilt turrets of Prabhupada's Palace of Gold shimmer and shine.* <small>DAVID FATTALEH</small>

for the passing hawk. Below and all around, the silent hills ring this dream experience like prostrate worshippers. Up the landscaped terraces, blinking in the glare of sunlit glass and gilt, you arrive at last at the **Palace of Gold.**

This splendid mountain-top kingdom is a far, far cry from the small farm community built on a dump site in the late sixties by Swami Bhaktipada, follower of the first messenger of Krishna consciousness to the West, Srila Prabhupada. Arriving in New York at the age of 69 in 1965—with only $7.00 in his pocket and a fervent vocation—Prabhupada established a Hare Krishna movement that swept the world. Within ten years thousands of his converts built 120 temples on six continents. This palace in New Vrindaban, a memorial to Prabhupada, was constructed between 1973 and 1979 with the unskilled labor of a tiny band of Krishna devotees; an incredible feat by any standards. The community today numbers about 200 residents who maintain the 5,000-acre farm and palace complex, conduct tours, manage the conference facilities and, most important for them, follow the rigorous prayer and study life ordained for followers of Hare Krishna.

Tours begin about very half hour. While you wait, take advantage of the video presentation of the life of Prabhupada–an excellent orientation.

The **west gallery** is an overwhelming introduction: dazzling chandeliers, brilliant stained-glass windows, mirrored ceiling and gleaming marble floor and walls. Each of the four radiant-blue peacock windows contains 1,500 pieces of hand-shaped stained glass. The peacock motif, associated with Lord Krishna, is carved and etched throughout the palace. Walls and floors in the tenroom tour represent over 50 varieties of marble from 17 countries, weighing 250 tons. Twenty-one thousand crystals twinkle overhead, reflecting the filtered sunshine. In corners and flanking doorways, fresh flowers fill enormous enamelled brass vases.

In the lavishly decorated **study,** a lifelike image of Prabhupada sits at the desk. A massive, ornately carved teakwood altar supports deity images under a gold wainscoting of lion heads. Marble walls, silk brocades, crystal and paintings compete for the eye's attention.

The **bedroom** is a warm, golden, sensual delight. Italian marble walls inset with amber onyx meet a gold-leafed canopy. On the ceiling, nearly a thousand hand-painted flowers match the burnished tones of the embroidered silk couch. Fixtures in the adjoining bathroom are 22-karat gold plate.

At the south end of the temple hall some of the 8,000 square feet of palace gold-leaf emblazon arches and frame teakwood doors carved with Indian designs—scrolls, lotuses, birds and flowers.

Devotees gather twice a day to perform their kirtan (chanting) in the **temple room.** If you miss this ritual, you'll at least hear a tape of Prabhupada chanting the Hare Krishna mantra. Green and bronze-hued inlays on the floor and gold-capped marble pillars leading to the altar present a classic theme, recalling Versailles and other European masterpieces. Murals depicting scenes from Lord Krishna's life and 4,000 crystals cover the 25-foot-high dome. Dominating the room, the altar and golden jewel-studded throne hold a regal statue of Prabhupada. His accoutrements—some velvet, fur-trimmed and lavishly decorated—and flower garlands are changed daily.

To ease your return to reality after this intoxicating assault on the senses, go downstairs and eat a relaxing lunch in the cheerful restaurant, which serves a variety of vegetarian cuisine. Or browse through the gift store, stocked with many intriguing items from India.

No less breathtaking than the splendid interior are the terrace gardens, waterways and fountains from where visitors view the hills of three states beyond. In season, marigolds, canna lilies and lotuses prevail, accented by geraniums and red and blue salvia. The crown jewel, however, is the prize-winning **Garden of Time** rose garden. From miniature and tea roses to climbers that cascade from wrought-iron archways, more than 3,000 bushes blossom profusely at these pure heights. The oval-shaped Interfaith Garden encloses a 30-foot statue of Prabhupada, which eventually will be accompanied by figures of other great spiritual masters such as Moses, Jesus and Confucius. A short, flower-bordered drive takes you past a swan lake to a conference center and the **Interfaith Temple of Understanding** where religious ceremonies are conducted several times daily. The beautiful stained-glass ceiling is the largest of its kind in North America. Plans are underway to complete an elaborate adjoining complex of formal gardens, arboretums, waterfalls, fountains and a temple of majestic proportions.

Although still devoted to the teachings of the Krishna faith, the religious emphasis of the New Vrindaban community is shifting more to an ecumenical welcome and, through interfaith festivals, drawing followers of many beliefs to worship God in this magnificent, mystical, mountain miracle.

**Tip**: Plan plenty of time here. Depending on your interest in participating in or observing religious activities, allow at least half a day. The gardens and restaurant provide areas for resting or contemplation. Because you will be required to leave your shoes at the door before taking the palace tour, bring or wear socks. Take time to talk to the friendly residents who are more than willing to share their knowledge and faith.

**Admission**: Adults $5.00; ages 6-18 $3.00; under 6 free.

**Hours**: April through October 9:00 A.M. to dark; November through March, 10:00 A.M. to 5:00 P.M. Restaurant open May through October, 12:00 to 4:30 P.M. during weekdays, 12:00 to 8:00 P.M. Saturday and Sunday.

**Directions**: Take I-70 to I-470 to Bethlehem, Exit 2. Take Rt. 88 south 8 miles to Rt. 250. Turn left and follow 250 south 2 miles for signs to palace. Turn left and go 3 miles. For group tour reservations call (304)843-1812 or (304)845-1207 or write Palace Tours, RD 1, NBV #24, Moundsville, WV 26041.

# Wellsburg
## *Brooke Glass Company*

During Wellsburg's heyday, there were at least five glass companies in town, the first foundry being established in 1814. Today only one remains: the Brooke Glass Company, owned for four generations by the Rithner family.

Your tour of this factory is not an opportunity to see how fine crystal or fancy one-of-a-kind-art pieces are crafted, but you do get an A-Z overview and step-by-step explanation of how a small, hand-operated factory produces lighting fixtures, lamps, bells and candle holders. You'll learn what makes glass (70% sand, 20% soda ash and the rest, chemicals determining color), how the molten liquid is heated in a 2,500-degree furnace, press-blown, cooled, shaped into cast-iron molds, then decorated, etched and painted. Colored glass—28 shades—is a specialty. After cooling, each piece is inspected for flaws. At the acid-etching station, an employee hand dips pieces one at a time into a basin of acid to achieve that frosted look we see on light shades. In a separate room filled with shelves of decorated glassware, skilled artists apply free-hand painted designs and flowers, each one a different creation. Here you'll see decals applied and learn to appreciate the difference between this effect and the one-of-a-kind painted process. The company also specializes in filling tailor-made orders, like matching antique pieces. The tour starts at the gift shop where many items made on the premises are sold.

**Restrictions**: Visitors under the age of 15 are not allowed on the tour unless accompanied by an adult. Groups of school age children are not permitted.

**Hours**: Tours Monday through Friday at 10:00 A.M. and 2:00 P.M. Closed most holidays. Reservations requested for groups of 15 or more: call (304)737-0619. Gift Shop: Monday through Saturday 9:30 A.M. to 5:00 P.M.

**Directions**: Located at 6th and Yankee Streets. From Wheeling, take Rt. 2 north about 15 miles to downtown Wellsburg and follow Rt. 2 to 6th Street. Store is across from a CITGO station.

# Wheeling

## Independence Hall

Nearly six years before President Lincoln signed the proclamation making West Virginia the 35th state in the Union, construction began on the Wheeling Customs House, headquarters for federal offices for the Western District of Virginia. Its completion, coinciding with the beginning of the Civil War, provided a facility for heated political discussions and constitutional conventions that led to eventual statehood in 1863. Here issues dividing Virginians—slavery being one of many—were thrashed out, debated, compromised and shaped into the skeleton of statehood. Serving as the capitol for the Restored Government of Virginia (aligned with the Union) from 1861 to 1863, it is appropriately known today as West Virginia's Independence Hall.

The three-story, hand-cut sandstone building is notable as much for its architectural and engineering significance as for the historic debates that took place within its walls. Ammi B. Young,

Costumed guide in Independence Hall portrays Mrs. Busbey and her times, 1860s' Wheeling during the Civil War.   MICHAEL KELLER an experienced urban architect with the U.S. Department of Treasury, used a balanced and stately Italianate Renaissance revival design that, with a skeletal structure of wrought-iron beams and cast iron columns, presaged the skyscraper. Now on the National Register of Historic Places, the innovative building incorporated gas lighting, an air circulating system and flushing toilets—a first for Wheeling.

When originally opened in 1859, the building housed federal offices of customs collections, postal services and the district court for the Western District of Virginia. During the Civil War debates over taxation, boundaries, representation and emancipation of slaves were conducted in sessions of the Legislature and the Constitutional Conventions which met in the third floor federal court room. After the long debates ended and the constitutional requirements were met, West Virginia became known as the "Child of the Storm," the only state to be created as a result of the Civil War.

Following statehood, the new government moved to other quarters, and this building eventually passed into private hands. In May 1964, the state purchased the structure and renovations began to return it to its original appearance. Maintained by the state Department of Culture and History, the hall offers special exhibits and programs highlighting the West Virginia legacy.

Start your visit on the lower level with the award-winning 20-minute film, *For Liberty and Union*, which dramatizes the struggle for statehood during the terrible war years. Exhibit photos of old-time Wheeling capture the excitement of the "Gateway to the West" during its prime. Then take the elevator to upper floors for changing exhibits and restored period rooms that interpret the formation and development of the Mountain State. The Court Room, on the third floor was the scene of many rousing debates. Note the *trompe l'oeil*, the original pseudo-fresco painting, grained light oak columns, capitals, iron shutters and grained mahogany benches and desks. Throughout the building, rooms boast massive 13-foot wooden doors, 20-foot ceilings and decorative iron work.

**Mrs. Busbey tours** are a dramatic way of introducing history to groups of any age, but with special appeal to children. Elizabeth Busbey, a colorful 19th-century character, who was mother to a large family and wife to the proprietor and owner of a carriage/wagon company once housed next door to the hall, is portrayed by a living-history tour guide.

Dressed in period clothing and speaking in dialogue scripted from Wheeling newspapers during 1862–63, Mrs. Busbey tells about the painful debates over Secession that took place in this hall. Her first-person narrative allows interactions with guests as she explains Wheeling daily life during the war, her anxiety and hopes for her children, the new State of West Virginia and for her country. History lessons stick when a "real" person from those times shares them. To make reservations call (304)238-1300; self-guided tours anytime during open hours.

**Tip**: Combine this tour, which you can do in about an hour, with a Historic Walking Tour or a tour of Victorian mansions (see entry).

**Admission**: Free if self-guided. Group tours with Elizabeth Busbey require a minimum of ten people; $2.00 per person.

**Hours**: All week long 10:00 A.M.–4:00 P.M. Closed on Sunday during January and February.

**Directions**: Located on corner of 16th and Market streets. From I-70 take 1A south on Main St. to 16th. Parking is available in back. Call (304)238-1300 or write West Virginia Independence Hall, 1528 Market Street, Wheeling, WV 26003.

## Oglebay Complex

Wheeling's *piece de resistance*—and by far its biggest tourist attraction—is the vast Oglebay complex of resort, zoo, mansion, golf course, arboretum, garden center and 1,500 acres of municipal park. Bequeathed to the city in 1926 by industrialist Earl W. Oglebay for "as long as the people shall operate it for purposes of public recreation and education," the initial 750 acres became the nucleus of the park, and his marvelous summer home is now the mansion museum. The initial gift has expanded to accommodate over four miles of hiking trails, amphitheater, nature center, tennis courts, swimming pool, 204-room lodge, the largest floating fountain in the U.S., a 2½-acre lake for fishing and boating, and one of the most spectacular and longest light festivals in the country.

Depending on the time of year and how selectively you plan, it is possible to see much of what Oglebay offers in a day. If you're with children, start in the morning with the zoo while the animals (and kids) are frisky.

### Good Children's Zoo

Open since 1977, the 65-acre natural habitat for North American animals is the only accredited zoo in the state. A gift of the Good family in memory of their son Philip, the zoo and its activities are designed specifically for children. But don't let this discourage animal lovers of any age from visiting this wooded, cheerful park. A paved trail around and past the animal exhibits is an easy 7/10 of a mile walk, but if weather is poor or children are cranky, take the little train ($1.25) that departs every 20 minutes near the bird house.

*Llamas are among the animals children can pet at the Good Zoo at Oglebay.*  <small>Courtesy Good Zoo</small>

There is a Children's Farm where goats, pigs and donkeys–even a llama—can be fed and petted. Ducks and geese always welcome a handout at the Waterfowl Pond. Bison and deer graze in spacious enclosures, and the black bear peer through the viewing windows with uninhibited curiosity, giving visitors a close-up appreciation of ursine paws and teeth. These are no cuddly teddies!

A favorite for many is the exhibit of otters. These playful creatures, swim, dive, cavort and amuse with indefatigable energy. But the zoo's pride is its precious population of the handsome red wolf. Under a project to save and reintroduce this rare species to the wild, red wolves are mated here and their cubs sent into designated wilderness areas with successful survival rates.

When you finish your walk, enjoy a movie at the **Benedum Science Center,** which usually has a free presentation on some aspect of science. Special programs are scheduled throughout the year such as summer camp activities, laser shows, an Easter hunt and spooky Halloween train rides. Before leaving, take the kids to see the miniature "O"-gauge railroad and village display in the main building. Turn-of-the-century scale models—a blast furnace, wooden trestle bridge, drive-in movie theater, gristmill, river with steamboats, logging operation and small mill town— all help re-create the heyday of the steam locomotive. Open every day of the year.

**Restrictions**: No food may be brought into the zoo.

**Tip**: Rental strollers available for small fry.

**Admission**: Adults $4.25; children 2 to 17, $3.25, under age 2 free. Family membership $25.00. Group rates available.

**Hours**: Summer weekdays 10:00 A.M. to 6:00 P.M., winter weekdays 11:00 A.M. to 5:00 P.M. Weekends, 10:00 A.M. to 7:00 P.M. For more information call (304)243-4030.

### Oglebay Mansion Museum

Originally a summer residence for Cleveland industrialist Earl W. Oglebay, the 1846 neo-classical Oglebay Mansion perches on a hill where summer breezes passed through the enormous rooms, cooling visiting VIPs before the age of air-conditioning.

Now a museum, the mansion has eight period rooms furnished with antiques, Oriental carpets, family portraits, glass and china collections. A Victorian parlor represents the 1860s, a Federal style bedroom, the early 1800s. A replicated frontier kitchen, with spartan furniture and table set with simple pewter utensils, contrasts sharply with the elegant Hepplewhite dining room (1790–1810) and its glittering crystal and china display. In the Waddington Room, look for the priceless silver service made especially for the Oglebay family. Two years to hand craft, the coffee/tea service depicts different scenes of family homes and places of worship.

An extended wing, added through the generosity of the late Oglebay grandson Courtney Burton, provides a spacious gallery for ever-changing exhibits of many media.

**Admission**: Adults $4.00, seniors $3.50, students $3.00. Ages 12 and under free with an adult.

**Hours**: Year-round Monday through Saturday 9:30 A.M. to 5:00 P.M., Sundays and holidays 1:00-5:00 P.M.

## Carriage House Glass

Nearing completion, next to the Visitor Center and a short walk from the mansion, is the Carriage House Glass building, designed after an historic estate structure which was destroyed by fire nearly 50 years ago. The building houses china and glass items never publicly exhibited before and a priceless collection of Midwestern one-of-a-kind glass masterpieces, including the magnificent Sweeny punch bowl, reportedly the largest piece of cut glass ever produced. The bowl, if put to use (heaven forbid!), could serve 21 gallons—400 people—before going empty. Another case holds an eye-catching collections of "whimsies" and "riggers," unusual or experimental objects that tested the skill of the glass blower: pipes, needles, rolling pins, eggs, chains and pens whimsically colored and shaped in swirls and stripes. From Cranberry to Carnival glass, these showcases and their breathtaking contents document the art of glassmaking that helped make Wheeling so prosperous during its heyday. Plans are to show working artisans plying the glass trade that was a mainstay of the Ohio Valley economy. There is an admission charge for entrance to this floor. Entrance to the retail level is free: Here you will find exceptional glass products mainly from West Virginia, Pennsylvania and Ohio glass companies.

**Hours**: Retail store is open 9:00 A.M. to 5:00 P.M. Monday through Thursday, 9:00 A.M.-9:00 P.M. Friday, Saturday and Sunday. During spring and summer months, store is open until 9:00 every evening. For more information call (304)243-4100.

Outside on the grounds stroll through the **Wigginton Arboretum** and **Waddington Gardens** and consult with experts at the Civic Garden Center. The flower beds, hanging baskets and water displays are meticulously maintained with seasonal specialties: thousands of tulips in spring, brilliant annuals in summer and chrysanthemums in fall.

Rent a boat, pack a picnic and share crusts with the ducks at the lake or treat yourself to lunch at the lodge. Freshen up with a swim in the pool after a game of miniature golf. End your day with a family nature walk or a star gazing session at the A.B. Brooks Nature Center (304)242-6855, or with a concert at the amphitheater. But before going home be sure to include one of the light and music shows at the **Cascading Waters** on Schenk Lake. These free half-hour spectacles take place daily at 6:30, 8:00 and 9:30 P.M. The tallest free-flowing fountain in the U.S. is computer programmed to "dance" to a medley of taped musical selections; jets propel waters 200 feet high, gushing, splashing, tumbling to trickles, changing colors, shape and volume as they interpret marches, movie themes and Western favorites.

**Tip**: Check your calendar for a full moon and plan ahead for a splendorous lunar backdrop. Dogs on a leash welcome.

## Festival of Lights

Early November through February the park is a multi-colored riot of lights as part of the city-wide Festival of Lights. Over 500,000 lights encircle and emblaze 300 acres of trees, lake, roads and pathways. More than a million visitors jam the roads to see this fairyland extravaganza. Lights blink, wink and twinkle, outlining holiday themes like the 30-foot candy canes, the 45-foot poinsettia wreath and the animated Jack-in-the-box that jumps and waves to admirers.

**Tip**: Weekend traffic is particularly heavy. Avoid peak holiday crowds.

**General Directions to Oglebay**: About a 10-minute drive from downtown Wheeling. From I-70 take the Oglebay exit and follow Rt. 88 north for about 2½ miles. Follow signs. For visitor information call 1(800)624-6988 or (304)243-4000/4088 or write Oglebay, Wheeling, WV 26003.

## Stifel Fine Arts Center

Located four miles from the park but part of the Oglebay Institute, the Stifel Fine Arts Center sponsors changing art exhibits as well as instruction in arts, crafts, music and dance. The stately 30-room mansion, once called Edemar, was a gift from the Stifel family, civic-minded industrialists. A stained-glass window at the top of the grand staircase depicts the family's ancestral castle in Bavaria. To guarantee that the mansion would be fireproof, builders made its walls of concrete eight inches thick.

Downstairs the enormous living room and dining room area are paneled in walnut. The library holds a collection of art and music books and formal portraits of the original owners. Studios and offices upstairs have replaced former bedrooms. Don't expect elegant furnishings or formal gardens, although there is a pretty perennial bed. The 1912 house is notable primarily for exhibits and special activities and should be on the list of "must-sees" for art enthusiasts interested in investigating local talent.

**Admission**: Suggested donation of $1.00.

**Hours**: Monday through Saturday, 9:00 A.M. to 5:00 P.M., Sunday 12:30 to 5:00 P.M.

**Directions**: 1330 National Road, one mile from I-70, Exit 2B. For information on exhibits call (304)242-7700.

# Valley Voyager

Even now, with its banks lined with a mish-mash of houses and tumbling factories, Wheeling's frontage on the Ohio River is lovely. How much more beautiful it must have been when the Indians shared the waterway with elk, before French explorers in 1749 discovered its pristine majesty and named it La Belle. Soon settlers came, claiming prize sites and establishing businesses, and the river became a major transportation artery for those heading west and south. Many built simple rafts, stocked up with supplies, and ferried south passing the infant community of Cincinnati to the confluence of the great Mississippi and the wilderness beyond. Arriving at their destinations, or forced ashore, pioneers used these simple rafts to build their first shack dwellings and stayed, changing history and this continent forever.

To get a feeling for the excitement of river adventure and to appreciate the Ohio's strength and beauty, have a bon voyage on one of the many cruises offered by the *Valley Voyager*. All year-long this authentic sternwheeler glides up and down both sides of the river, giving a good overview of river history and the rise and fall of its industries. You'll learn that in the last century coal barges supplying factories were so numerous one could almost step from West Virginia to Ohio without getting wet. You'll see Victorian mansions built with the wealth the barges made possible as well as modest structures that document the demise of the great industrial boom. Ask to see the marker near the dock that shows the high point of the 1936 flood, when the Ohio crested 55 feet into the streets of downtown Wheeling. You can choose a Gambler's Paradise Cruise (including on-board Bingo and an evening at the dog races), an all-day Playhouse Cruise with lunch in Wellsburg and theater entertainment at the Brooke Hills Playhouse, a fall Foliage Cruise, an all-day shopping spree, a luncheon, sunrise breakfast or Sunday brunch cruise or a romantic moonlight dinner dance cruise. Christmas is a special time in Wheeling, and the *Voyager* will take you past decorated riverside mansions to see the famous Festival of Lights, particularly impressive when reflected in the water. The sternwheeler turns into Santa's Sleigh Boat, with a seven-foot Santa on top and green and gold garlands of lights gleaming on all three decks. Or, almost anytime of year, just take a short scenic sightseeing tour—reasonably priced and free to children 10 and under who are accompanied by an adult.

**Tip**: If you are sitting on deck, choose a spot near the loudspeaker so you can hear the tour guide clearly.

**Admission**: Reservations required for all trips. For sightseers only, a one-hour cruise is $5.25; one and a half is $6.50, two hours, $7.50 and three hours $9.85. Call for current prices of special cruises as they change without notice 1(800)237-1867 or (304)233-1010.

**Directions**: From I-70 take the Downtown Exit that puts you on Main Street. At the corner of 12th Street and Main (the fourth set of lights), turn right onto 12th and go 1½ blocks to a large parking garage. *The Valley Voyager* docks at Lou's Landing right behind the garage.

## Victorian Wheeling House Tours

Called the "Gateway to the West," Wheeling in its 19th-century heyday was the terminus of eastern "civilization," the last stop for adventurers heading for the Wild West or those rafting southwest on the Ohio to unknown, uncharted territories. Merchants grew rich from supplying those moving on and built mansions near their factories on the river. Drawing on the talents of newly-arrived immigrant artisans—German, Scottish-Irish, Italian among them—the nouveau riche spared no dime to tint their temples with the finest tiles, stained glass, wood and iron work. Most materials were Wheeling made, down to the bricks and nails. Between 1837–1905 more than 600 houses representing the different stages of Victorian architecture graced the thriving city. Fortunately, many have survived its decline, and those that have suffered abuse and neglect are being rediscovered and restored.

Because so much of the glorious detail of these mansions was handcrafted, each dwelling was unique, each banister a little masterpiece of carving, each window a tribute to sunlight. Since lots along the river were deep and narrow—often located near manufacturing locales—houses were understated on the exterior. Inside they were lavished with expensive embellishments. Tiffany glass, bird's-eye maple and mahogany trim, marble mantels, ceramic-tiled fireplaces, filigree cast-iron, lacy wooden screens— all testified to the owner's taste and success. All contributed to the aura of opulence and prosperity required for tea parties, social climbing and comfortable family life.

Happily for Victorian fans, some of these bejeweled residences are polished and poised for public applause. On a two-hour guided tour sponsored by Yesterday's Ltd., a private group, you may peruse four of the loveliest homes and marvel at the workmanship that peaked with the economic boom of river trade.

Starting with the 1858 Italian Renaissance **List House** (827 Main Street) your costumed guide, properly attired in period dress, parasol and bonnet, will explain the history and highlights of each residence.

At 823 Main Street, the **Hazlett-Fields** Queen Anne-style house is three stories of smooth brick finish dating from 1893. The

The dining room of the Hazlett-Fields House shows off a magnificent inlaid floor and a cut, beveled and zinced fanlight
window. Courtesy Victorian Wheeling Landmarks Foundation

round front window and fabulous beveled and zinced glass on
the door are the only exterior frills. Inside, note the rare spindle
screen, stair rail, walk-in fireplace and feminine parlor, whose
dainty colors and details are typical of the times. Frosted with
floral patterns and soft pink tones, this room was used for the
ladies' retreat after formal dinners. In contrast, the dining room,

where men lingered over post-dinner political talk and cigars, usually stated a masculine motif, as in this house: heavy furniture and dark wood trim carved with fruit motifs. The sun-filled Billiard Room with its triple-hung windows gives a splendid overlook of the Ohio River.

For a good example of the clever lincrusta technique, take special note at the **Christian Hess House** at 811 Main Street. The hall is decorated with trim resembling wood. In fact the material is made from linseed oil and wood pulp hand shaped into molds and applied to walls, an inexpensive alternative to handcarved wood. This elegant 1876 mansion in a French Renaissance style incorporates many of the details that exemplified state-of-the-art Victorian Wheeling: the marbleized mantel, iron window boxes, plaster roses on ceilings, art nouveau pansy design on stained-glass windows—all bespeak an era bursting with growth, wealth and genius.

The 1885 **Holiday-Schaefer House** at 2307 Chapline Street boasts a spectacular array of fretwork and woods—maple, oak and beech—exquisitely worked in mantels and balustrades.

Epitomizing a composite of period styles, and the latest of the four residences on the tour, is the 1905 **L.S. Good House**, the first to acquire indoor plumbing (at 95 14th Street). The lighting fixtures document the transition from gas light to electricity. Ingeniously crafted built-in furniture, 22 art nouveau stained-glass windows, baronial mantels and mirrors and the double set of cut, beveled and zinced glass doors mark the culmination of Wheeling craftsmanship and Victorian pomp.

There are many more historic buildings in Wheeling, most of which are closed to the public. But you can admire many exteriors by following the walking tour published by the Wheeling Historic Landmarks Commission. Copies are available at the Stone and Thomas Department Store at 1030 Main Street or by writing Friends of Wheeling, P.O. Box 889, Wheeling, WV 26003.

**Admission**: $12.00 for a tour of four homes; $10.00 for three.

**Hours**: Saturday at 11:00 A.M. and 1:00 P.M. and Sunday at 12:00 and 2:00 P.M. By appointment any day. Special teas, luncheons, and dinner tours available. Call for reservations, (304)233-2003 or write Yesterday's Ltd., 827 Main St., Wheeling, WV 26003.

**Directions**: From I-70 West, enter right lane east of Wheeling tunnel. After leaving tunnel, exit right (Main St. 1-A). Turn right on Main St. You'll see 827 directly across the street on left. Park behind this building. From I-70 East, cross the Ohio River, go through Wheeling tunnels and take the Oglebay Exit 2-A. Immediately re-enter I-70 west back through the tunnels; then follow directions for I-70 west.

An innovative building for its day (1859), the Wheeling Customs House, now Independence Hall, was the scene of many political debates that lead to statehood for the "Child of the Storm."

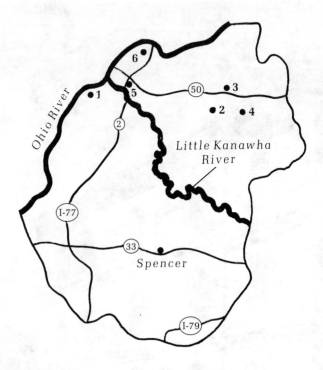

## MID-OHIO VALLEY

1. ***Blennerhassett Island***
   ***National Historical Park***

2. ***Cairo***
   North Bend State Park

3. ***Ellenboro***
   Mid-Atlantic Glass

4. ***Harrisville***
   Berdine's Five & Dime

5. ***Parkersburg***
   Blennerhassett Hotel
   Cook House
   Gas and Oil Museum
   Smoot Theatre
   Trans Allegheny Books

6. ***Williamstown***
   Fenton Art Glass Company
   Henderson Hall

# Mid-Ohio Valley

Man has been lured to the natural riches and beauty of the Mid-Ohio Valley for over 11,000 years. Among the treasures you'll discover there today are:

• an island paradise where lovers sought to shed a scandalous past;

• a vaudeville masterpiece restored to its glamorous youth;

• a mansion time-capsule filled with five generations of memories, memoirs and memorabilia;

• a Victorian hotel where "oil boomers" plotted to change a small river port into an industrial crossroad, while nouveau riche and would-bes rode the streets on horseback;

• exquisite one-of-a-kind glass art created while you watch;

• a five-and-dime that still sells penny candy.

Whether you're seeking romance, culture, natural beauty or a day-trip through history, you have a big choice in the Mid-Ohio Valley. Parkersburg, the center of most attractions, throbs with civic enthusiasm and commitment to preserving the community's rich heritage through museums, restorations and handcrafts. Closeby, on dozens of river islands, the first national wildlife refuge in the state is off to an exciting start. A short drive from the city, a state park with facilities just for them welcomes the handicapped. If you do your research, you can cover a number of diverse sites in one day, but allow time to enjoy the scenery and that beautiful Ohio River along the way.

For more information on visiting the Mid-Ohio Valley, call or write: Parkersburg–Wood Co. Convention and Visitor Bureau, 215 First St., Parkersburg, WV 26101, phone 1(800)752-4982 or (304)428-1130.

## Cairo

### North Bend State Park

Spacious, serene, sprawling over 1,400 beautiful acres, North Bend State Park offers complete overnight and recreational facilities, from a 29-room resort lodge overlooking the valley to 8 fully-equipped deluxe cabins and 75 camping sites.

Day trippers can use the tennis and game courts, pool and miniature golf at a nominal cost and picnic, hike and bike for free. The ambitious explore the Rails to Trails, formerly an old railroad line, stretching 60 miles over 32 bridges and through 12 tunnels passing scenic landscape and small towns. The less athletic have several trails two miles long or less to choose from. A special paved trail, the Extra Mile, designed specifically for the physically impaired, has Braille interpretive signs. There are other sports facilities for the handicapped including bikes for the blind.

Nature films and programs are offered during the summer, and there are special packages throughout the year like the Sweetheart Weekend for Valentine's Day or the Square Dance Weekend in August. A sampling of other events: Gospel Song Festival, Quilters Getaway, International Sports Jamboree and, for you hunters, even a Turkey Calling Seminar.

**Hours**: The lodge and cabins are open year-round. Camp grounds are open from the last weekend in April through October 31. Park hours are dawn until 10:00 P.M., but the office in the lodge is open 24 hours a day.

**Directions**: From Parkersburg take Rt. 50 east to Rt. 31, about 20 miles. Follow to Cairo and then signs to park. For reservations or further information call 1(800)CALL WVA or (304)643-2931. Write North Bend State Park, Cairo, WV 26337.

# Ellenboro

## Mid-Atlantic Glass Factory

If you are in the area of Ellenboro and would like to see a small glass factory in operation, stop at Mid-Atlantic Glass, just a few minutes off Rt. 50. Though the tour schedule is flexible, the best time is morning, starting whenever visitors arrive and when someone is available to guide them through. Many of the basic glass-making procedures you'll see in action here are the same as those covered during the Fenton Art Glass tour (see entry). Mid-Atlantic Glass is known for its colorful marbles and small hand-made and blown items like bells, vases and wine glasses. A factory outlet store is on the premises. Arrangements for bus tours should be made in advance.

**Hours**: Best time to stop in for a tour is from 8:00 A.M. to 2:00 P.M. Monday through Friday. Outlet hours are 9:00 A.M. to 4:30 P.M. Monday through Friday and 9:00 A.M. to 2:00 P.M. on Saturday.

**Directions**: Coming from Parkersburg take Rt. 50 east about 30 miles to the Ellenboro exit, making a left after exiting and crossing over a bridge. At the Y, take a right (Rt. 16) and the factory is about ¾ mile on right. For more information call (304)869-3351 or write Mid-Atlantic of West Virginia, PO Box 279, Ellenboro, WV 26346.

# Harrisville

## Berdine's Variety Store

If you are over 55, you'll love Berdine's, West Virginia's (and perhaps the nation's) oldest five-and-dime, because you'll remember one just like it and feel you've stepped back into your youth—a time of fifteen-cent movies and penny candy. If you are under 12, you'll love Berdine's because you'll be able to afford all the candy you can eat, a Halloween costume and a comic book without blowing your allowance. And if you are somewhere in between, you need Berdine's for that rare kitchen item, hard-to-find gift or special colored thread.

Preserving the 80-year Berdine tradition of stocking old-time and difficult-to-find ware at reasonable prices is the deliberate decision of the present owners, who took over the store from the Berdine family in 1983. They want to continue a town treasure and pass on the fun to a new generation of penny-candy seekers. And "variety" is the right name for this store. Everything from knitting needles, musical instruments, school supplies, glass figurines, mechanical and stuffed toys, jacks, marbles, pots and pans, baskets, mouse traps, cow bells, oil lamps, hair do-dads, paper dolls, greeting cards, cap guns, fake flowers, mirrors and magic.

The dazzling array of "things" keeps growing and growing, as a few "new-fangled" items are added to the inventory. Hence, you must look carefully here, above, below and around the walls, counters, shelves and glassed candy case so as not to miss that green fingernail polish or monkey mask.

The history of this local landmark, that has supplied three generations with licorice sticks, started in 1908 when two brothers opened a variety store in a nearby location. In 1915, Berdine's, under K.C. (Kit Carson) Berdine, came to a new building on Court Street and has remained little changed since, with its original pressed tin ceiling, oak counters and shelves. Those were the days when ladies' hats were a dime and nothing in the store cost more.

The new owners are intent on preserving the tradition of offering old-time favorites at old-time prices. Their bookmark ad states that Berdine's is "where prices are born and not raised. . . ." Kids can still press noses against glass cases of penny sweets and deliberate whether to splurge on jawbreakers, chewy kisses or bubble gum.

*In 1908 the most expensive items sold at Berdine's were ladies dress hats—ten cents each.*     <small>Courtesy Berdine's Variety Store</small>

The owners confess to a special weakness for the glitter and joy of Christmas and display a limited sampling of Santas and decorations throughout the year. But come early November, they start feeling that Yuletide itch and drag out ever so stealthily (so as not to be accused of preempting the season) boxes of ornaments, Victorian cards, ribbon and wrap, Old World decorations, twinkling angels and shiny stars, and transform the store into a holiday explosion of music, garlands and good cheer. Though this is Berdine's jolliest season, a stop here any time of year is a treat and trip to another time.

**Tip**: Combine a visit here with an outing to North Bend State Park a few miles away (see section).

**Hours**: 9:00 A.M. to 5:00 P.M. all week long except Sunday and major holidays.

**Directions**: From Rt. 50 take Rt. 16 to Harrisville. As you pass through the downtown area turn right onto Court Street (drugstore on corner). Berdine's sits at #106. For further information write them: zip code 26362. Call (304)643-2217.

# Parkersburg

Most of the tourist attractions in the Mid-Ohio section of West Virginia center around Parkersburg, and what a fine town it is. Even without knowing much about its rich history, the first-time visitor to this city senses a strong civic pride as evident in the number of museums, historical sites and cultural facilities boasted and toasted by a supportive public. People here seem to know and like each other and enjoy living here. The physical setting at the junction of the Ohio and Little Kanawha rivers framed by rolling hills is still remarkably pretty, despite nearly 150 years of commercial development. Its riverside location, however, has cost the city and its citizens incalculable loss over the years from flooding. This hazard was put under control in the late 1940s with the building of a floodwall, a major city landmark.

Human history in the area, as you'll learn at the **Blennerhassett Museum,** goes back to at least 11,000 years ago, when Indians lived and grew corn along the river. In the mid-1600s European explorers passed through, and in the 1770s settlement began in earnest. By 1800 a log-cabin town was properly laid out and in 1810 received its name, Parkersburg. When oil was discovered along the rivers, the economy exploded and continued to surge, after the disruption of the Civil War, until the early 1900s. Fortunes from the oil and gas industries were made and lost and made again, some financing the Victorian mansions you'll see on the walking tour. Today, with other industries based here, the economy is relatively stable and prosperous.

You should start a day trip here at the **Visitors and Convention Bureau** at 215 First Street. Open Monday through Friday 8:30 A.M. to 4:30 P.M., the office has a good supply of brochures, up-to-date information and an Historical Walking Tour Map. It is also close to Point Park and the floodwall, where you can see the levels of the three highest floods marked on the wall at the Second Street opening. The worst flood occurred in 1913 when the river crested at 58.9 feet (the norm is 20 feet). Point Park is the sternwheeler departure point for Blennerhassett Island.

**Directions**: From I-77, follow Rt. 50 West (7th Street) into the city and turn left at Avery Street. Follow Avery Street to intersection with Second Street; turn right and continue to floodwall.

Many of the sites on the walking tour, like the Victorian homes in the pretty Julia-Ann Historic District, are not open to the public. Two that are: **St. Francis Xavier Church** and the Gould-Gerwig House at 720 Juliana Street, the headquarters of the Parkersburg Chamber of Commerce (you can get a walking tour map here also).

Dating from 1870, the church has the spiritual inspiration and elegance of a Romanesque cathedral. The bells in the tower chime with a particularly pure and joyous tone that's heard all over the city. A brochure, available at the back of the church, outlines a self-guided tour. Note the beautifully carved altar, stained-glass windows and Stations of the Cross hand-painted on copper

*This view of the east front of Blennerhassett Mansion shows the Italian Palladian style with semi-circular porticoes chosen by George Washington for Mount Vernon.*     BRIAN B. SCHROEDER

plates. *Tromp l'oeil* paintings depicting the life of Christ, his mother, saints and apostles have been described as "the most significant examples of ecclesiastical art in West Virginia." The church is open to the public from 9:00 A.M. to 5:00 P.M. For more information call (304)422-3142. Other important stops on the walking tour are described in detail in the following pages.

## Blennerhassett Island Historical State Park

### The Blennerhassetts

No other love story in West Virginia history approaches its fame, passion, mystery, glamour and adventure, nor holds the enduring appeal of the Blennerhassetts' romance. Their saga—in terms of star-crossed fate and lost fortune—reached the drama of a Greek tragedy. Yet, their story is deeply American, connected inextricably to events that shaped this country's history, the most celebrated tale in Ohio Valley folklore.

**Harman and Margaret,** both from British/Irish aristocracy, seemed doomed to misfortune from the beginning of their love match. She was tall, beautiful, educated, athletic, and twenty-two when she married her uncle in 1794. He was tall, musically talented, highly educated, an elegant dresser and the very rich scion of a landed gentry family. Details of their flight from Ireland where their odyssey began are murky, but most researchers agree that the "incestuous" marriage so outraged Irish society and their relatives that they were forced to flee scandal and seek a new start elsewhere. Another important factor hastening their departure was Harman's awkward involvement in Ireland's independence movement, a foreboding of his weakness for political intrigue that proved his eventual undoing.

The couple crossed the Atlantic on a difficult, prolonged voyage to New York in 1796, evidently well equipped with servants, family heirlooms, scientific instruments, books, china, linens and many other accoutrements needed for setting up a manor house in the grand style to which they had been bred. Drawn by the romantic notion of living in the Wild West, they traveled via Pittsburgh to Marietta, Ohio, then on the fringe of the frontier. Within a short time, the Blennerhassetts bought land on an island in the Ohio River (in what soon would be Wood Country, Virginia) and prepared to build their estate. The splendid **mansion** took 2 1/2 years to complete and rivaled Mount Vernon in grandeur, even sharing a similar configuration with a central section, covered porticoes and flanking wings. In its day it was proclaimed the most beautiful private residence in the Ohio Valley.

What they hadn't brought with them to furnish the interior, the newcomers purchased, spending extravagantly on the best furniture, rugs and paintings from eastern cities. The Blennerhassetts established formal grounds with exotic trees and plants, hothouses and flower gardens on a grand scale. Here they set up court and entertained lavishly, sharing their cultural interests and accomplishments with their many prominent guests. In addition to writing poetry (she is officially the state's first published poet), Margaret, an accomplished equestrian, struck a stunning figure on horseback, while Harman in his library wing pursued his interest in scientific research and experimentation. Their lives were not all frivolity. He was also an important entrepreneur in the area, operating a store on the island and owning shares in others, and Margaret carried out the first program of smallpox innoculations in the Mid-Ohio Valley.

Acknowledged as the most glamorous and cultured of their peers, they were popular with local neighbors as well as gentile society. Hosting balls, conducting cultural salons, entertaining guests from near and abroad—these were the good years in Eden (1798-1806). To complete their happiness, three children were born to them during this time and despite dwindling resources, they relished their new life.

Enter the dark antagonist in the persona of **Aaron Burr**, who first called on the Blennerhassetts in May 1805. Whatever mysterious attraction sealed their fate during their early meetings (Burr's stature as ex-vice president may have seemed prestigious), the result is a matter of historical record. As the alliance deepened, Burr's powerful personality seduced Harman into a decision that ruined his life.

Embittered over losing the presidency to Thomas Jefferson and already a pariah for killing Alexander Hamilton, Burr conspired to set up his own empire by seizing Spanish territory in the Southwest. Enlisting Harman in the financing and aid of the treasonous project, Burr set up his headquarters at Blennerhassett Island. When the plot was uncovered the Wood County authorities prepared to attack the island and arrest the perpetrators. Forewarned, Harman escaped down the river under darkness, leaving his family to cope with the invading militia. Within days, Margaret, with her children, fled also, never to return. Life in paradise was over.

After Harman was arrested, indicted and released, he joined his family and attempted a new life on a Mississippi cotton plantation. But fortune refused to smile. As though scripted into the tragedy by an evil magician, the mansion, only 11 years old was accidentally set on fire and burned to the ground in 1811.

After the cotton market collapsed and he failed to secure a position in Canada through personal connections, Harman returned to England where he spent the rest of his life pursuing one unsuccessful venture after another. Following his death on the Isle of Guernsey in 1831, Margaret, badly strapped for funds, returned to America to visit her sons and seek financial help. Although the couple had five children, two daughters died in infancy and no son left heirs. Their eldest son, a wastrel and alcoholic, literally disappeared on the frontier. The second son, a failed artist, died in poverty, as did Margaret herself in 1842, leaving behind—at her sad expense—one of the most romantic legends in American history.

The Blennerhassett drama did not end with the actors' deaths. Not long ago, a camper spending a foggy night on the island awoke to the aroma of strong perfume. Leaving his tent, he saw a lady staring at him in the fog. He offered her a cup of coffee, but she remained silent and then slowly and eerily faded away. During the night the camper heard noises outside his tent and in the morning found his books removed from his knapsack, stacked in neat piles. His description of the lady is consistent with other accounts of Margaret's ghost, perhaps returning to the grave of her infant daughter who is buried on the island, a fitting epilogue to a timeless, moving story that continues to fascinate and unfold.

### Blennerhassett Island

That the island was a wild place, inhabited by predators, shrouded many mornings in mist, isolated from the mainland by a fickle river, and, only a few years previously, released from hostile Indian control makes this an appropriate setting for the Blennerhassett legend. Nearly 4 miles long, with 8 miles of shore-line and consisting of 500 acres, Blennerhassett Island floats on the horizon like an enchanted Bali-Ha'i, a mile and a half south of the mouth of the Kanawha and Parkersburg's Point Park.

Archaeologists have proved by unearthing weapons, tools, jewelry and other artifacts that Indians lived here 9,000 years before Christ. In fact, the island is ranked as one of the richest Indian sites in the Midwest. Early European explorers and traders passed through in the mid 18th century, some staying to grow crops on the fertile bottom soil. When the Blennerhassetts arrived, the Indian wars had been settled for only a few years (following a bloody massacre on the nearby shore), making it safe for permanent settlement. In the later part of the 18th and early 19th centuries, the island was farmed and used as a private park for sporting competitions and celebrity gatherings. In 1970 the island was placed on the National Register of Historic Places, and the state passed legislation creating the **Blennerhassett Historical Park Commission** to preserve the island's heritage—a history long celebrated in painting, poetry and literature. The park was an immediate success, and in the early 1980s West Virginia decided to reconstruct the mansion. Permanent electricity was first brought from the mainland in 1986. In just 12 years the island was transformed from a neglected overgrown tangle of weeds to the gorgeous manicured park and estate you see today. You can explore its natural wonders on foot, on a rental bicycle or on a leisurely, horse-drawn wagon ride along the wooded trails. Of particular note is the magnificent stand of black walnut trees. Facing the mansion on your left near the shore is a giant tulip poplar, 8 feet in diameter, more than 24 feet in circumference and 76 feet tall—one of the largest trees in the state.

A naturalist group has identified 112 different species of birds (including ospreys) and suggests the wetland area at the western side for spotting them. Deer and other small mammals like raccoon are plentiful. Near the water, look for freshwater mussels, an important part of the river's ecosystem (as a food source and water filter) and of history: Indians ate mussels and used the shells for ornaments and weapons. Although the Blennerhassett gardens, gazebos, fish pond and pathways are long gone, you can see where the exquisite flower beds spilled over two acres, rimmed with fruit trees and fragrant vines. The rich soil also produced wheat, corn and other edibles, including apples planted by "Johnny Appleseed."

The island is accessible to the public via sternwheelers, which operate every half hour in season (May through October, including weekends) from Point Park in downtown Parkersburg. The trip takes about 20 minutes and the lovely views along the river add a bonus to the outing.

### The Blennerhassett Museum

Begin or end your tour of the island at the museum, on the mainland near the sternwheeler boarding point. On the bottom level of this recently renovated, spacious building a background 12-minute video on the Blennerhassetts sets the stage for your island visit.

Displayed in glass cases, ancient relics uncovered by archaeologists, prove the island was long prized and used by man and beast. One case holds the enormous bones of a mastodon, an ice age mammal. Three floors of displays chronicle man's occupations, dating back 11,000 years ago, from Indian petroglyphs, arrowheads, pipes, pottery, weapons and ornaments to fine Blennerhassett furniture, china and glass. In addition to a railroad exhibit, other interesting period pieces unrelated to the Blennerhassetts include 19th-century clothing and furniture, Civil War items, a Victorian mourning wreath made from human hair, a display on Parkersburg's "Golden Era," and antique farming equipment. Allow at least an hour to see everything. Gift shop attached.

### The Blennerhassett Mansion

After many years of research and archaelogical excavation, the Blennerhassett mansion was reconstructed on its original site in

The entrance hall of Blennerhassett Mansion welcomed guests to many lively evenings of lectures, concerts, dinners and dances given by Margaret and Harman Blennerhassett. BRIAN B. SCHROEDER

the mid-1980s. The half-elliptical shape follows the Italian Palladian style much admired and used by both George Washington and Thomas Jefferson for their own homes: a two-story central section connected to two flanking wings by covered semi-circular porticoes. The vertical lines are balanced by massive brick chimneys that seem to anchor the mansion to the ground. Because Harman feared earthquakes, he had the house constructed from native hardwoods (instead of brick) and painted it white so it would gleam brilliantly for admirers to see as they passed by on river boats; the foundation was cut from river rock. In the main section, costumed docents explain the history and contents, room by room, retelling how the mansion tragically burned: a candle lit in the wine cellar set hemp afire and the conflagration spread.

The mansion held over 7,000 square feet of floor space. Most day-to-day activities took place in the **central building,** composed of two parlors, two drawing rooms, a library, dining room, entrance hall, winter kitchen and four bedrooms. The walls, painted in rich, bright, happy tones, reflect the ample light from large windows: this was one of the first homes in this part of the country to have glass panes. Notice the Venetian sunshades, remarkably contemporary looking but actually a discovery Marco Polo brought home from China. Oil paintings, Oriental rugs and opulent antiques furnish the rooms, including exquisite Italian alabaster vases once owned by Harman and Margaret. Some original Blennerhassett pieces were luckily retrieved from local families whose ancestors had bought items at the 1807 auction of mansion contents. An intriguing circular glass object in the dining room functioned as a fly-catcher. Around the table, stood 14 black-and-gold cane-seated chairs handmade in Baltimore. The downstairs drawing room, paneled in walnut, exudes a masculine, clubby feeling. On the top floor, the ballroom with its marbled wallpaper witnessed many a gay evening of music and dance. Heart of pine floors, ceiling medallions and detailed carved moldings throughout draw the rooms together in a harmonious style.

The **south wing** served as the summer kitchen, and the restoration is reportedly one of the best-equipped 18th-century kitchens in the country. A huge hearth, at least five feet wide, was tended by some of the Blennerhassett slaves, but Margaret, an accomplished cook, prepared many of the meals herself. Clever contraptions like the small-fowl roaster and coffee roaster document how well guests dined. Utensils, casks, pewter dishes, oversized mugs, tables and chairs, some original to the house, complete the authentic scene. Outside an herb garden fills the air with appetizing scents.

The **north wing**, where the fateful fire started, was Harman's sanctuary. Here he flirted with chemical experiments, kept accounts, read and fiddled with his scientific instruments. Note the handsome bookpress and original table. A "magic message machine" in each wing explains the room.

Take time to stroll through the grounds. Although their population boom is a nuisance, the white-tailed deer add a touch of tranquility and timelessness to the pastoral scene. Allow at least three hours to absorb all the visual and cerebral rewards of this magnificent site, truly the jewel of the Ohio.

**Tip**: If you are in the area in early December, call the park for details on special Christmas events. In summer, inquire about the August outdoor musical drama *Eden on the River*. On-going craft demonstrations take place in season.

**Hours**: Sternwheeler rides leave on the half hour from 10:00 A.M. to 5:00 P.M. every day except Monday from the first week of May to Labor Day weekend; weekends only during September and October. No schedule from November 1 to April 30, except for special events and private arrangements. The park is closed to all visitors from November 1 to May 1. Call Ruble's Sternwheelers at (304)428-2415 or (614)423-7268. The museum is open 9:30 A.M. to 6:00 P.M. Tuesday through Sunday year-round.

**Admission**: Ride to island only: Adults $4.00, ages 6-12 $3.00, under 6 free to all facilities. Boat ride, mansion and museum: adults $6.50, ages 6-12 $4.00. Mansion tour: Adults $2.00, 6-12 $1.00. Museum admission: Adults $1.00, 6-12 $.50. Wagon rides: Adults $3.00, 6-12 $2.00.

**Directions**: Board the sternwheeler to the island at Point Park, at the foot of Second Street in Parkersburg. The museum is at Second and Juliana. For further information write Blennerhassett Historical State Park, P.O. Box 283, Parkersburg, WV 26102 or call 1(800)CALL WVA or (304)428-3000.

## Blennerhassett Hotel

Passing through the brass-handled wooden doors to the lobby of the Blennerhassett Hotel, the visitor feels the aura of another era—horse-drawn carriages, gas lights, rustling skirts and that special spark generated from a town and people making fast money. Indeed, Parkersburg in 1889 was such a rough and ready place that steel guards were placed in front of the hotel's lobby mirror to protect it from street shootings. Built by banker Colonel William Chancellor to accommodate travelers drawn here by the booming oil industry, the new hotel was an immediate success, a showplace bringing a veneer of gentility, sophistication, elegance and above all a respectable meeting place to this wild port.

Businessmen made deals at the bar, ladies exchanged gossip over tea, and vaudeville stars kept guests up all night rehearsing their acts in their rooms. In its day, the 50-room hotel was considered the grandest in the state. To accommodate the needs of brisk business, a bank was even established downstairs.

Almost one hundred years later, the building, now expanded, renovated and reopened, recaptures the charm and glamour of its early days. Although not original to the hotel, antique chandeliers, wall sconces, doors, mirrors and furniture recreate the heydays of 19th-century Parkersburg. Some of the clocks, like the one in the entry lobby, are over 100 years old. Charming English prints on the guest floors are typical of the originals. The exterior lights, resembling period gas lamps, shed a soft welcoming glow. **Harman's** restaurant off the lobby serves the best cuisine in town. The hostess greets diners from a 90-year-old ship clerk desk from England. The sconces in the lounge come from the Dunn & Bradstreet Building in New York. Spacious guest rooms are furnished with reproductions of Chippendale furniture and fabric. The crown molding reproduces the design in the wallpaper that was stripped out of the hotel prior to remodeling.

For many, the Blennerhassett Hotel is still the place to meet, and even the casual stroller, just peering through the window, feels the pulse of activity. Go in for a drink, dinner or just to hear the echo of an exciting part in Parkersburg's past.

**Tip**: This is a good central point for starting a walking tour of many interesting sites and a resting spot for a refreshing meal or drink after the trip to Blennerhassett Island.

**Directions**: The hotel is #28 on the Historical Walking Tour at Fourth and Market streets, three blocks from the floodwall. Coming into town on Rt. 50, take a left on Market, follow to Fourth. For reservations or further information call 1(800)262-2536 or (304)433-3131 or write Blennerhassett Hotel, Fourth and Market Streets, Parkersburg, WV 26101.

## The Cook House

If you are touring in a car, you must look closely for the Cook House—over 160 years old and one of the oldest existing buildings in Wood County. It's better to see this beautifully preserved 1825-29 farmhouse as part of the Parkersburg walking tour (#12) or you may miss the quaint, cozy home among the modern buildings, traffic and general hub-bub surrounding it. Thanks to the tender loving care of the Junior League, to whom the site was deeded by a Cook descendant, this little gem is preserved as an important historical site and is particularly well used and valued by local fourth graders. Under the tutelage of Junior League docents, these Parkersburg children are learning from living-history field trips just how a frontier family lived in the early half of the 19th century.

Even a superficial glance at the exterior tells you the structure was unique among other homes of the same period. The Cook family were Quakers from New England, heavily influenced by Puritan severity. There are no frills in the economy of construction and interior details. No fancy moldings decorate windows or doorways, no ornamentation adorns the mantle. The style could be considered modified Federalist except for the inverted T-plan and one-story wings on either side of the two-story center core, which are very unusual. There is grace and understated elegance in the vertical symmetry, the handsome Flemish bonding in the bricks, the stately chimneys, the balanced nine-over-six windows accented by an arched fanlight in the gable.

**Tillinghast Cook** came from a frontier family who arrived in the Mid-Ohio area in 1795, when he was five years old. His father, Joseph, subsequently bought and bequeathed to him large and strategic tracts of land around Parkersburg, then a crude settlement of log cabins at the confluence of the Kanawha and Ohio rivers. Like other settlers who had to depend on their own ingenuity and skills to survive on the edge of civilization, Tillinghast was a jack-of-many-trades and talents: farmer, merchant, surveyor, politician, land speculator. After marrying Betsey Russell in 1820, Cook built his home on a 108-acre lot from bricks made on site (presumably with slave help) and hardwood timber

162

harvested from virgin forest nearby. In this dwelling the Cooks spent 50 years of married life, rearing seven of their eight children to adulthood. During these eventful years, Parkersburg burgeoned from a small crossroad to one of the richest cities in the new state of West Virginia, and their once-rural farmhouse became part of an urban boom.

It is a bright, welcoming house inside, furnished with some items belonging to the Cooks and others authentic to the times. The entrance room, or parlor, with fireplace was a busy living area. In keeping with the economy evident throughout the house, the fireplace was enclosed with a stenciled screen in summer and used as a storage for woolens. Above the mantle a dignified oil portrait of Tillinghast surveys the comings and goings of visitors. A corner staircase leads to three upstairs bedrooms, a luxury for the times. An open-Bible pattern on the door reflects the family's religious leanings. In Tillinghast's bedroom to the right hangs a New England sampler. The tiny, fine stitching illustrated here was exemplary of the medium used by young girls to prove their domestic skill. Visitors are shown the wick trimmer and explained the value of a candle and the importance of keeping the wick properly trimmed after each use. The kitchen to the left holds authentic period pieces and a collection of irons that demonstrate the evolution of this household tool through the shape and material of the handles. Perhaps most interesting to children (besides the hidden potty chair) is the collection of handmade toys—corn cob dolls, carved animals, puzzles—some of which, like Job's Ladder, were only allowed on Sundays.

Cook descendants lived in this house until the 1950s—another reason for its excellent condition. A family photo album documents every generation. During the Christmas season, League docents in period costumes show off the open house, bedecked with traditional greens and candles.

**Tip**: If you are driving, park in the adjacent shopping mall parking area.

**Hours**: Make arrangements for a tour at least a day ahead by calling (304)485-1122, by leaving a message on the Cook House tape (304)422-6961 or by contacting the Convention and Visitor Bureau at (304)428-1130.

**Admission**: $1.00; under age 12 free. All fees are returned to the community through League service projects.

**Directions**: From Rt. 50 west turn onto Market St. then left on Murdoch. Go about ½ mile. For more information write the Cook House, 1301 Murdoch Avenue, Parkersburg, WV 26101.

## The Henry Cooper Log Cabin Museum

Relocated, log by log, in 1910 to the City Park in Parkersburg from its original site nine miles away, the Cooper Museum is fun to browse through on a summer Sunday afternoon. Kids resistant to seeing yet another place filled with "old things" can use the playgrounds or feed ducks while their parents browse through an eclectic array of historical paraphernalia. But most children do love exploring the nooks and crannies, fantasizing living in this cozy log home Henry Cooper built for his family in 1804. His descendants are still active in maintaining it as a museum under the auspices of the Daughters of American Pioneers, to whom it has been deeded. Their slogan describing the cabin as "where time is stored in Parkersburg" couldn't be more apt.

Remarkably large and accommodating for its time, the two-story structure is chock full of antique 19th-century Americana: photos (including Henry and his wife), Civil War and WWI uniforms, stuffed birds, rope beds, old sewing machines, potting and spinning wheels, quilts, vintage clothing, baby carriages, cradles, farm implements, a table original to the house, period hats and an astounding collection of some 45,000 buttons. Ask to see the red-white-and-blue eagle-patterned coverlet.

**Hours**: Sunday afternoons from 1:30 to 4:30 P.M., Memorial Day to Labor Day. Special arrangements can be made for group tours. Call (304)422-7122 or 442-7841.

**Admission**: Adults $1.00, children 6–16 $.50, under 6 free.

**Directions**: From Rt. 50 heading into Parkersburg, turn right onto Park Ave. at the Park Elementary School and go two blocks to City Park. For further information write Curator, Daughters of American Pioneers, 3310 Kim St., Parkersburg, WV 26104.

## Little Kanawha Crafthouse

Since its opening in 1988, this cute craft house tucked into the floodwall, has featured high-quality handmade items from nearly 800 artisans—most representing Mid-Ohio heritage. Quilts, wooden furniture and toys, baskets, ironware, stained glass, paintings, coal figurines, dolls, ceramics and a year-round collection of Christmas crafts offer visitors a wide choice of unique gift items. You can spend as little as a dollar for a kitchen magnet or several hundred for a large quilt. Items are on consignment, so you will be supporting artisans directly through your one-of-a-kind purchases. It's easy to combine a shopping visit here with a trip to Blennerhassett Historical Park since the store is next to the boarding point for the sternwheeler. Call 48 hours in advance to arrange for a craft demonstration.

**Hours**: May to October 10:00 A.M. to 6:00 P.M. Monday through Saturday and 11:00 A.M. to 6:00 P.M. on Sunday. From October through April, hours are 9:00 A.M. to 5:00 P.M. Monday through Saturday.

**Directions**: Between First and Second streets on Ann Street at the floodwall. For more information call (304)485-3149 or write Little Kanawha Crafthouse, 113 Ann Street, Parkersburg, WV 26101.

## Ohio River Islands National Wildlife Refuge

In May of 1992 the first national wildlife refuge in the State of West Virginia was formally dedicated. This landmark occasion celebrated over a decade of efforts on the part of naturalist groups and political supporters to acquire funding and the appropriate legislation to establish the refuge and staff a permanent office.

Managed by the U.S. Fish and Wildlife Service, the Ohio River Islands National Wildlife Refuge acquisition area stretches along 362 miles of the Ohio River from Shippingport, Pennsylvania, to Manchester, Ohio.

The initial acquisition of **eight islands** is an exciting beginning to the new naturalist haven. In time, when other islands are purchased from private holders, the refuge may consist of up to 38 islands ranging in size from less than an acre to more than 400 acres (most of them physically located in West Virginia), and encompass up to 3,500 acres of fish and wildlife habitat. Areas along the mainland that provide excellent natural environments will be valuable additions in the future.

For years naturalists have prized the Ohio River Islands and their back channels for the high quality of wildlife ecosystems used by migratory and resident waterfowl, shorebirds, songbirds, warm-water fish and rare freshwater mussels. More than 130 species of birds have been identified, including 11 species of raptors and 87 species of songbirds. Two of the four great blue heron rookeries in the state are located on two of these islands (Grape and Fish Creek). Bald eagles and peregrine falcons make regular visits. Mammals also proliferate here, including beaver, rabbit, mink, muskrat, opossum, raccoon, woodchuck and white-tail deer. Some of the over 50 species of fish breeding in these waters are drum, channel catfish, bluegill, largemouth bass and spotted bass. Over 30 species of freshwater mussels inhabit the sand and gravel bars around the islands. The refuge's primary goal is preserving, restoring and enhancing the diversity and abundance of these fish and wildlife populations.

The islands played an important role in human history and the development of this part of the country, supplying and harboring Indian populations, early settlers and surveyors (like George Washington), and pioneers headed west. Civil War soldiers fought strategic battles nearby. In this century, the islands witnessed the growth of commerce and served primarily navigation and industrial purposes. Now again they will serve man, this time for recreation and nature activities. Most of the islands have sandy beaches, good for picnics and fishing. Visitors wanting to explore the interior will find terrain forested with bottom-land hardwoods and some relic plant communities that are unusual for low elevations. Because there are no bridges connecting them to the mainland, the islands remain relatively undisturbed: a wild and wonderful spot for a getaway day.

As more islands are purchased from private owners, the Fish and Wildlife Service will encourage hunting, fishing, hiking and wildlife observation. At the present time, the islands in West Virginia are clustered around the Sisterville, Paden City and St. Mary's areas and are accessible only by private boats. They are open to the public year-round during daylight hours, but you should consult the refuge manager for current regulations before landing.

For information on how to rent boats, call Ray Maxwell at the Sisterville Boat Club (304)652-2039, or you can rent a pontoon boat by the hour or day from Flotilla Boat Rentals, 1413 First Avenue, Parkersburg, WV (304)485-0164. For more information on the refuge, call (304)420-7568 or write Ohio River Islands National Wildlife Refuge, P.O. Box 1811, Parkersburg, WV 26102.

## Oil and Gas Museum

Don't leave Parkersburg without seeing this museum even if you think you don't have an interest in the subject. Its contents document the history, growth and character of Parkersburg so fascinatingly that even kids will like it.

The museum's intent is "Dedicated to preserving the rich heritage of individuals from West Virginia and southeastern Ohio who created the oil and gas industry in the U.S. and who have played a major role in its management and development from the 1800s to date. The theme is truly a history of rugged, resourceful inventive, persistent and dynamic individuals who developed an industry that made our country a world leader." For a museum less than three years old, it accomplishes this aim admirably.

Housed in a spacious, old brick hardware store near Point Park, the museum owns adjacent land to accommodate enormous pieces of drilling equipment and a 1905 steam engine too big to put in a building. A complete 84-foot derrick soon will join the imposing pump and boiler already in place.

Inside, through historical documents, the statement is firmly made that the Parkersburg area was the first producer of oil and gas in the U.S., starting with the major boom in oil in 1859. Even before then, Indians and early settlers knew about oil and used and sold it for medicinal and industrial purposes. The slimy substance was so abundant and close to the surface that it oozed into the rivers. George Washington also knew about the oil supply and owned land from which the rich deposits at Burning Springs were later extracted.

Early artifacts and equipment, engines, pumps, tools, models, letters, legal and business documents and exhibits trace the story of oil from its earliest use through the Civil War days (when Confederate soldiers burned out the major oil field) to the present.

Following the war, the industry recouped and exploded when **Standard Oil** came in the 1870s and built a refinery and transportation facilities. The first congressman, senator and governor of the state were oil men and in a position to encourage the rapid growth of that industry, and consequently Parkersburg. A fascinating model of the Parkersburg Pumpers shows exactly how the drilling process worked.

One of the most informative items is a wall-sized geologic map proving the vast extent of exploration. Tens of thousands of wells have been drilled in the state since 1860. The eclectic collection of photos, clothing, memorabilia, many donated by old Parkersburg families associated one way or another with the industry, demonstrates the industry's impact on the social and political history of the city. Photos and lithographs capture 19th-century street scenes, buildings, floods, river traffic and the colorful personalities who made Parkersburg—in its prime— one of the most dynamic cities in the country.

**Hours**: Saturdays 10:00 A.M. to 6:00 P.M. and Sunday 12:00 to 6:00 P.M. Weekdays and evenings by appointment. Call (304)485-5446 or 428-8015.

**Admission**: Adults $2.00, children $1.00.

**Directions**: Number #24 on the Historic Walking Tour, one block from Point Park in historic Smith Hardware at 119 Third Street. For more information write Oil and Gas Museum, Box 1685, Parkersburg, WV 26102.

## Parkersburg Art Center

The Art Center, established in 1938, is one of the oldest visual arts organizations in the state. Moved to its bright, cheerful location in 1974, the center sponsors shows of local artists as well as nationally recognized favorites like Winslow Homer. Exhibits span many media and interests, including such imaginative themes as a "Touch and Feel" exhibit designed for the blind to "see" celebrities by feeling their life masks, a life-size dinosaur show, wood engravings from children's classics, a photographic documentary of the Sioux, a competitive exhibition focusing on American Realism, children's art as well as more conventional portraits and landscapes. Once a year there is a show of regional artists living within 75 miles of Parkersburg. You can fit this visit in with the walking tour of the city because it is convenient to the Smoot Theatre and Blennerhassett Hotel.

**Hours**: Tuesday through Friday, 10:00 A.M. to 4:00 P.M., Saturday and Sunday from 1:00 to 4:00 P.M. Closed Mondays and major holidays. Docent-led tours are available on request.

**Admission**: Adults $1.00, children $.50.

**Directions**: From Rt. 50 coming into Parkersburg, bear right onto Eighth Street. The center is at 220 Eighth, between Market and Juliana streets. For more information, call (304)485-3859 or write Parkersburg Art Center, P.O. Box 131, Parkersburg, WV 26101.

## Point of View Restaurant

Even if the food weren't delicious and the service so extra pleasant—which they are—a stop at this restaurant is a must if only for the magnificent view. From the glassed-in dining area you look down and out to the south side of Blennerhassett Island and for miles up and down the Ohio River. In fall colorful leaves, reflected in the water, bejewel the riverbanks, and in winter, with the view unobstructed by trees, you see Blennerhassett Mansion and Parkersburg landmarks. River traffic and an occasional osprey add a dynamic dimension to the picture. At night the lights of the city twinkle like Christmas ornaments, but the view is best during the day, particularly from the small observation deck attached to the restaurant.

**Tip**: Try the homemade crab and lobster bisque.

**Hours**: Lunch 11:30 A.M. to 2:00 P.M. and dinner from 5:30 nightly. Closed on Sunday. Reservatons are required for Friday and Saturday. Call (304)863-3366.

**Directions**: From downtown Parkersburg take Rt. 50 (Seventh Street) west and turn left onto Rt. 68 south (in front of hospital). Follow Rt. 68 out of town and go 1¼ miles turning right onto Star Avenue, then make an immediate left onto Marrtown Road. Go ¼ mile to Point of View sign, turn right and follow for 1½ miles. For more information write Point of View, Blennerhassett Heights Road, Parkersburg, WV 26101.

## The Smoot Theatre

If you think Tinkerbell was a fictional fairy with no earthbound siblings, arrange a tour of the Smoot Theatre and meet Felice Jorgeson. With the wave of her magic wand and (she will emphasize this) the generous wallets of local supporters, volunteers and the invaluable memory of a colleague, dynamic Felice rescued an historical treasure from the demolition crew and mobilized support for its transformation from shabby movie house into an architectural gem and now Parkersburg's showpiece for

In 1932 the Smoot Theatre promised to provide nurses and smelling salts to patrons feeling faint from watching Frankenstein.

ARTCRAFT STUDIO, PARKERSBURG

performing arts. The story is a variation of the ugly toad to handsome prince, with Felice providing the magic kiss.

Built in 1926 at the peak of **vaudeville** verve and at a cost of $250,000, the Smoot was the inspiration of the Smoot Amusement Company, who thought that building a new glitzy theater would attract famous acts to booming Parkersburg. And for a while it did. In the best of vaudeville tradition, the new stage hosted such outrageous scenes as saxophone-playing Siamese twins, dancing midgets, prancing elephants and saw-wielding magicians as well as conventional entertainment like Guy Lombardo's band and beauty pageants. At its prime during the Roaring Twenties, audiences packed the house every day of the week for five shows a day, from 1:00 to 11:00 P.M.

Sadly, however, the days of vaudeville ended. With the coming of the silent screen and later the "talkies," the nation's theaters designed to house live acts were dismantled, mutilated and reshaped to accommodate movie screens, popcorn machines, projector rooms and efficient (and ugly) street-side ticket booths. Like its peers that were stripped to woo the fickle public to the new fad, the Smoot, too, surrendered its glorious glitter to become a movie house, and thus it served for the next fifty-plus years. After it closed to mall competition and fell into disrepair, plans proceeded for tearing it down and concreting its colorful past into a parking lot. At this crucial point, Felice and her band of local elves (mostly musicians, theater buffs and concerned citizens) recognized the grand dame for her classic charms and restoration potential. Reversing the aging process, the group raised money to buy the building and opened its doors for a historical big band concert in May 1989.

Three years later, with the help of private donations, public grants and a great deal of elbow grease and volunteer manpower, the Smoot shines again. The water-stained ceiling is repaired and painted, the walls repapered, new carpets installed, seats reupholstered, wooden doors and brass fixtures replaced and polished, and chandeliers shined and relit. The curtain once again rises to live performances.

This miraculous rebirth seems destined to have happened since so many important characters who made it possible turned up serendipitously at the right moment, as though cued for the role. Take Tom Piatt, for instance, who worked at the Smoot as an usher when he was ten years old for twenty-five cents an hour. Now in his mid-seventies, he remembers the thrilling days of touring companies, temperamental stars and, most important, how the old theater looked and operated. With his recollections, plus old photos and documents, the original colors were matched and applied to gold-gilt art deco designs on walls and ceiling. Soft tones of beige, mauve, jade and blue accent complementary colors in the magnificent stained-glass chandeliers. Another patroness won the lottery just in time to pay for the return of the original 1928 pipe organ to its rightful location up front, stage right. When sufficient donations come in, it will be put back into working order.

To tell you about all this is Felice herself, former high-school band teacher, now present fixer, director, fund-raiser, manager, inspirer—full of a thousand ideas for creatively using and sharing the theater for all kinds of projects and performances. With inexhaustible enthusiasm, Felice will show you a superb slide show of the history of the theater and some of the gimmicks and ads for early vaudeville shows and movies. A standout is a 1932 newspaper photo showing nurses standing beside an ambulance in front of the marquee advertising *Frankenstein*. The ad promised that if you felt faint from the horror of the movie, the theater would provide nursing, smelling salts and transportation to the hospital.

Felice takes you up on **stage** and demonstrates the original lights and dimmers, points out the six curtains and the floors made from pine and maple to bring out the unique sounds of tap dancers, the trap door and loft at a dizzying height (to which she climbs with the confidence of a high-wire artist to clean from time to time). You'll hear how the 1937 flood entered the theater during a performance and covered the stage with three feet of water.

She'll take you to the **projection room** and explain the 1930 projectors and the tricky task of changing movie reels quickly every 18 minutes, the cleaning of the chandeliers with Tide and ammonia, and why the acoustics are so fine and every one of the 720 seats are good. She'll show you the dressing rooms downstairs and tell you how the local high school art students painted and decorated the walls and how apprentice plumbers repaired and re-installed old brass shower fixtures. She'll tell you about the summer vaudeville camp here that teaches young people dance and music and what she will do to finish the interior and stage when the money comes in. But mostly she'll enchant, charm and weave her magic so you too will want to help her vision materialize: to recreate, through the Smoot, the wonderful world of early 20th-century live theater. Her contagious spirit spearheaded the restoration, but she is quick to give credit to the volunteers who man all performances, anonymous donors and grants, material and labor from local citizens and businesses.

Felice will tailor-make almost any kind of tour you want depending on the interest of the group. One specialty is a **dessert tour** that seats guests at tables on the stage and serves them scrumptious goodies. No tour, of course, can unleash the full impact of Smoot's power to transcend reality. Do try to catch a performance: jazz, ragtime, opera, bluegrass, rock, children's theater, comedy or dance. All the hard work, the fund-raising, the begging come together for the big payoff when those crystal lights dim, the music begins and the curtain goes up.

**Hours**: You must make advance reservations either through the Visitor and Convention Bureau at 1(800)752-4982 or (304)428-1130 or directly with the theater at (304)422-PLAY.

**Admission**: Depends on what kind of tour is requested. Full dessert tour with slide show is about $10.00 per person; regular tour $3.00.

**Directions**: Five blocks east of the flood wall, the theater is #31 on the Historical Walking Tour: 213 Fifth Street. For further information write the Smoot Theatre, P.O. Box 886, Parkersburg, WV 26102.

## Trans Allegheny Books

Book worms, beware! Allow lots of time and bring lots of money when you visit Trans Allegheny Books. And take note of the closing hours, for this is one library you won't mind being locked in overnight.

On the National Register of Historic Places, this seductive, addictive used/rare/new book store and its fascinating contents occupy the 1906 Parkersburg Carnegie Public Library, which be-

The Andrew Carnegie Public Library in Parkersburg now houses Trans Allegheny Books and their large selection of used, rare and new books. COURTESY TRANS ALLEGHENY BOOKS

came available for another purpose when the new public library was built in 1976.

Typical of the turn-of-the-century elegance of other Carnegie libraries, the stately brick neo-classic structure has retained its original glass insets in the floor, giving a feeling of light and space between the levels of stacks. A spiral iron staircase, adding a bit of art deco flair, winds up three stories to a special section on West Virginia history and literature. Marble on the exterior trim and on counters inside adds a touch of classicism and scholarship, so appropriate for book browsing. Behind the staircase and dominating the light source, a stained-glass window properly honors the philanthropist patron with the Carnegie coat-of-arms.

The idea for a rare book store was the dream of the present owner whose passion for historical volumes led to a personal collection of over 8,000 titles. Renovation and restoration costs topped $300,000 before the store opened its doors in 1985. Catering to all book lovers, Trans Allegheny specializes, through their contacts with other book collectors and vendors, a search service for out-of-print books. Although the company is probably the best retail source for books on West Virginia in the state, they fill hard to find requests for all kinds of books from all over the country.

Spread over four floors of shelves, the inventory ranges from new regional titles to children's books, magazines, newspapers, postcards, sheet music, old photographs, prints, hymnals, records. Over 200,000 hardcover and paperback volumes—most acquired from auctions and estate sales—cover every category imaginable: how-tos, poetry, biographies, references, manuals, fiction, cookbooks, travel guides, art and historical collectibles—and on and on and on.

With the price of new books escalating and the growing appreciation for second-hand first editions—and, above all, a popular demand for affordable reading material of all kinds–this second-hand book business is enjoying phenomenal growth—an average of 50 percent a year.

Beyond the marvelous surprise of discovering a new interest or an underpriced antique, much of the reward in exploring the stacks is in feeling old leather, sniffing that indescribable aroma of old paper, and reading the personal messages inscribed inside so long ago. Knowing the book was originally given with a special sentiment or purpose can enhance its value to the new owner—like recycled romance.

After you satisfy your own lust for *le livre*, keep in mind what a great opportunity this is to find the perfect gift for a new baby (nursery rhymes from the 1920s), a birthday (matching the date to an old magazine) or holiday (old Valentines and Christmas cards). If you can't find what you're seeking, ask the people working there, most of whom are "worms" too and seem to know just where what book is waiting to be claimed.

It's also possible to bring in your own books for trading. Just remember that, according to Trans Allegheny guidelines, "Paperbacks are traded two for one of like kind. Romances must be no older than 1990." So much for love eternal!

**Hours**: Tuesday through Saturday, 10:00 A.M. to 6:00 P.M. Open most Mondays, but call first. Private tours can be arranged.

**Directions**: The former Carnegie Library is #36 on the Parkersburg walking tour at 725 Green Street, Parkersburg, WV 26101. Call (304)422-4499. As you come into Parkersburg on Rt. 50, turn right onto Green Street.

# Williamstown

## *Fenton Art Glass Factory and Museum*

If you have time and interest for only one glass factory tour, this should be it. Fenton Glass has been a thriving business for over

85 years, outlasting other glass companies in the area that have come and gone, victims of fickle fate and the erratic economics of Ohio Valley industry. The secret for Fenton's endurance and growth is apparently the successful marriage of old-time hand glassmaking techniques, modern technology and business acumen. With about 350 on full staff, Fenton runs a very efficient enterprise, including their comprehensive tours of the factory.

Since 1907 when two Fenton brothers pooled $284 and built their Williamstown plant near a cheap source of gas, the company has produced high quality handmade glassware using innovative techniques for such classic favorites as Carnival Glass, hobnail, milk glass, Cranberry and Burmese. The brothers later persuaded two more siblings to join them, and thus began the Fenton Glass dynasty that is now in a third generation of ownership and management.

On entering the showroom, you're confronted with a dazzling choice of lamps, vases, goblets, eggs, pitchers, dishes, figurines, paperweights in a multitude of colors, shapes, glazes and textures. Don't dawdle long here, for you'll have a chance to browse after the tour when you can better appreciate and judge the selection.

Start with the movie and **museum** upstairs—an excellent orientation to the glass industry particularly along this part of the Ohio—well worth the nominal charge. A 24-minute film shows the step-by-step glassmaking process at the Fenton factory. The adjacent museum is a fascinating chronology of the art in the Ohio Valley, showcasing irreplaceable pieces from early Fenton years as well as from other famous, now defunct, glass companies. Some beauties like the amethyst "Goddess of Harvest" are valued at thousands of dollars, and their stunning delicacy, translucence and artistry make one gasp. Glass objects are arranged categorically and labeled with such romantic names as "Diamond Optic in Ruby," "Daisy & Button in Cape Cod Green" and "Love in White on Ruby." You'll learn here that Burmese glass is valuable for its contents (uranium and gold), that milk glass contains fluoride and that Carnival glass gets its unique iridescence from a spraying of metallic salts. The awesome beauty of these amethyst, orange, jade, sapphire and ruby jewels is all the more overwhelming when you realize a human being made these with just sand, soda and a few selected minerals.

This miraculous process takes on meaning and relevance when you go downstairs and join a 45-minute **tour of the factory** floor. As you move through the different stages of production you'll see that because each vase is handmade, no two are exactly alike. The tour varies slightly from hour to hour depending on what is being made, but skilled craftsmen usually follow the steps below.

The "batch" or basic ingredients are mixed from sand (75%), soda ash (15%) and lime (9%) plus remaining materials to give color. Uranium, for instance, is added for a yellow glass, cobalt for blue, iron for green, sugar and iron for amber, selenium, cadmium and sulphur for Ruby Red and gold for Cranberry. The mixture is then loaded into a large gas-fired melting furnace at about 2,500 degrees F. Next a "gatherer" collects a gob of the molten liquid on a hollow blow pipe or steel rod (called punty). Rotating the mixture to form a perfectly sized ball, he drops it into a mold, which has been hand carved with Fenton designs and patterns. The "presser" next performs the exacting science of snipping off the molten glass in the mold and flipping the cut end to prevent a shear mark with just the right amount of pressure to prevent shattering.

If the piece is to be blown, the gatherer delivers the gob on a blow pipe to the "blocker," who cools it before shaping it into a wooden block placed in soapy water and gives the piece its first bubble. Next the blower reheats it, rolls the gathered ball onto a flat plate and then blows the hot mass into the mold and its final shape.

Before the liquid cools the "finisher" quickly smooths the object with a traditional cherry wood paddle to refine final shape, then crimps edges and straightens stems. The tricky task of attaching the handle is the province of another expert, the "handler." With a lightning-fast twist of the wrist, he hooks the ribbon of glass onto one side of the basket, forms a loop and attaches the other end. After working and shaping it into a perfect arch, he affixes his own personal stamp to the base of the handle. This mark identifies exactly which handler finished the piece.

Other variations, such as crystal edges on milk glass and crimps, are executed in yet other procedures. When the piece is cool enough, it is placed onto a slow moving conveyor belt and allowed to reach room temperature before being inspected, judged and packaged. At this time all defects are recognized and the item rejected or labeled a "second." If the piece is to be hand decorated, it goes to a room where artists paint on designs with inorganic pigments of mostly crushed glass that are fused into the glass through a heating process. Each piece is individually signed by the artist. Etched, or sand carved, pieces receive their frosted pattern through a high-powered spray gun that applies grit over a stencil-like covering. Competence at any of the jobs comes only after years of training and experience. At each stage the confident worker must perform quickly and flawlessly.

After the tour, equipped with a deeper appreciation and respect for the glassmaking process, you're prepared to admire and purchase final products in the **gift shop** and factory outlet where seconds are discounted. You should never again take for granted the fluted edges of a Cranberry vase, the perfect symmetry of a goblet, the delicate etching on a beer stein nor forget the talented men who created them. A visit to Fenton is truly a marvelous, enlightening experience.

**Restrictions**: No children under two years of age permitted on factory tour. However, they are allowed in museum, movie and gift shop.

**Admission**: Entrance to the museum, movie included, is $1.00 for adults and $.50 for children. Tour of the factory is free.

**Hours**: Tours begin about every 45 minutes from 8:30 A.M. to 2:30 P.M. Monday through Friday. There is a limited tour at 3:45 P.M. When tours are not available (on weekends, national holidays or during the two weeks in July when the factory is closed), a visit to the museum and a free movie are substituted. The tour schedule is subject to change. Call for exact dates and for making arrangements for groups of 20 or more, (304)375-7772.

Gift Shop and Factory Outlet: Monday through Saturday 8:00 A.M. to 5:00 P.M. and Sunday 12:00 to 5:00. Extended evening hours some days in summer, spring and fall. Call (304)375-7772.

**Directions**: Williamstown is about 10 miles north of Parkersburg (take Rt. 14 North) and just across the Ohio River from Marietta, Ohio, (accessible by I-77, Exit 185). After entering Williamstown, Fenton Glass signs pointing the way to the factory are clearly visible, directing you to turn right on Henderson Avenue. For more information write Fenton Art Glass Company, 420 Caroline Avenue, Williamstown, WV 26187 or call (304)375-6122.

## Henderson Hall

After a tour of Henderson Hall, you'll understand why this manor has been called the most significant historic site in the Mid-Ohio Valley. Stepping across the threshold of the elegant, three-story Italianate Villa style mansion, the visitor intuitively grasps its unique value: an intact time capsule of 18th-century life along the Ohio River.

Because the house has been occupied and owned by family members since its initial construction in 1836, the structure and original contents have been preserved in superb condition. Another blessing adding to its authenticity and value, and acknowledged by the present owner, is the fact that his ancestors were pack rats, throwing almost nothing out. Hendersons saved shopping lists, business accounts, bills, wedding dresses, candy boxes, children's shoes, Christmas decorations and letters from everyone they knew including Robert E. Lee.

Correspondence, deeds and documents of all kinds stuffed into envelopes, and heirloom linens folded haphazardly fill drawers throughout the house. These priceless relics not only document

*Henderson Hall as viewed by travelers between Parkersburg and Williamstown before the turn of the century (photographed by E. Thorla, 1891) and its builders, George Washington Henderson and his wife Elizabeth Ann Tomlinson, circa 1859.*

the history of the house they once served but provide a continuous thread to the past for us all to unravel, interpret and delight in. The original grant to the land, for instance, was signed by Patrick Henry. Diaries list everyday events as well as the names and descriptions of slaves working the 2,000-acre plantation, where cash crops and horse breeding kept the Hendersons in style and substance.

Portraits and photos of previous generations hang in almost every room; wonderful strong faces peer with expression from their frames as though they are still concerned with the daily caring and loving of the house. These marvelous likenesses alone elevate a visit here to much more than a trip to an old house-museum. You are visiting a family and sharing their very lives— from household trivia and business transactions to secrets, scandals, weddings and wakes.

The Hendersons, through their long association with the area and intermarriages with other prominent settlers, were large land owners, shaping much of the local lore and commerce along this stretch of the river. Of course, having George Washington as a personal friend and surveyor of the property was a good beginning for the family legacy, which began with Alexander Henderson, Sr. On a tip from his friend he acquired 25,000 acres of land in Western Virginia in the late 18th century. Henderson Hall's first structure, a two-story brick house built in 1836 by his grandson, was added onto in 1856–59. The enlarged mansion, whose original plans by architect J. M. Slocomb remain in the house today, is made from material on site: handmade and fired bricks, stone cut from a quarry and wood logged from nearby virgin forest.

Following an Italianate design, the symmetrical structure boasts fine window and molding detail, an entrance porch flanked by sandstone columns and a belvedere crowning the central roof. From this eagle nest, the view encompasses 65 acres remaining from the thousands that originally composed the farm, the flowing river beyond, and rolling slopes leading down to it, on which, as captured in an old painting, cows grazed in pastoral bliss.

Unlike other mansions that perched (and perished) too close to the river, Henderson Hall sits high enough to have survived the worst floods, yet close enough to transportation and trade routes on both land and water to be strategically accessible. The rich soil that supported corn and the fine horses once bred here gave generously again and again. Later, the lucky family hit oil on the property.

The tour begins in the spacious **entrance hall** where a marvelous curved, cherry staircase circles 35 feet upwards to the third floor. Here you'll be introduced to portraits of the early

Hendersons and be briefed on general background. A rare clock from 1815 has told the Hendersons time for six generations. Ceilings on the first floor are 12 feet high, allowing in maximum light through the tall, round-headed windows, graciously draped and framed and some embroidered by Aunt Rosalie, a gifted artist who died in 1966. Many of her hand-painted ceramics are displayed throughout the mansion. Seventeen rooms, excluding the attic, basement and halls are in general use: more than a dozen others are shut off.

The **parlor** holds two marvelous antiques. The 1875 rosewood box piano has never been moved from where you see it. On a table in the corner a delightful Symphonian instrument made in Germany is in mint condition, an 1800 version of a compact disc player with comparable sound quality. When the large metal discs, stamped with note holes, play those Viennese waltzes, you'll feel an irresistible urge to roll up the rug. The music, startlingly pure, echoes the eras when the family entertained such famous guests as Johnny Appleseed and Stephen Foster. The wallpaper was brought by horseback from Cincinnati in 1870.

The **dining room** is chock full of heirloom silver, china and linens accumulated by generations of resident collectors. The small china set hand-painted in a floral pattern is an Aunt Rosalie contribution and required multi-steps of glazing and firing before the subtle, shaded tones blended smoothly. In the sitting room you can ogle the glass paperweight collection and the photos and memorabilia from an ancestor who served for 39 years as the Fifth Commandant of the U.S. Marine Corps, Brigadier General Archibald Henderson.

The **front room** holds a collection of old books, some dating from the 1600s, shelved in a handsome cherry bookcase, and a stunning 12-foot gilt mirror that draws admirers like a magnet, to assess its own beauty as well as their own.

You'll see Jane Henderson's wedding dress from 1801 in the upstairs **boys room**. A message scratched on the window, "George Henderson April 11, 1893," attests to a young boy's curiosity to test the theory that diamonds could cut glass. The lad, grandfather of the present owner, used his mother's engagement ring to affix his lasting signature. A cradle, looking lonely for an occupant, has comforted Henderson babies since 1802. Note the shaving stand. Another like it is in Mount Vernon and dates from 1798. Ask about the broad hatchet on the bedside table and the "Mammie's Bench," designed for rocking a baby and shelling peas at the same time.

Almost all the decorations you see in **Rosalie's room** were designed and made by her: curtain, canopy and bedspread. Her imaginative and feminine flair lends a refreshing contrast to traditional Victorian furnishings in other parts of the house.

The original part of the house, the **kitchen**, is still a good place for drying herbs. Every room holds too many interesting antiques, mementoes, photos and stories to be appreciated in just one visit, but the longer you stay the more you'll feel the warmth and continuum of the Henderson heritage, a living tribute to a remarkable family and their marvelously chronicled contribution to history.

**Admission**: Adults $3.00; children $1.50. Special group tours can be arranged with a minimum charge of $45.

**Hours**: Open Sundays, May through October 1:00 to 4:00 P.M.

**Directions**: From Parkersburg follow Rt. 14 north towards Williamstown. Approximately 4.5 miles beyond the Vienna line you will see a sign for River Road indicating a sharp, reverse left turn for Henderson Hall. For further information call (304)375-2129 or 295-4772 or write Henderson Hall, Route 2, Box 103, Williamstown, WV 26187.

If the Henderson antiques spur interest in acquiring your own, continue on Rt. 14 into Williamstown and see the beautiful selection at the **Williamstown Antique Mall**. This cream-colored, two-level mall showcases quality glassware, decorated stoneware, china, furniture, quilts, toys and other collectibles from 18 dealers. Items are attractively displayed, and the variety fascinates even novice antique hunters.

**Hours**: 10:00 A.M. to 6:00 P.M. Monday through Saturday; 12:00 to 6:00 P.M. Sunday.

**Directions**: From Parkersburg take Rt. 14 to Williamstown and turn right at the traffic light. The mall is located at 439 Highland Ave. (Rt. 14) on your left. Coming from I-77, take the Williamstown exit (Exit 185) and follow onto Rt. 14. For more information call (304)375-6315 or write the Williamstown Antique Mall, PO Box 351, Williamstown, WV 26187.

Quickly, deftly, expertly a handler at Fenton's factory fixes a ribbon of glass to each side of a basket, shaping it into a perfect arch.  COURTESY FENTON ART GLASS

## METRO VALLEY

1. **Belle**
   Samuel Shrewsbury, Sr., House

2. **Ceredo**
   Pilgrim Glass Corporation
   Z.D. Ramsdell House

3. **Charleston**
   Capitol Complex
   Craik-Patton House
   P.A. Denny Sternwheeler
   Sunrise Museum
   Watt Powell Baseball Park

4. **Cross Lanes**
   Tri-State Greyhound Park

5. **Dunbar**
   Wine Cellars Park

6. **Huntington**
   Camden Park and C.P
      Huntington Sternwheeler
   Heritage Village
   Huntington Museum of Art
   Huntington Parks
   Railroad Museum and New
      River Train Excursions
   Huntington Walking Tour

7. **Malden**
   Cabin Creek Quilts

8. **Milton**
   Blenko Glass

9. **Point Pleasant**
   Battle Monument State Park
   Krodel Park
   West Virginia State Farm
      Museum

10. **Scott Depot**
    Hamon Glass Studio

11. **St. Albans**
    Chilton House Restaurant

12. **South Charleston**
    South Charleston Mound
    West Virginia Belle

13. **Williamson**
    The Coal House

# Metro Valley

As its name implies, the southwestern Metro Valley region contains larger cities than found elsewhere in the state, including the state capital, Charleston, and Huntington. You'll find here those amenities that come with most urban areas: an airport, fine restaurants, large multi-purpose government centers, big city entertainment, sophisticated shops and cultural attractions. Put the State Capitol Complex on your list to visit: a tailor-made one-day trip, from the gold dome of the Capitol Building, to the Governor's Mansion and the impressive Cultural Center where galleries and a plethora of interesting programs attract visitors. The Sunrise Museum brightens the cultural mix here as well. Fifty miles west on I-64, practically to the Ohio border, lies Huntington, another cultural center. Don't miss the Huntington Museum of Art or the state's only amusement park, Camden Park.

Even with the size of these cities, the wild and wonderful beauty of West Virginia's outdoors is never more than a stone's throw away—inside or out of town. Instead of pounding the pavement to tour Charleston and Huntington, consider seeing their sites from aboard any of the several paddleboats plying the mighty waters of the cities' boundaries, the Kanawha and Ohio rivers. Or take to the air and see Huntington from a hot-air balloon. Back on terra firma, a day spent in Huntington's parks proves nature can be enjoyed even within the city limits. And railroad buffs will delight in the old engines chugging out of Huntington each October.

Surrounding the cities are a wealth of attractions from which to pick. Of special note are the region's four glassmaking factories, each with a different appeal. The South Charleston Mound looms mysteriously, raising visitors' curiosity as to the area's earliest settlers. Culture here is in no way strictly urban. A pleasant reminder is the down-home country music at the Mountaineer Opry in Milton. Point Pleasant Battle Monument State Park is one of many sites that will satisfy fans of history, and the West Virginia State Farm Museum, also in Point Pleasant, is a sure bet for a family outing.

Your trip to this area can be big-city-lights and a fast-pace (the Tri-State Greyhound Park in Cross Lanes just outside Charleston), or it can be quiet and serene. (Pack a picnic and unwind at the intriguing remains of the Wine Cellars in Dunbar, for instance.)

Whatever route you choose—river, road or rail—and whatever your day's desire—culture, cuisine or quilts–you'll find the metro region "has it all."

For more information on the Metro Valley contact:

Charleston Convention and Visitors Bureau, 200 Civic Center Dr., Suite 002, Charleston, WV 25301 or phone 1(800)733-5469 or (304)344-5075.

Cabell-Huntington Convention and Visitors Bureau, PO Box 347, Office 13, Huntington, WV 25708, 1(800)635-6329 or (304)525-7333.

Putnam County Convention and Visitors Bureau, 1 Valley Park Dr., Hurricane, WV 25526, (304)562-0518.

# Belle
## *Samuel Shrewsbury, Sr. House*

Six miles past Cabin Creek Quilts on Rt. 60 East lies the Samuel Shrewsbury, Sr., House, also known as the Old Stone House. Unfortunately dwarfed by a large, neighboring chemical plant, the circa 1800 house is the oldest in Belle. It was built by two of the town's first settlers, Samuel Shrewsbury and his brother, John, who were active in the salt business. Made of hand-cut sandstone with hand-hewn walnut interior walls, cupboards and woodwork, the home has been continuously occupied. It now houses the office of the Belle Historical Restoration Society who purchased the building in 1980 and completed its refurbishment.

The period-furnished house may be toured by scheduling an appointment in advance. Of interest are photos and exhibits of local history and a time capsule dedicated in 1987 that will be opened in 2045. A history book of the town may be purchased at the house.

**Admission**: $1.00 children, $2.00 adults
**Hours**: By appointment. Call (304)949-2380 or 2398.
**Directions**: On old Rt. 60 East 10 miles from Charleston.

# Ceredo
## *Pilgrim Glass Corporation*

The Pilgrim Glass Corporation located in Ceredo just 500 yards down the road from the Tri-State Airport, attracts thousands of visitors annually to its factory and show room. Famous world-wide for its exotically colored, hand-blown glass, Pilgrim Glass is especially noted for two difficult-to-make forms of glass, Cranberry Glass and Cameo Glass.

Rare and special, **Cranberry Glass** is fashion's richest, ripest color and the hardest of all to produce. Glassmakers must fuse solid gold with lead crystal to achieve the desired result. Its price reflects its gold content.

**Cameo Glass** is also expensive. It is created by "casing" one layer of molten glass on top of another and repeating the colors one layer at a time. After the glass cools, artists delicately carve down into the different levels. The long process requires that the layers of glass be chemically compatible and have the same rate of expansion; if not, the glasswork shatters or shows flaws. Pilgrim artists have successfully carved as many as nine layers of glass in one piece! Any Cameo Glass bought here is signed by the artist, documented in the Pilgrim Registry and accompanied by a notarized Certificate of Authenticity. In a day when foreign competition can dominate an American market—in 1986 the imported glass business commanded a staggering 92 percent share of the U.S. market—a visit to see Pilgrim's innovative glass being mouth-blown and hand-shaped is very satisfying. It makes one want to applaud Pilgrim's mission: "Handmade glass is a part of America's past. Pilgrim is making it a part of America's future."

The company was purchased by its current CEO and owner, Alfred Knobler, in 1949. A former New York businessman, Knobler had been the main buyer of the glass being produced by Walter Bailey and his small glass factory in Huntington before deciding to acquire the company himself. With no room to expand at the original location, Knobler built a new facility, site of today's factory, in 1956. The colored glass made in the early years were primarily ruby, tangerine, amethyst, smoke, amber, sapphire, green and crystal. Three Italian artists, all related, have contributed outstanding artistry to the company. Alessandro Moretti, who trained at the famed Murano Glass Center in Italy, joined Pilgrim in 1953, and his brother Roberto, also trained at Murano, joined in 1957. A testament to his work, Roberto received commissions from such notables as Chagall, Picasso, Cocteau and Paul Jenkins. A brother-in-law of the Morettis, Mario Sandon, who joined the company in 1963, is well known for his tiny, handmade glass animal collections. Sandon is the last of the three still making glass.

New developments in the company's Cameo Glass production began in the 1980s. It was a New England graphic designer, Kelsey Murphy, who discovered in 1981 that a sandblasting technique she was using on signs was very effective for sanding designs on glass. Andy Rainey aided her by designing equipment that could accelerate production, and a full-service architectural furniture and giftware corporation, Glass Expectations, was born. Robert Bomkamp, a machinist who had worked on such projects as the B-1 Bomber and the Viking *Mars Landers*, came aboard in 1982 and further improved the machinery. In 1984 Murphy and Bomkamp showed their portfolio of sand-carved glass to the Pilgrim Glass Corporation, and the seeds for yet another partnership were planted.

Pilgrim Glass contracted with Glass Expectations in 1985 for 100 each of 12 various-size vessels and solid-glass eggs. Market reactions far exceeded anyone's expectations—there were orders for a whopping 30,000 eggs alone! Murphy and Bomkamp quickly met the demand and came up with further mechanical refinements. Think of trying to build a machine that can hold many sizes of delicate glass and function under considerable air pressure, with fine particles of sand getting into its moving parts, and you get an idea of the challenges. Included in the group of first successful Cameo pieces was the Liberty Vase, made for Lee Iacocca and presented to him on July 4, 1986, in honor of the Statue of Liberty's centennial. And the rest is history.

Murphy and Bomkamp—and their equipment—combined forces with Pilgrim in West Virginia in 1987. And now after years of development, including a first year when breakage ran at 95 percent, their art glass division is producing editions of up to 250 pieces of Cameo ware.

**Hours**: Observation deck is open Monday through Friday 9:00 A.M. to 5:00 P.M. Call (304)453-3553 if you plan to come with a large group. You can see all kinds of Pilgrim's glass being made in their factory. Finished pieces are displayed and for sale in a handsome gift shop gallery, open Monday through Saturday 9:00 A.M. to 5:00 P.M. and Sunday 1:00 to 5:00 P.M.

**Directions**: Take Exit 1 off I-64. Turn away from Ceredo on Rt. 52 North and follow signs to the left. The factory is on the left on Walker Branch Road before you reach the Tri-State airport.

## Z.D. Ramsdell House

A few miles west of Huntington, on the flatlands of the Ohio River flood plains, lies the small town of Ceredo. Named for "Ceres," the Greek goddess of grain, the community was founded in 1857 by Eli Thayer, an abolitionist who believed steam power could replace slave power in developing industry.

One of the many supporters who followed Thayer to Ceredo was the bootmaker Z.D. Ramsdell. His house, built a year after the founding of the community, was the first brick house erected in Ceredo. It has been preserved by the Ceredo Historic Landmark Commission and is available for you or your group to tour.

Random plank floor, cut nails and horsehair plaster walls provide the backdrop for display cases in the museum room where

Civil War artifacts, many of them recovered from the attic, are shown. At special events, military re-enactment groups portray Civil War camp life in recognition of Captain Ramsdell's service. Military fife-and-drum music and authentic attire are emphasized. Post office delivery boxes from the time Ramsdell served as a postal service special agent, reflect his post war work. From time to time there are displays of old-time arts and crafts, demonstrations and period music performances.

**Hours**: Open only by appointment and for special occasions. Lunches, dinners and other parties can be catered for groups of 25 to 40 guests. Call (304)453-2482 to arrange a tour and request a schedule of events.

**Directions**: From I-64, take the Kenova/Ceredo exit and go toward Ceredo. Turn onto Route 60 East. After the third traffic light turn left on B Street. The house is located at 1108 B Street.

# Charleston
## Capitol Complex

### Capitol Building

From whichever vantage point you approach the West Virginia **State Capitol Complex,** your eye will likely be drawn first to the brilliant, gold dome of the main capitol building. Recently re-gilded, a laborious three-year-long process completed in 1991, the 293-foot-high dome stands five feet higher than the United States Capitol dome in Washington, DC, and marks the home of the West Virginia State Senate, the State House of Delegates and the governor's office. Even when the legislature is in session, this mammoth stone and marble building, covering more than 14 acres of floor space, lends a feeling of accessibility to the visitor. Your only challenge during busy times may be finding a parking space.

Today's building is the state's sixth capitol building. The first, The Linsly Institute Building in Wheeling, gave way to a legislative vote to make Charleston, a more central location, the capital city in 1870; however, a subsequent vote returned the capital to Wheeling just five years later because Charleston's building was too small. Still dissatisfied with the location, the state's lawmakers decided to let the citizens choose, which they did once and for all with a vote that returned the capital again to Charleston in 1885. With so many moves up and down the Kanawha and Ohio rivers, the capital became fondly known as the "floating capital." In 1885 a new capitol building was dedicated in downtown Charleston. Covering one block, this building

The brilliant, gold dome of the main Capitol Building dominates Charleston's skyline. STEPHEN J. SHALUTA. JR.

served as the state capitol building until 1921 when a fire stemming from the ignition of confiscated dynamite hidden in the building caused the structure to burn down. The fire lasted three days. For the next six years West Virginia's state government was run from a temporary structure, which also succumbed to fire in 1927. The present building, resting on a 16-acre site with a commanding view of the Kanawha River in Charleston's east end, was designed by Cass Gilbert, who also designed the U.S. Treasury, Supreme Court and Chamber of Commerce buildings in Washington, DC. Constructed in three stages beginning in 1924, the Renaissance-style building was completed in 1932 at a price of $10 million.

When you arrive for a tour, go to the information desk on the lower level and request a tour. Should Louise Burke, the desk's supervisor, be your guide, consider yourself lucky—she's as affable as she is informative. Your tour will likely begin with a welcome to the "**marble building.**" Six types of marble (Imperial Danby, Italian Travertine, Tennessee, white Vermont, black Belgian and pink Georgian) are lavishly used throughout the building. Limestone pillars, weighing 86 tons each, support porticos at the north and south entrances. If you think that's heavy, consider the 2,800-pound brass and copper sliding doors. They are decorated with oak, elm, hickory, beech and maple leaves representing West Virginia's native hardwood trees. The focal point of the rotunda is a gorgeous 4,000-pound, eight-foot-wide chandelier hanging 54 feet down from the capitol's dome. Made of 10,080 pieces of hand-cut Czechoslovakian crystal and lit by 96 bulbs, the chandelier is lowered via a stout gold-plated chain and ¾-inch cable to the floor and each piece of crystal cleaned every four years in time for the Governor's Inaugural Ball. The chandelier is also partially lowered each year at Christmas time to serve as a star above a decorated tree. Halls on either side of the rotunda hold portraits of West Virginia's past governors.

Also at the capitol, you can watch the **state legislature** in action. Galleries are available for visitors on a first-come-first-served basis in both the Senate meeting room, located in the west end of the capitol, and the House of Delegates chamber, located in the east end. While the two chambers are similar in design, you will observe some symbolic differences because the Senate, with its 34 members, is considered to be the upper house to the House of Delegates, with its 100 members. Notice the ceiling of the Senate chamber is domed whereas the House chamber is flat; and the carved eagle in the Senate chamber has its wings spread, while the one in the House chamber has its wings closed. You can watch each senator and delegate at his or her own hand-carved walnut desk complete with electronic voting devices and phones connected to their respective offices. The chandeliers, also of Czechoslovakian crystal, are the same in each chamber as are the hand-carved cherry replicas of the Great Seal bearing the state motto, "Montani Semper Liberi"—Mountaineers Are Always Free.

Before leaving the building, stop to see where the governor comes to work each day—a truly impressive office. And before leaving the grounds, pause at any of the numerous fountains and historic statues including those honoring Stonewall Jackson, Booker T. Washington, a Union Soldier, a Union Mountaineer and Abraham Lincoln, the man who signed West Virginia into statehood. The *Lincoln Walks at Midnight* statue is especially poignant. In front of the Capitol Building and dedicated in 1974, it was inspired by the Vachel Lindsay poem of the same name.

**Hours**: 9:00 A.M. to 3:00 P.M. Monday through Saturday.

**Directions**: From I-64/77 take Exit 99, Greenbrier Street, and follow towards the Kanawha River. The Capitol Building will be on your left. Phone: (304)558-3809. For more information write The Rotunda, Guide's Desk, Main Capitol Building, Charleston, WV 25305.

## The Cultural Center

Also part of the Capitol Complex and only a stone's throw away from the Governor's Mansion is the Cultural Center. Opened in 1976 to serve the people of West Virginia and to showcase their artistic, cultural and historical heritage, the sprawling, contemporary building is perfect for visitors who want to see many attractions under one roof. But beware. You may not want to leave—there are that many wonderful art and historical exhibits, research libraries and performances to see throughout the center's many spaces. There is literally something here for everyone.

The goings-on at the Cultural Center are the responsibility of two main groups, the West Virginia Division of Culture and History and the West Virginia Library Commission. The Division of Culture and History has several sections here including The Archives and History Section, the Arts and Humanities Section, the Historic Preservation Office, the Museums Section and a quarterly folklife magazine called *Goldenseal*, all of which serve to bring together the state's past, present and future. The Library Commission maintains more than a quarter of a million volumes for public use. Among its facilities here are the Library Reading Room, Microfilm Library, Film Library, Video Studio and Blind and Physically Handicapped Division.

You will likely marvel at the fact that all of this together with the State Museum, the State Theater and the State Archives Library is in one building. But your biggest surprise may come upon realizing that all of what you see is indigenous to the state.

Relish first the focal point of the Center, the **Great Hall.** A variety of receptions, festivals and exhibits are held in this grand room with its marble floors and towering marble walls. If your visit is during the summer months you will see a popular quilt exhibition hanging here. Next you can move on to the State Museum's exhibit areas which cover three floors. You can see permanent exhibits on the lower level that trace West Virginia history from Indian migration to the early 20th century. Included are a settler's cabin and a general store complete with life-like resemblances and a wonderful collection of artifacts—all of which have been donated to the museum. The artifacts have been painstakingly researched and are correctly placed in the time represented by each exhibit. During a two-week period in December these exhibits are manned by real people—a special treat for youngsters. Also popular with young people at Christmas time is the exhibit with a telephone callboard where believers can place calls to Santa Claus and give him their wish lists.

Elsewhere in the Museum, Lobby and Balcony Galleries you can expect changing displays of West Virginian art and craft work and special collections of West Virginian subject matter. Among the most popular and most anticipated is the biennial West Virginia Juried Exhibition. Cash prizes are awarded to the best of this impressive all-West-Virginian event, which features everything from paintings, photography and basketry to weavings, ceramics and mixed media. Says one smiling docent, "Our best resource is our talented people." She also adds, "West Virginians love to celebrate." And this event is no exception and not without cause. Its opening is the hottest ticket in town and always very exciting.

Still another popular show can be enjoyed here most Sunday afternoons in the intimate, 468-seat, two-level, wheel-chair- accessible State Theater. The show, **Mountain Stage**, an interesting and eclectic mix of cutting-edge popular musical styles, is produced by West Virginia Public Radio for American Public Radio and is broadcast live across the country. Call (304)558-3000 for tickets so you can be part of the fun. Other performances in the theater, ranging from jazz, dance, theater and traditional music to gospel, films and lectures are featured as well. Check the calendar at the information desk in the Great Hall for an event that suits your taste and schedule.

Not everything at the Center is for groups or deals with the arts. Some are for quietly pursuing on your own. And it's hard to imagine a setting more ideal for research than here in the **State Archives Library.** Everything from state and public records and documents, and private manuscript collections to photographs, film and video collections are here for you to explore. If you want to trace a West Virginia family line, this is the place to do

191

it. The Archives and History Library is West Virginia's genealogy research center and is complete with exhaustive printed and microfilmed records.

Don't leave the Cultural Center without stopping by The Shop, located next to the Great Hall, for a remembrance of your visit. Here you can purchase the works of West Virginian artists, crafts-people, musicians and writers. Especially notable are the quilts and the exquisite hand-made glass items.

**Hours**: Shop's hours are 9:00 A.M.–5:00 P.M. weekdays and 1:00–5:00 P.M. weekends. Phone: (304)558-0690. The hours for the Cultural Center are 9:00 A.M.–8:00 P.M. weekdays and 1:00–5:00 P.M. weekends. The Archives Library hours are 11:00 A.M.–6:00 P.M. Monday through Friday, and 1:00–5:00 P.M. Saturday. The Archives Library is closed on Sunday. The State Museum is open 9:00 A.M.-5:00 P.M. weekdays and 1:00–5:00 P.M. For more information on the Cultural Center, call (304)558-0220 or write Marketing/Communications, West Virginia Division of Culture & History, The Cultural Center, 1900 Kanawha Blvd. E., Charleston, WV 25305-0300.

**Directions**: Take Exit 99 (Greenbrier Street) from I-64/77. The Capitol Complex is visible from the exit. Turn left into the complex at the light.

### Governor's Mansion

Part of the Capitol Complex, the 30-room Governor's Mansion is only a few steps west of the Capitol Building. The 30-room home of the governor and his family (the second floor of the mansion is their private residence), this large, handsome Georgian-style building, provided by the people of West Virginia, stands as a symbol of their history. Designed by prolific Charleston architect Walter F. Martens, who designed 89 churches in West Virginia alone—the mansion proudly faces the Kanawha River and is distinguished by red Harvard brick and a two-story portico supported by four white Corinthian columns.

The First Family has not always lived in such elegance. During the first 30 years of statehood, the governor was on his own to find a place to hang his hat. However, in 1893 outgoing Governor Aretas Fleming changed the tide by netting $22,000 from the legislature for his successor William MacCorkle to buy and furnish a home. In 1921, after the capitol building burned, proceeds from a new sales tax provided money not only for a new capitol building but $100,000 for an executive mansion as well.

Because the two important buildings were to be next to each other, architect Martens checked with Cass Gilbert, the capitol's architect, to be sure the mansion would complement the new capitol. He discovered, interestingly enough, that his plan was practically identical to one Gilbert had already prepared. Construction began in 1924 and one year later Ephraim Morgan became the first governor to occupy the mansion—albeit for only one week before his term expired. The garage, service wing and garden you see were added in 1926 and, 20 years later, to conform to the original plans, a slate-covered mansard roof was added.

On first entering the mansion, you'll face two fabulous Georgian staircases flanking either side of the entry room. The second level of the mahogany staircase gives the appearance of being suspended in mid-air. The flooring is black Belgium and white Tennessee marble, and the finials on the newel posts are solid, cut crystal. All the carpets in the state rooms feature motifs that relate to symbols found in the capitol building. Among them, the Ballroom's rug boasts the state bird, the cardinal, and the state flower, the rhododendron. The public rooms are maintained by the West Virginia Preservation Foundation, Inc. The Foundation has retained as many pieces original to the mansion as possible and has given many others, including a Chinese screen now found in the Drawing Room. The artwork hanging throughout the state rooms includes pieces original to the mansion as well as others on loan from various museums.

Be sure to take note of the Ballroom's chandeliers. They once hung in Scott's Drug Store on Capitol Street in Charleston. Also notable among the treasures here are the circa 1820, 22-seat banquet table with its beautiful needlepoint chairs, the State Dining Room's unique 18th-century knife urns; the Drawing Room's chandeliers from Charleston's old Kanawha Hotel and the Library's warm, butternut-wood paneling from Randolph County, West Virginia. All are meticulously preserved. Curious adults may want to pause in the Library for a quick look at the urns displayed in the bookshelves. The figures are now three-dimensional thanks to a re-glazing process that added clothing to the previously *au naturel* figures.

Check to see if your visit coincides with a current event of the mansion's **Arts and Letters Series,** a program launched by the governor and his wife featuring prominent musicians, authors, artists and craftspeople. Aficionados of the arts will be delighted to learn that this series is not a typical figurehead's acknowledgment of the arts. First Lady Rachael Worby knows whereof she speaks, she is an experienced musician and a conductor of the Wheeling Symphony.

**Hours**: Because the mansion's ground floor state rooms are now used so frequently for such a wide variety of functions, tours are available only on Thursdays and Fridays from 9:30 to 11:30 A.M. However do try to fit this into your schedule; this is an antique-lover's dream house and not to be missed. You need to call (304)558-3809 or stop by the guide's desk in the capitol rotunda to schedule a tour. Tours last about 20–25 minutes.

**Directions**: Leave the Capitol Building by the west door. To your left is the Governor's Mansion.

Before leaving the Capitol Complex, return to the Governor's Mansion for a view west beyond its far hedge. Here you can see **Holly Grove** also known as the Daniel Ruffner House. Built by Ruffner in 1815 on what was then a plantation east of Charleston, the mansion served as an inn for a period of time. Well-known figures, including John James Audubon, Daniel Boone, Henry Clay, Samuel Houston and Andrew Jackson came here for room and board. The mansion is now an office complex for the Commission on Aging.

## Craik-Patton House

The lives and times of two prominent West Virginia families have been preserved in this Charleston historical treasure, the Craik-Patton House. Completely and authentically restored by the National Society of Colonial Dames of America in time for the 1976 Bicentennial and listed on the National Register of Historic Places, the Greek-revival style building contains countless pieces representing the Craiks and the Pattons including many original to the home. Most rooms are furnished as they would have been during the Craiks' tenure here in the 1830s with the exception of the Patton Room, which looks as it did around 1865. Also of note are the numerous "windows" cut out in the house to reveal period types of construction used. With original floors, doors and hardware in place and one room after another full of antiques and history, lovers of old houses and their histories will feel like kids in a candy store here.

One of the first homes in Charleston to be erected with sawed lumber from early sawmills, the two-story house, known then as Elm Grove, was built by James Craik in 1834 near what is now Virginia and Dunbar streets. Craik was named for his grandfather, Dr. James Craik, who was not only George Washington's friend, neighbor and personal physician, but was also married to Washington's cousin. James Craik's father, George Washington Craik, was the president's personal secretary during Washington's second term. James Craik practiced law in Charleston from 1833 until 1839 when he became a deacon in the Episcopal Church. In 1841 he was ordained a priest and served as pastor of Charleston's St. John's Church until 1844 when he was called to Christ Church in Louisville, Kentucky. There he served until his death in 1882. Craik and his wife, Juliet Shrewsbury, were the proud parents of a total of 11 children, seven of whom lived here at Elm Grove.

After the Craiks left, the home continued to attract lawyers. Isaac Reed, a lawyer, purchased the home for $2,200 in 1846, and in 1858 **George Smith Patton**, also a lawyer, and wife Susan

*Beautifully restored, the 1834 Craik-Patton House is furnished with many pieces belonging to its early owners.* RICK LEE

purchased the home for $2,900. Like Craik's, Patton's relatives were notable as well and included a Revolutionary War general and a former governor of Virginia. Patton distinguished himself prior to the start of the Civil War when he formed the Kanawha Riflemen and, as their leader, rose to a colonel's rank. He and the Riflemen became a part of the Confederate Army and fought in the 1861 battle at Scary Creek. He died of wounds in the Battle of Winchester in 1864. Patton's family subsequently abandoned this Charleston home, and his son settled as far away as California, where the five-star General George S. Patton, Jr., of later World War II fame was born.

The home then passed through many hands until it was donated to the Colonial Dames of America by the estate of Dr. H. H. Smallridge in 1970. It has twice been moved, each time in three sections. The first time, in the early 1900s, was to Lee Street and the second time, in the early 1970s, was to its present location.

**Admission**: $2.00 for adults and $1.00 for children.

**Hours**: Docents in period clothing lead tours of the house each Thursday, Friday and Sunday from 1:00 to 4:00 P.M., May 1 through September 30. Special tours may be arranged by calling the house in advance at (304)925-5341.

**Directions**: In Daniel Boone Park on US Rt. 60 East (2809 Kanawha Boulevard).

To see what homes were like before the introduction of sawmills, visit the **Ruffner Log House**, also located in Daniel Boone Park. One of the earliest known buildings built in what is now Charleston, the log house is possibly the oldest in the area dating back to as early as 1820. Interestingly enough, its owner, Joseph Ruffner, established a sawmill and built this building as an office before later letting his son move into it. The Kanawha Valley Historical and Preservation Society saved the house and moved it here where it is now maintained by the Colonial Dames of America.

## P.A. Denny *Sternwheeler*

Unlike other paddlewheel boats constructed as replicas of the early transport ships that reigned supreme on the Ohio and Kanawha rivers, the *P.A. Denny* Sternwheeler is the real thing, an authentic sternwheeler made right here in Charleston in 1930.

There's no need to re-live the past. This ship is a living history, continuing to work its home waters. A celebrated centerpiece of the Sternwheel Regatta Festival, Charleston's popular annual river celebration held the week before Labor Day, the *P.A. Denny* is available for public and chartered cruises including luncheons, dinners, dances, meetings and parties. She is operated by the Charleston Festival Commission as a public tour boat.

Originally christened the *Scott*, the *P.A. Denny* served the U.S. Corps of Engineers until 1954. She was then purchased and moved to Alabama where, due to neglect, she fell into disrepair. In 1973 Charleston riverman P.A. Denny purchased the *Scott* and brought her home. Denny rebuilt the ship from the hull up and renamed her in honor of his granddaughter, Robin D. Too. Following Denny's death only two years later, Charleston businessman Lawson Hamilton bought the boat and renamed it again for his long-time friend P.A. Denny.

The white, red-trimmed boat with its big red paddlewheel has three tiers and can accommodate up to 200 passengers. Its first level and most of the second are enclosed and heated for year-round comfort. The third deck is entirely open save for the captain's control room. The lower deck has a cash bar for legal beverages and features an old juke box. If you're on a tight time schedule that doesn't coincide with the sternwheeler's, you can at least get on board and visit this lounge. It is open nightly while the *P.A. Denny* is docked.

**Admission**: For complete price list, hours and schedules for public cruises and/or private charters call (304)348-0709.

**Directions**: Location of the boat will change due to construction of the New City Park. Call for exact directions.

## Sunrise Museum

Venture across the Kanawha River from Charleston and climb up the hill to the Sunrise Museum. The museum is actually spread between two large mansions, one on either side of Myrtle Road, and features a wealth of entertaining things to see and do.

Especially enticing are the children's areas, which include **Playscape**, a large room loaded with equipment for climbing, sliding and other creative fun, and a five-room, hands-on exhibit called Pre-Historic People of the Kanawha Valley. Here youngsters get a feel for Indian life by making pottery or tools, wearing Indian clothes and perusing artifacts uncovered from the South Charleston Mound that are on loan from the Smithsonian Institution (see South Charleston Mound entry). Across the street in **Torquilstone Mansion** adults with or without children will want to take in an art exhibit or two, as the museum has become Charleston's art center and boasts both a wide variety of changing exhibits and an excellent permanent collection of art. And all ages will want to visit the Nature Center's environmental exhibits and discover secrets of the sky in the **Planetarium**. Programs in the 65-seat Planetarium are presented on a weekly basis, usually the first and third Saturday of each month and the second and fourth Friday evening. In late 1993, the first floor of Sunrise Mansion will be transformed into a hand-on Science Center.

With so much to see and occupy one's imagination at the museum, it may be easy to overlook the history that led up to today's prize. In fact, had it not been for William A. MacCorkle, there may not have been a museum at all—at least not here. The ninth governor of the state (1893–97) and a long-time devotee of promoting both its natural resources and industrial development, MacCorkle built the larger of the two mansions that make up today's museum as his home in 1905. Made of natural stone, the 36-room, neo-Classical revival-style home was named Sunrise in honor of MacCorkle's birthplace, his family's plantation in Virginia. During his lifetime, MacCorkle developed a reputation as a collector of antiques, art, historical documents and curio. He filled Sunrise with his collection making it a showcase in the region. Among MacCorkle's treasures is the fireplace in the **Drawing Room**. It contains stones acquired from antique structures worldwide including 75 stones inscribed with places of origin ranging from the Great Wall of China, the Tower of London and the Appian Way. One Egyptian stone is 2,000 years old. In addition there are a few furnishings original to the home including the long table, large arm chair and secretary in the Drawing Room. Also of note are the balconies built into the third-story portico pediments from where musicians entertained guests when this room was a ballroom in MacCorkle's day. Today it serves as a library.

Following MacCorkle's death in 1930 the home passed among several owners until its acreage was threatened with subdivision for real estate lots. In 1961 the Sunrise Foundation, Inc. stepped in to save the home and, together with the Children's Museum of Charleston and the Charleston Art Gallery, moved to Sunrise.

Today's museum is not only for indoor, rainy-day pursuits. Its 13 acres of lovely, mostly wooded grounds are ideal for a picnic or for just absorbing the view of the river and Charleston. Of special interest are the **Rose Garden** and its statue of Christa McAuliffe, who died in the *Challenger* explosion, and the shrine on the carriage trail for MacCorkle's daughter, Isabelle, who was killed in an auto accident in 1926. At William MacCorkle's request, his ashes were placed in this shrine following his death.

**Admission**: Adults $2.00, students, teachers and seniors over 60 $1.00. Fee includes access to both buildings. Free admission is available Tuesdays from 2:00–5:00 P.M. and at all times for children three and younger. The Planetarium shows are $2.00 per person or $1.00 per person with a museum admission ticket. Children under 12 must be accompanied by an adult in the Planetarium and throughout both museum buildings.

**Hours**: Tuesday–Saturday from 10:00 A.M.–5:00 P.M., Sunday 2:00–5:00 P.M. The museum is closed on Mondays and major holidays. Phone: (304)344-8035.

**Directions**: From Rt. 60 turn away from the river on Thayer Street and make an immediate left paralleling the river. Turn right on Bridge Road and right on Myrtle Road to 746. For further information write Sunrise Museum, 746 Myrtle Road, Charleston, WV 25314.

## *Town Center*

Charleston is also home to one of the largest enclosed inner-city shopping malls in the United States, the Charleston Town Center. Shopping fanatics who grow tired of sight-seeing may want to leave their non-shopping friends at another site while they check out the offerings here. This is truly a place to shop until you drop. There are more than 150 shops together with four major department stores to choose from. If you need a break or just want to rest your feet, go by the Center Court Atrium and recharge in the lush surroundings of its three-story waterfall. The mall is next to the Charleston Civic Center Complex in downtown Charleston and is bordered by Clendenin, Court, Lee and Quarrier streets. The phone is (304)345-9525. To add to the fun, take one of the trolley buses to the mall. Shuttling throughout the downtown area, these replicas of old-fashioned trolleys are available Monday through Saturday, 11:00 A.M. to 7:00 P.M. for a nominal charge.

### Watt Powell Baseball Park

And if the crack of the bat and the pounding of the glove of America's favorite pastime are your ticket for a good time on a summer evening, then head to the 7,500-seat Watt Powell Baseball Park and cheer for the Charleston Wheelers. The Wheelers are a single-A farm club for the Cincinnati Reds and are no slouches—they're former Sally League Champs. If you've never been to a minor league game, do give it a try. These young ballplayers play their hearts out while delivering good baseball. You'll enjoy the chance to pick out tomorrow's big-league stars.

**Directions**: The ballpark is at 35th Street and MacCorkle Avenue, SE, in the Kanawha City area. Call (304)348-6848 or 348-6840 for a schedule of when the team is in town.

# Cross Lanes

### Tri-State Greyhound Park

If you expect to pocket any winnings, you need to bring both luck and skill when you come to watch and bet on purebred greyhound racing at Tri-State Greyhound Park in Cross Lanes. Purported experts say you need a little bit of each for success.

Depending on the weather and your depth of pocket, there are several ways to enjoy the races. During fair weather you can get right next to the sights and sounds of the action on the outdoor patio. You'll best appreciate the dogs' speed from this up-close vantage point. There is also seating for more than 3,000 people in the enclosed grandstand section where a casual environment rules and where floor-to-ceiling windows allow a full view of the track and giant computerized tote board. Legal beverages and snack items from concession stands are available. And for those who want to take in the races while dining in a more formal atmosphere, there are an additional 1,200 seats available in the

An evening out in Cross Lanes means "going to the dogs" at Tri-State Greyhound Park.                                    STEPHEN J. SHALUTA. JR.

clubhouse. Each table has its own personal cable TV that allows a closed circuit replay of each race. Phone (304)776-5000 for dining room reservations.

**Tip**: Purchase a $1.00 program. It is loaded with information including how to wager (the minimum bet is $2.00), which dogs are running in each race and a report on each dog's past performance.

**Admission**: No charge for the outdoor patio or seating in the grandstand; nominal per person and per table charge for the clubhouse. For more information, including special group rates and party planning, call (304)776-1000.

**Hours**: Located just ten minutes west of downtown Charleston, the large, modern facility is open rain or shine year-round for 7:30 P.M. races Wednesday through Saturday and 1:30 P.M. matinee races Saturday, Sunday and holidays. (The track opens 90 minutes before post time.) Youngsters under 18 are admitted to the track with proper parental supervision but are not permitted to wager or cash tickets.

**Directions**: From Charleston take I-64 west to Exit 47, Cross Lanes, and follow the signs ½ mile to the park. There's plenty of free parking.

# Dunbar

## *Wine Cellars Park*

As you make your way west from Charleston to Huntington on I-64, stop in Dunbar, just outside of Charleston, for an unusual attraction: a recreation area that is listed on the National Register of Historic Places, the Wine Cellars Park.

In the mid-1850s, Thomas Friend began a promising winery on a 448-acre tract of land once owned by George Washington. Hundreds of acres of "big blue" grapes (probably Catawba) were planted, lining both sides of this hollow and extending to the next for half a mile or more. Three wine cellars were built to store and age the wine after the grapes had been picked, pressed and set in the sun to ferment. Newspaper accounts indicate the winery flourished commercially but, as was the case with so many businesses of the day, success was cut short by the Civil War. The property passed through many hands—first at auction to settle Friend's bad debts—and the wine cellars were soon thereafter abandoned.

In 1974, the City of Dunbar purchased 316 acres of the property including the cellars and began an ambitious restoration project. Completed in 1982, the job not only refurbished the cellars, but it added a caretaker's house, three covered picnic shelters (with fireplaces, tables and grills), restrooms, parking lots, a playground, nature paths and hiking trails, cross-country skiing trails, camping areas, a game refuge and a seven-acre lake stocked with trout, bass, bluegill and catfish. There's no shortage of things to do at this attractive, pleasant park, overseen by the Parks and Recreation Department of Dunbar.

Before you leave the park, pause to consider an interesting footnote to the wine cellars here. Although not confirmed by historians, popular legend has it that during Friend's tenure, the cellars were part of an underground railroad for runaway slaves. Purportedly, they found their way to the vineyard, mixed in with the other workers and then escaped hidden in the wine shipments. Abolitionists could then pick them up and care for them.

**Hours**: The park is open daily, sun-up to sunset. (Night fishing is available by checking in advance with the caretaker.) Arrangements for handicapped and/or elderly persons can be made by phoning ahead (304)766-0223. You can also receive information on indoor basketball and an olympic size swimming pool in Dunbar.

**Directions**: Take Dunbar exit off I-64 and go west on Rt. 25. Follow signs to park.

# Huntington

## *Camden Park and the C.P. Huntington Sternwheeler*

For a sure-fire family hit, head to Camden Park, West Virginia's only amusement park. A tradition since 1902, the park features 28 rides ranging from the Big Dipper roller coaster and the new, looping Thunderbolt Express to Splash Down and the powerful G-Force generating Magic Rainbow. Cowabunga, dude!

There's also a merry-go-round, Kiddie Land for tots, roller-skating rink, batting cages, arcade loaded with games, miniature golf course and gift shop.

Hot dogs and cotton candy are of course mainstays. You can have a meal in the air-conditioned full-service cafeteria or bring your own food and spread out in the huge picnic area. There's space enough for 10,000 guests. For birthdays and other occasions, catering is available. On holidays and during special events, the park blasts off fireworks and brings in big-name entertainment to perform in the amphitheater. Also at the park is the third largest Indian burial mound in the state. Still not excavated, the flat-topped, conical burial mound is the biggest in the Huntington area. It was built by the Adena People between 1,000 B.C. and A.D. 1.

While at the park, take a ride aboard the sternwheel excursion boat *C.P. Huntington*. The packetboat boards at the Camden Park landing located at the western extreme of the park. Like the other cruise boats running the river (see also the *P.A. Denny* Sternwheeler and the *West Virginia Belle*), the *C.P. Huntington* has no propellers. What makes it go is often referred to as the churning "lawnmower on behind."

Painted white with white railings, red trim and two big black stacks, it is licensed by the U.S. Coast Guard to carry 100 passengers. It has two decks, the lower enclosed and the upper open for sightseeing and dancing. Both are equipped with a sound system that pipes narration and music. Don't forget your camera so you can have your picture taken at the vessel's large steering wheel. The *C.P. Huntington* is available for private charters as well, both during the park's season and afterwards up until November.

**Admission**: You can pay one price, $9, and ride all day or purchase individual tickets for the rides of your choice. Admission is $.50. Tickets for rides cost $.20 each. Most rides require between three to five tickets. Call for group discounts. Fares for the *C.P. Huntington* are $2.50 for adults and $2.00 for children and are separate from admission to the park.

The Big Dipper roller coaster is a favorite ride at Huntington's Camden Park, West Virginia's only amusement park.

**Hours**: Camden Park is open on Saturday and Sunday in April and September, and seven days a week May through Labor Day. Hours are 10:00 A.M. to 10:00 P.M. The park stays open one hour later on Saturday. No alcoholic beverages are permitted. Phone: (304)429-4231. One-hour tours along the Ohio River on the *C.P. Huntington* are from 10:00 A.M. to 8:00 P.M. daily, May through Labor Day.

**Directions**: Take Exit 6 off I-64 to Rt. 60 West. Go three miles to the entrance on your right.

## Heritage Village

On the mid-section of the Ohio River at a point where West Virginia, Ohio and Kentucky meet is Huntington. Begin your visit here at **Heritage Village**, the award-winning shopping and entertainment complex opened in 1977 that serves as a tribute to the city's historic railroad past. The village owes its origin to the Cabell-Wayne Historical Society and the Collis P. Huntington Railroad Society. Centrally located downtown at 11th Street and Veterans Memorial Boulevard, the village contains many reminders of the time around the turn of the century when this was the transportation center of the east. Chief among the sites to see is the larger than life bronze statue of Huntington's founder, railroad magnate Collis P. Huntington. Moved here from its original home several blocks away and presented to the city by the Huntington family, the statue now stands atop a granite pedestal in the courtyard of the village. It was sculpted by Gutzon Borglum, the creator of the four presidential heads at Mount Rushmore.

In 1869 **Collis Huntington** built the city of Huntington to serve as a western terminus for the Chesapeake and Ohio Railway, a company that he built, owned and operated. This area was ideal because of the availability of nearby timber tracts, coal fields, oil and natural gas and because it offered the important advantage of the Ohio River steamboat connection with Cincinnati. Huntington further connected his operations by completing a long, seven-year task of pushing his line through the mountains to link it with the Union Pacific line, thus establishing the long-dreamed-of Transcontinental Railroad. In 1884 he became the first man in the United States to ride his own railroad car from the Atlantic Ocean to the Pacific over tracks he either owned or controlled.

The city of Huntington was planned around the development of the railway system. Tree-lined, 100-foot-wide avenues (big enough for four carriages abreast plus passing space) ran horizontally, numbered streets ran vertically and the railway ran through the center for easy access. The railways in turn brought all sorts of things to Huntington. Dry goods, candy, food, hardware, furniture, equipment and animals came by rail. So did foreign entrepreneurs, farmers making their twice-annual buying trips and caskets bearing the heroes of three wars. Presidents Teddy Roosevelt, Garfield and Eisenhower all stopped in Huntington to give speeches from their campaign trains.

An example of the kind of steam locomotive used during Huntington's railroad heyday is preserved at Heritage Village. You can sit at the throttle of old B&O 4559, a Mikado-class locomotive built in Ohio around 1911. Large engines like this often pulled a sleeper car together with the rest of its load, especially on transcontinental trips. The development of the **Pullman Sleeper,** named in 1864 for its inventor George Pullman, not only made the long journeys much more comfortable but revolutionized rail travel. Two types of Pullmans were manufactured, the sleeper and the parlor car, equals to luxurious living rooms. Both types were made outside of Chicago in a town also named for the inventor, Pullman, Illinois. The Pullman Sleeper at Heritage Village was built for the Great Northern Railway's Oriental Limited in 1925 and named Larpentuer. It has 12 open sections for sleeping and a drawing room. Used and later retired by the Southern Railway in 1965, the sleeper was donated to the Railroad Historical Society who again donated the prize to the Park and Recreation District. Following its installation here, the car was renamed Collis P. Huntington. It was completely restored in 1988.

If reliving Huntington's life on the railroad doesn't seem exciting to you, then try this. Imagine being the teller at the Bank of Huntington on September 8, 1875, just two months after the bank has received its charter. Three bandits enter the building and rob it—the **Jesse James Gang!** According to local folklore, the gang fled south into Kentucky and beyond and were never caught. The grill work on the original teller's cage is one of many interesting period pieces in the old brick bank building.

There are an attractive plaza, gazebo and boxcar filled with curio shops to peruse; also visit the popular Heritage State Restaurant for lunch or dinner. Transformed from the restored 1890s train station, the Victorian-style eatery is furnished with antiques and decorations from the day. Be sure to have a look at the countless photos lining the stairway to the upper level. The smiling faces in these photos as well as the faces of current customers suggest that many happy travelers have come through here including many who begin their journey into marriage here. The smiles warm the heart and signal a good time at Heritage Village.

**Hours**: Shops open at NOON.

**Directions**: From I-64 take Exit 8, 5th Street. Follow to 8th Street and turn left. Turn right on Veterans Memorial Boulevard. Heritage Village will be on your right. For more information call (304)696-5954 or write Cabell/Huntington Convention and Visitors Bureau, PO Box 347, 13 Heritage Village, Huntington, WV 25708.

# Huntington Museum of Art

A visit to West Virginia's largest art museum, nationally acclaimed Huntington Museum of Art, is anything but a boring, rainy-day escape. Containing outstanding collections of 18th–20th-century European and American paintings as well as Ohio River Valley historical glass, contemporary art glass, Georgian silver, Oriental prayer rugs, American furniture, Appalachian folk art and contemporary sculpture, this museum also provides studio art classes, workshops and lectures, a hands-on **Young People's** gallery, a 10,000-volume art reference library, an auditorium for the performing arts and a museum store. In addition the museum boasts something few others can: more than 50 acres of land surrounding its handsome building complex. It has taken full advantage of the lovely hilltop locale to combine nature trails, herb gardens, outdoor amphitheater, a sculpture courtyard and spring and fall festivals into a vibrant cultural center with a broad range of offerings. Put a visit to this museum at the top of your list.

The museum opened its doors in 1952 thanks in large part to Herbert L. Fitzpatrick who donated the wooded site (now part of the Park Hills area of Huntington), together with his private collection of fine art. Since then the museum has often been helped by generous benefactors. Rufus Switzer, one of Huntington's early successful businessmen who was the driving force behind the creation of Ritter Park (see entry), donated money to the museum in its early years when it was known as Huntington Galleries. In 1970 a large addition to the museum was made possible by the Henry L. and Grace Rardin Doherty Foundation. Designed by Bauhaus architect Walter Gropius, the addition houses the 300-seat **Doherty Auditorium,** home of the Huntington Chamber Orchestra and host to other performers and lecturers.

As recently as the fall of 1991 Joseph and Omayma Touma and their family donated an impressive collection of more than 180 Near Eastern art objects. Included are 15th-century metal bowls, vases and weapons from Persia, Syria and Egypt; Roman and Syrian glass from 200–400 A.D.; Egyptian ceramics from 3,000 B.C.; and 18th- and 19th-century Russian icons. The carpets given by the Toumas, plus many given by Herbert Fitzpatrick and other donors, make the museum's collection of prayer rugs rank as one of the country's finest.

Permanent exhibits range from guns to glass. The **Herman P. Dean Firearms Collection** traces the development of firearms from the 13th century, when gunpowder was invented, through the mid-19th century when the Kentucky rifles and Colt guns held sway. The collector drew obvious satisfaction from learning the story behind each firearm: who owned it, when and where it was used and how it was made. Other highlights are The Daywood Collection of American paintings, prints and sculpture from the 19th and early 20th century and one-of-a-kind Ohio River Valley historical glass.

Outdoors, 2.5 miles of marked nature trails crisscross the museum's grounds. Informative docents give tours past a wide variety of trees, foliage and wildlife; or you can head out on your own with good maps and guides to help. There are picnic areas and restrooms on the trails.

**Admission**: Adults $2.00, students and senior citizens $1.00. There is no charge for museum members or children 12 and under. Wednesday is a free day for everyone. Group tours of 10 or more may be arranged by calling ahead.

**Hours**: 10:00 A.M. to 5:00 P.M. Tuesday through Saturday and NOON to 5:00 P.M. Sunday. Closed Mondays, Christmas Day and New Year's Day, Independence Day and Thanksgiving. Call ahead for a schedule of events and exhibits or to make arrangements for a group tour (304)529-2701. The museum is handicapped accessible.

**Directions**: Follow the signs off I-64 Exit 8 or, from downtown Huntington, take Eighth Street away from the river to the museum. For more information write Huntington Museum of Art, 2033 McCoy Road, Huntington, WV 25701-4999.

## Huntington Parks

By all means spend at least part of your day trip in one of Huntington's many beautiful landscaped parks. Few cities can boast as many diverse, well maintained and equipped open spaces. Maps as well as additional information on programs, facilities, special events and rental fees for all of the parks that follow may be obtained from the Greater Huntington Park and Recreation District, PO Box 9361, Huntington, WV 25704. Their phone is (304)696-5954. If you prefer, you may stop by their office at 1 Heritage Village. Pack your jogging shoes, throw in a basketball or soccer ball, bring your tennis racquet, carry your fishing pole, plan a picnic, tote a favorite book and don't forget your camera for a day in the park!

Directly in front of Heritage Village at 10th Street and Veterans Memorial Boulevard is the **David Harris Riverfront Park**. Opened in 1984 and situated on a wide section of the Ohio River, it is the newest of the city's parks. The sightseeing cruise boat, *West Virginia Belle*, docks here (see entry); power boat races speed by to the delight of racing fans; picnickers enjoy grass-covered areas while youngsters give playgrounds a workout; and at night concert-goers fill a popular riverfront amphitheater complete with a floating stage.

The park is also home to the largest river gala between Pittsburgh and Cincinnati, the Tri-State Fair and Regatta. Held during the last two weeks of July, it features live entertainment, arts and crafts, ethnic foods, powerboat and jet ski races. For a schedule of what is taking place in the park, call (304)696-5954.

There's also family fun within walking distance of the Riverfront Park at **Riverfront Recreation**, located at 201 Tenth Street. The phone is (304)525-5577. You can enjoy horse-drawn carriage tours of downtown Huntington nightly from April through November and by special arrangement at other times. Pony rides, a petting zoo and a miniature golf course are available as well.

Turn to place the river at your back and go to the opposite side of Heritage Village to find Huntington's most famous park, **Ritter Park**. Designed with the family in mind, the 100-acre park includes many sources of outdoor fun. Three of its attractions are unique: a nationally recognized rose garden with upwards of 1,500 plants and more than 80 different varieties of roses, an award-winning children's playground listed in *Child* magazine as one of the "ten best playgrounds in America," and a new tennis center.

The park could very easily have been named Switzer Park. Rufus Switzer, twice-elected mayor of Huntington, also served as the director of the First National Bank of Huntington and gave strong financial support to numerous local causes, including Huntington Galleries, now the Huntington Museum of Art (see entry). As a city councilman in 1908, Switzer was the first to propose that 55 acres of land alongside Four Pole Creek be used for the city's first public park. Switzer continued to push for his idea and by 1909, as the city's new mayor, won the support of businessman Charles Lloyd Ritter that would bring the realization of his vision.

Ritter was building an estate on a hill overlooking the land in question. Obviously preferring to see a park instead of an incinerator in front of his home, which had been proposed, he offered to deed the city 20 additional acres of his land if they supported Switzer's park idea and built a road through the property. In 1925 the park was finally constructed and named Ritter Park.

By the 1970s the park needed repairs and revamping. Among the improvements was a mile-long, tree-lined oval jogging track, especially popular now. The 1,200-seat amphitheater was renovated, a new picnic shelter and a fabulous children's playground added. "There's nothing like it anywhere," says James McClelland of the Park and Recreation District. Cut into the hillside with bigger-than-life stone columns, arches and triangles to climb on and hide in, it challenges the imagination that only children can bring it. There is also a pioneer cabin to explore. Parking is available.

Be sure to see the large stone **Memorial Arch** located at the western end of Ritter Park at the intersection of 11th Avenue West and Memorial Boulevard. One of Huntington's most prestigious landmarks, it is dedicated both "to the glory of God and the men of Cabell County who served faithfully in the Great War."

Several other neighborhood and roadside parks, both inside and outside of the city are maintained by the Parks and Recreation District. At **Altizer Park** you find softball and soccer fields, large group picnic shelters, a basketball court, children's playground and restrooms. The park is at the easternmost end of Altizer Avenue and is the District's newest neighborhood park. The same features, with the exception of restrooms, are at **Westmoreland Park** on Vernon Street in the Westmoreland section of Huntington. In addition, **Prindle Field**, next to Marshall University's Fairfield Stadium and framed by Charleston Avenue and Park Street, has a Little League field and regular size baseball field. Both fields double for soccer and football use. **Kiwanivista Park** is a popular roadside picnic stop between Barboursville and Milton on Rt. 60 East outside of the city. Three picnic shelters, restrooms and parking are available.

**Rotary Park**, Huntington's largest park, offers a terrific view of the city's east end from a tall observation tower. The only park in the system with such a tower, it also has two ballfields, a basketball court, playground and picnic shelters. Follow the signs off I-64 Exit 15 to the park.

Huntington's "athletic park," **St. Cloud Commons Park**, is home to the Huntington Cubs semi-pro baseball team. A notch below West Virginia's other professional team, the Charleston Wheelers (see entry), the Cubs play a slightly shorter summer season. Call (304)429-1700 for a schedule. There are numerous other ballfields, basketball and tennis courts as well as a playground, wading pool and large stone clubhouse with kitchen and meeting rooms at the athletic park. The facility is at 1701 Jackson Avenue off I-64 Exit 6.

There are two tennis courts at **Wallace Park** located off Spring Valley Drive five miles west of Huntington. Also of note here is the garden space for the District's novel Gardens for All program and home of the park's nursery containing 2,500 seedlings.

**Camp Mad Anthony Wayne**, named for the frontier army general, is special for its lodge and four rustic rental cabins hidden in a wooded area eight miles west of Huntington. Be sure to call in advance if you expect to secure a cabin reservation for an overnight stay. The same is true for the lodge which is often used for parties, workshops and various reunions. The camp is at 2125 Spring Valley Drive off I-64 Exit 6.

Finally, the westernmost point of West Virginia is also a park, **Virginia Point Park**. The Ohio and Big Sandy Rivers merge at this point where West Virginia, Kentucky and Ohio meet. Overnight campgrounds are available as are a boat launching ramp and the park system's largest group picnic shelter. The park is at the end of Laurel Street in Kenova off I-64 Exit 1.

## Huntington Railroad Museum and New River Train Excursions

Railroad buffs delight in the many activities of the Collis P. Huntington Railroad Historical Society. Founded in 1959 as a chapter of the National Railway Historical Society, the Huntington-based, not-for-profit society is devoted to preserving, promoting and inspiring railroad history. Though railroading has long since been overtaken by other modes of transportation, society members keep it alive—and running—here.

At the **Huntington Railroad Museum**, the Society maintains several impressive engines and railway cars resting on short tracks in the park. You are invited to climb aboard and peruse a large locomotive, the ex-Chesapeake & Ohio Railway Company's Mallet #1308. Made in 1949, this is one of two in its class still in existence today. The last made, #1309, is now on display in the B&O Museum in Baltimore, Maryland. You may walk inside an ex-C&O caboose for an up-close look at what life on the railroad was like. The fenced-in, outdoor museum also boasts a handcar, available for a hand-cranked ride.

Many groups—the C&O Railway, CSX Transportation, Norfolk & Southern Railway, CONRAIL and the city of Huntington and the Huntington Park Board—have contributed to the museum since it was established in 1962. It costs money to maintain it, however. Individual contributions are gratefully received, and membership in the society is also encouraged.

The tours are lively, inviting and nostalgic. Among other things you learn how a steam engine works. To schedule a tour you need to call (304)525-5884 in advance.

**Directions**: On the fringe of Ritter Park at 14th Street West and Memorial Boulevard. From I-64 take Exit 6; go right three blocks to traffic light at 14th St. Go about ¼ mile and take a right through underpass. Park on right.

Since 1966 on two weekends each fall, using a variety of vintage railroad engines and cars, the society has run day-long trips through the scenic "Grand Canyon of the East," the New River Gorge. When the fall colors are at their most spectacular, the old engines and cars puff along the entire length of the gorge giving passengers one of the most exciting train rides in America.

Called **The New River Train Excursion**, the round trip begins in Huntington's old C&O Station early in the morning, picks up passengers in St. Albans and Montgomery and arrives about six hours later in Hinton, site of one of the oldest surviving train stations on the C&O main line. Along the way, you can use a mile-by-mile guide provided by the society to recognize points of interest, including Gauley, where a restored New York Central Depot houses town offices and a rail history exhibit, and **Hawks Nest State Park,** the most spectacular point in the canyon. The guide also gives a roster and history of the railway equipment being used for your trip. The train makes a stop for trackside photos.

**Admission**: You have a choice of Coach, Deluxe Service or Premium Service class. Coach fares range from $55 for children to $75 for adults but do not include meals. Food service is available on board or you may bring your own picnic. Deluxe Service, a new accommodation with very limited seating, includes continental breakfast and box dinner at your seat in a lounge car, day Pullman or other special car. The fare is $115 per person, adults or children. The Premium Service includes all three meals in the diner car plus seating in a special car or a dome car, which permits most visibility. The fare is $135 for adults and children alike. Be sure to dress for the weather as heating is limited in the railcars. No alcoholic beverages are sold or permitted on board. The excursions run rain or shine. Handicap access is very limited. Smoking in designated areas only.

**Hours**: Call (304)453-1641 or 1(800)553-6108 for schedule information. The two trips generally start in mid-October. The same number may be used for reserving tickets. Some tickets, however, need to be purchased through the mail; so be careful to plan ahead.

**Directions**: Downtown Huntington at the old C&O depot, 7th Ave. and 9th St. Maps enclosed with tickets.

## Huntington Walking Tour

Several sights and activities in Huntington can be enjoyed on foot. Among them is a very nice **Streets of Style** self-guided walking tour of downtown Huntington prepared by an organization known as Huntington Main Street. The group's tour takes you by 13 of Huntington's venerable buildings, all within a five-block range. The walk begins and ends on Tenth Street and Fifth Avenue. A copy of the tour brochure, which includes a map and information on the buildings, may be obtained by calling (304)529-0053.

Among the highlights: The ornate Keith Albee Theatre, which opened in 1928 with the film *Good Morning Judge* starring Reginald Denny; The Hotel Frederick, West Virginia's largest hotel when it opened in 1906 complete with 250 guest rooms, Turkish baths, hot vapor rooms and a frieze-painted bar room; Reuschlein's Clock, the four-faced cast-iron timepiece made by the famous clockmaker, Seth Thomas, around 1800, and still running today; the Old Post Office, built around 1909; the Carnegie Library, named for steel tycoon and philanthropist Andrew Carnegie and now home to the Huntington Junior College of Business; and the Central Huntington Garage, one of the state's first indoor parking lots opened in 1927.

Though not included in the walking tour, there are two other points of interest along the tour's path. At Ninth Street and Fifth Avenue in the Old Federal Building you'll find an exhibit on West Virginia's coal industry featuring a mine from the hand-loading era, an example of an early coal community and a company store. The exhibit is open 11:00 A.M. to 5:00 P.M., Tuesday through Friday. A suggested contribution is $1.00.

Antique lovers will want to take a one block detour to the plaza at Ninth Street and Third Avenue. There, in what was once an old department store is the **Huntington Antique Mall**. Twelve dealers display oak and other furniture, china, glassware, jewelry, quilts, postcards, baskets, lamps, clocks, toys, musical instruments, Victrolas and more. Normal business hours apply, including weekend operation. The phone is (304)522-6511. Still more antique shops beckon the browsers to Huntington's west end. Beginning at Jefferson Avenue and West 14th Street, the shops all but fill a five-block area.

Don't leave Huntington without seeing the asymmetrical, cable-stayed **East End Bridge**. If you take a sternwheel boat cruise on the Ohio River while here, you'll see this gem looking from the river much like an intricate, giant spider web rising to the sky. On land, you drive across its one-mile length (including the approaches) connecting Huntington's 31st Street and Ohio's Rt. 7 in Proctorville.

The idea of stringing up a steel bridge by cable is not new. However, the Huntington Bridge is only the second concrete cable-stayed bridge erected in the country and the first to utilize high strength concrete, nearly triple the usual strength. It was opened to traffic in 1985 after more than 20 years of planning and nearly ten years of construction at a cost of $38 million. Designed by Arvid Grant and Associates of Olympia, Washington, it consists of numerous segments, each weighing a staggering 200 tons. They were maneuvered into place by crane and fastened to a 360-foot-high A-shaped concrete tower well secured in the river.

## *Mountain State Balloon Company*

Although not sponsored by the Parks and Recreation District, there's an exhilarating one-day trip idea that lifts off from Ritter

Park. The Mountain State Balloon Company offers hot-air balloon rides from the park any time of the year.

In about an hour's time you can see all of Huntington from the air, swoop down near the Ohio River and ride over lovely countryside before settling down in any one of three states. "Depending on which way the wind is blowing," says the company's Steven Bond, "you can leave West Virginia, fly through Kentucky and Ohio and land again in West Virginia." A chase truck follows the balloon and returns passengers to Ritter Park. Flights are limited to two persons per ride in addition to the pilot and generally last between 60 and 90 minutes. The cost is $125 per person. You should call (304)523-7498 at least two weeks in advance to schedule a ride on any of the three balloons the company operates. A favorite time to go is in the fall when the trees' colors are at their peak.

# Malden
## *Cabin Creek Quilts*

Just five minutes east of Charleston lies the historically rich, quiet small town of Malden. On the National Register of Historic Places and declared an Historic District, it is an ideal one-day destination because of its colorful, interesting past. And if you're a quilter, you cannot miss the outstanding quilting cooperative Cabin Creek Quilts, West Virginia's most complete quilting shop.

In the early and mid-1800s, Malden, known then as **Kanawha Salines,** was the center of a thriving salt industry that helped open the door to westward expansion. (Salt making in this area had dated back to as early as 1755 when Mary Ingles and Betty Draper made salt for their Shawnee Indian captors.) Between 1842 and 1857 salt was king in the Kanawha Valley with upwards of three million bushels produced per year and shipped to markets in Cincinnati, Louisville, St. Louis, New Orleans and other river cities. Kanawha Salines was a commercial success and flourished with many homes, hotels, a bank, retail stores and service shops. Famous Americans reared here included, among others: the great educator Booker T. Washington; the Civil War Major General who later served West Virginia Constitutional Conventions for statehood, Lewis Ruffner; and the former chairman of the board of the F.W. Woolworth Company, James Leftwich.

The town also endured many not-so-distinguished times. Its salt industry faded following the Civil War when other more convenient sources were developed. Coal mining came and went, and fires claimed parts of the town in the early 1920s. Little more

Two U.S. presidents are among the many famous owners and admirers of Cabin Creek Quilts.  STEPHEN J. SHALUTA, JR.

than a ghost town in the hills was left here for many years. But a visionary VISTA volunteer from Boston, James Thibeault, changed the town's fortune when he helped establish the **Cabin Creek Quilting Cooperative** in 1970.

Thibeault had been taken in by area residents Lena Hawkins, her sister Grace Jackson and their great-aunt Victoria Haggerty whose passion was quilting. The three gave him food, shelter and friendship as well as something he had not seen before. "Women who could shoot rattlesnake, hunt, fish, paint murals, sculpt and quilt were unlike anyone I had known," wrote Thibeault. The group set out to solve the problem faced by quilters on Cabin Creek: not receiving a price that reflected the thousands of work hours put into their many quilts. Thibeault returned to Boston with several quilts—against the objection of a VISTA bureaucrat—and succeeded in selling them at previously unheard of prices. "I got $200.00!" exclaimed Stella Monk, one of the first co-op members from the area. "It was the biggest news on Cabin Creek. I told it to everybody I seen. Nobody had ever sold one for that price. The most women around here had got was $25.00," she said.

One thing led to another and soon Cabin Creek Quilters were flying on jet planes and riding in limousines on route to a "Today Show" television appearance. The town was again on the map. Orders for quilts, as numerous as the patches in their traditional designs, streamed in. Two U.S. presidents, a king, a premier, CEOs, show business celebrities and museums became customers. Yet even riding on this high, the co-op was not immune to troubles. In 1975 the cooperative's home burned to the ground destroying tens of thousands of hours' work. But the group persevered, never looking back, and has recently celebrated both its 20th anniversary and the dedication of its new home, the Hale House. One of the three oldest buildings in town (built in 1838), this two-story Federal-style residence (now painted pink) is the hub of the co-op's activities. Not only can you see fabulous quilts but you can find every supply needed to make your own. Classes, including weekend seminars, are available too.

Quilters should not hesitate to bring their families to **Malden**— there's enough to keep non-quilters busy. Walking tours of historic Malden are popular. (Copies of guides prepared by the Historical Society are available at Cabin Creek Quilts.) You can walk to several churches, mid-19th-century mansions, one of the oldest Masonic lodges in the state, a memorial park to Booker T. Washington and the ferry landing from which millions of bushels of salt were shipped. It may be a good idea to remember your fishing pole and swim suit too. Should you want to stay over in Malden, there is a reasonably priced, attractive bed-and-breakfast, the Rose Cottage, that boasts a Cabin Creek quilt on every bed. The phone is (304)925-6568.

**Hours**: Cabin Creek Quilts is open Monday through Saturday, 10:00 A.M. to 4:00 P.M.

**Directions**: Take Exit 96 (Rt. 60 east toward Belle) off I-64 south of Charleston. Go one mile and take the Malden/Rand Exit. Turn left after passing through the underpass and go three blocks where you'll see Cabin Creek Quilts. For more information call (304)925-9499 or write Cabin Creek Quilts, 4208 Malden Drive, Malden, WV 25306.

# Milton

Where do you find two glassmaking factories, a 125-year-old covered bridge, a country and bluegrass music hall, a huge flea market and access to one of the loveliest hiking trails in the state? Milton, West Virginia, of course.

Closest to the Milton exit off I-64 is the **Mountaineer Opry House**. Local and nationally known country and bluegrass stars from Ricky Skaggs and Skeeter Davis to the Seldom Scene have been coming here to play on weekend nights year-round since 1971. You can expect down-home fun with a no-alcohol policy in a large cinderblock building with theater-type seating. There is a great sound system, big concession stand and plenty of free parking.

**Admission**: Adults $7.00, seniors $6.00, children $2.00.

**Hours**: Year-round. Call (304)743-3367 for a schedule. Saturday shows begin at 8:00 P.M. Special shows on Friday or Sunday.

**Directions**: Take Exit 28 off I-64 and turn toward Milton. The Opry House is at the exit on your left.

If you are in the mood for bargains, then turn the opposite way from Milton off the interstate (toward Colloden) and follow Rt. 60 East to the giant indoor/outdoor **flea market**. Held Friday through Sunday during warm weather months, the market is the largest in the tri-state area having just about everything under the sun at one time or another. Call (304)529-4783 for more details.

Even though it is much smaller and without the history of its crosstown neighbor, Blenko Glass, **Gibson Glass** still pleases shoppers with its quality handmade glassware. Among the highlights offered at this residential-area shop are flower paperweights, a wonderful line of marbles, angels and other figures. Like snowflakes, no two of Gibson's pieces are exactly the same. Gibson Glass also sells seconds. There is an observation area for tours where you can get closer to the glassmakers than anywhere else.

**Hours**: Monday through Friday, 8:30 A.M. to 3:00 P.M. The gift shop is open until 4:00 P.M. Monday through Saturday. The phone is (304)743-5232.

**Directions**: Continue past Blenko Glass Company. At the "Y" intersection, make a left. Pass Wetterau on the left and the church on the right. Turn right onto West Mud River Road, go under the railroad bridge and turn right. Turn right again at the second road and follow to Gibson Glass.

If you still have energy left after a glass factory tour, head to Camp Arrowhead for access to the tranquil 32-mile-long foot trail called the **Kanawha Trace**. Of course hiking aficionados will likely begin their day in Milton here, but this is a delightful spot for any nature lover. So pack a picnic and throw in your hiking boots, fishing pole, camera and favorite book. A project of the Tri-State Council, Boy Scouts of America, the scenic trail runs all the way from Barboursville, at the junction of the Mud and Guyandotte Rivers, to Fraziers Bottom on the Kanawha River. For the serious hiker who would like to trek its entire distance, *A Guidebook to Hiking the Kanawha Trace* is available for $7.00 by writing the Council at 733 7th Avenue, Huntington, WV 25701. Phone: (304)523-3408.

**Hours**: Open year-round.

**Directions**: From Rt. 60 West, turn right on Blue Sulfur Road and follow to Camp Arrowhead.

## Blenko Glass Company

Glass factories are Milton's leading attraction. Especially noteworthy is Blenko Glass Company. Known throughout the world for its handblown glassware and blown stained glass, the company was started in Milton by a British glassmaker, William Blenko, in 1922. Blenko had failed with earlier attempts at glassmaking businesses in this country, including an 1893 effort in Kokomo, Indiana, a 1909 venture in Point Marion, Pennsylvania, and a 1913 operation in Clarksburg, West Virginia. However in Milton, joined by his son, William H. Blenko, and, seven years later, two experienced Swedish glassworkers, Blenko began exploring the field of handmade decorative glass. The rest is a history of success. Now into its fourth generation of Blenkos (including William H. Blenko, Jr., and Richard D. Blenko), the company has major installations around the world, including those in St. Patricks Cathedral in New York, the Washington Cathedral in the District of Columbia and Riyadh Airport in Saudi Arabia. Blenko Glass has also been shown in museums and cultural exhibitions worldwide and won numerous awards. Gift shops everywhere sell their glass.

Come see for yourself what all the excitement is about. The large, two-story Visitor Center, adjacent to the factory, bedazzles the visitor with beautiful shapes and colors. There is a factory outlet on its lower level and upstairs a glass museum, military exhibit and stained-glass showcase. Especially interesting and popular are the free factory tours. A special observation deck provides an excellent, up-close view of craftsmen practicing their art.

**Hours**: Tours are available 8:00 A.M. to NOON and 12:30 to 3:15 P.M. Monday through Friday. (Please note that the plant observes two-week vacations beginning on or about July 1 and during the week between Christmas and New Year's. If you want to watch glass being made and fear your schedules may conflict, phone ahead (304)743-9081).

The Visitor Center's hours are 8:00 A.M. to 4:00 P.M. Monday through Saturday and NOON to 4:00 P.M. Sunday. Both the Visitor Center and the plant close for holidays.

**Directions**: Take Exit 28 off I-64 toward Milton and turn right on Rt. 60 West. A left at the light in the town center will you lead you there.

After touring Blenko Glass Company, you can see something especially West Virginian, a covered bridge. Near Blenko, off Rt. 60 West on County Road 25, is the **Mud River Covered Bridge**. Built in 1876, the 112-foot-long bridge underwent extensive repairs in 1971 and continues to accommodate foot traffic over the river.

# Point Pleasant
## *Battle Monument State Park*

On October 10, 1774, the first battle of the American Revolution raged at the confluence of the Kanawha and Ohio rivers on this small parcel of land known by the Ayamdotte Indian phrase "tu-endie-wei," or "the point between two waters." So important was the day-long bloody Battle of Point Pleasant that it is considered a landmark in frontier history. Led by Colonel Andrew Lewis, 1,100 Virginia militiamen fought hand-to-hand against as many Indians led by Shawnee Chief Cornstalk. The Virginians' victory not only crushed the power of the Indians in the Ohio Valley but kept them from forming an alliance with the British that could possibly have changed the outcome of the Revolution. Also the peace with the Indians that followed the battle allowed settlers to continue pushing west.

The events leading up to this battle are indicative of the many struggles our forefathers faced in their search for independence. As they spread west they could not avoid encounters with the Indians, and they also had to contend with the will of the British. When Lord Dunmore was made Governor of Virginia in 1771, the British government ordered him to discourage settlement west of the Allegheny Mountains. The government wanted to maintain a lucrative fur trading operation with the Indians and appeased them by keeping settlers off their hunting grounds.

Yet settlers continued moving west and skirmishes with Indians occurred more and more often and with greater fierceness on both sides. For example, when a group of drunken settlers murdered the family of Logan, a friendly Mingo chief in Hancock County, Logan and his tribe retaliated. To organize the fight against the Indians, Lord Dunmore established a border militia with Colonel Lewis as its commander. Some historians believe this move was prompted to keep Virginians' attention away from the growing tensions with England; others believe the Indians had been purposely goaded by British agents to fight the settlers.

There is no denying the decisive battle that occurred when Lord Dunmore moved to meet with Lewis's army at Point Pleasant to take on Cornstalk's Shawnee, now together with Logan's Mingo. However Cornstalk moved quickly hoping to catch his opposition divided and engaged Lewis's army before Dunmore arrived. The colonists prevailed, proving to be stronger in the densely forested battlefield. Two hundred Indians lay dead alongside 50 fallen Virginia militiamen.

Standing in the two-acre **Point Pleasant Battle Monument State Park** today, it is hard to imagine such a violent fight taking place here. You see the two rivers meet in a wide peaceful expanse lined by tall trees, silent witnesses of what happened more than 200 years ago. Only the park's focal point, an 84-foot granite obelisk, erected early in the 20th century, will remind you of the history here. Other smaller memorials in the park include one dedicated to Cornstalk and another to "Mad" Anne Bailey, the widow of Richard Trotter killed in the battle, who lived to be past 80. The Indians had the opportunity to kill her but didn't because they thought she was "mad." She behaved unlike any other woman of her day, riding her horse through the woods while carrying a gun. A third plaque, not related to the battle, marks the place where French explorer Joseph Celoron de Blainville laid claim to this land for his country in 1749.

Of additional interest is the **Mansion House** located on the park's grounds. The first hewn log house in the county, it was built by Walter Newman in 1796 and first used as a tavern. Because it was large for its day and had two stories with glass windows, Mansion House was, believe it or not, a very suitable name. The building has been preserved as a museum by the Colonel Charles Lewis Chapter of the National Society of the Daughters of the American Revolution, who continue to meet here as they have since 1909. The 40 x 50-foot house feels spacious inside and contains countless artifacts from the era including a large, Indian flint-head collection, antiques and heirlooms and possibly the first square-leg piano carried over the Alleghenies.

**Admission**: Donations are appreciated.

**Hours**: Point Pleasant Battle Monument State Park is open year-round. The museum in the Mansion House is open from

May through October, 9:00 A.M. to 4:30 P.M., Monday through Saturday, and Sunday 1:00 to 4:30 P.M. Phone: (304)675-3330. Directions: The park is located in the southern end of the Point Pleasant at 1 Main Street. From I-64 you may choose to take either Rt. 35 or Rt. 62 north to Point Pleasant. (The two roads run on opposite sides of the Kanawha River with Rt. 35 being perhaps the faster.) The park is one mile north of the junction of US 35 and WV 2 or just west of the intersection of WV Rts. 62 and 2.

## Krodel Park

After touring the Point Pleasant Battle Monument State Park head to Krodel Park just one-half mile away on Rt. 62 west. On the site where Daniel Boone once had a trading post, the 44-acre complex, owned and operated by the City of Point Pleasant, is an ideal, quiet spot for a picnic. You may decide to linger and enjoy the park's 22-acre lake where you can rent paddle boats or fish for stocked trout, bass and bluegill. There is also an 18-hole miniature golf course and a playground. Those wishing to stay longer can take advantage of the campground, open mid-April through November. Fifty full hook-up rental sites near a bathhouse are available as is space for pitching tents. The park also has a clubhouse with kitchen and restrooms and two picnic shelters ready for groups to rent. Call the City of Point Pleasant at (304)675-2360 for more information and reservations.

**Admission**: Free. Mini golf, $1.00; paddleboats, $1.00; full hook-ups from $8.50; clubhouse, $25.00; picnic shelters, $15.00 and $30.00.

**Hours**: Open year-round. Phone at park (304)675-1068.

**Directions**: One-half mile east of the Point Pleasant Battle Monument on Rt. 62.

## West Virginia State Farm Museum

A highlight of any trip to Metro Valley is a visit to the West Virginia State Farm Museum, just six miles north of historic Point Pleasant. Consisting of 31 period buildings spread over about 50 acres, this living farm museum is a memorial to West Virginia's farm-life heritage. You can take guided tours throughout the buildings and see thousands of items used in the farm life of the area during the past 200 years, many of them restored to working condition and used now in demonstrations. Everything here has been donated by one source or another. One guide says, "There seems to always be something 'new' here." The museum is operated entirely by volunteers and admission is free.

The museum was started in 1976 when the majority of the buildings were moved to this site. Among them are a log house from the early 1800s furnished as it likely was then. Be sure to notice what looks like a large cabinet in the log house—it's actually a folding bed. There is a one-room school house from around 1870 complete with wooden desks, a pot-bellied stove and original copies of the standard text book of the time, McGuffey's Reader. In this school most farming children attended grades 1–8, which were free, but couldn't afford to go on to high school.

A replica of an old Lutheran church, said to be the earliest church of its kind west of the Allegheny Mountains, contains a safety balcony for women and children, a musket rack near the door for protection against Indian attacks and a pump organ that still works today. The church still offers an occasional service during the museum's special events.

There is also: a country store offering crafts and souvenirs, among other items cornmeal and molasses made on the premises; an old-time post office; a newspaper office with a variety of printers and gobs of hand-set type (be sure to pick up a sample of something printed on these old-time machines for a souvenir); a working blacksmith shop; and two big buildings loaded with an extensive antique collection of threshing machines, cultivators, tractors, carriages, sleighs, looms, sewing machines, bottles and jars, resourceful tools, a flint collection, caps and even an early Maytag seed cleaner. Morgan's Museum features an outstanding collection of taxidermy including a loon from 1905, the first bird ever mounted by Mr. Morgan, and the last elk killed in West Virginia (in 1912). You can also see a railroad boxcar and a caboose, a barnyard with farm animals and a country kitchen. The latter is really a snack bar serving lunches of cornbread and beans, hot dogs, cornmeal pie, ice cream and soft drinks.

Don't leave without seeing **General,** on record as the third largest horse ever to have lived. A registered Belgian gelding, General was the world's largest living horse from 1972 to 1981, standing 19½ hands high and weighing 2,950 pounds. He also wore the largest collar ever made—34 inches. After his death he was mounted by the same company that mounted Trigger for Roy Rogers.

The State Farm Museum organizes a number of special activities during the year when pioneer techniques like soap making, weaving, quilting, wood carving, broom making and blacksmithing are demonstrated. Call (304)675-5737 for a schedule of special events.

**Hours**: April 1 through November 31, Tuesday through Saturday from 10:00 A.M. to 4:00 P.M. and Sunday 1:00 to 4:00 P.M.

**Directions**: From Charleston, take I-64 west to Exit 45 and follow Rt. 62 north alongside the Kanawha River six miles past

Point Pleasant. Signs on Rt. 62 lead you to the museum. Or take Rt. 35 north to Point Pleasant, then Rt. 62 north to the museum. From Huntington take Rt.2 to Point Pleasant and Rt. 62 north. For more information write WV State Farm Museum, Rt. 1, Box 479, Point Pleasant, WV 25550.

# St. Albans
## *The Chilton House Restaurant*

You may want to plan dinner out when traveling near Scott Depot. One delightful, elegant stop, nearby in St. Albans, is the historic Chilton House Restaurant. Built in 1847, this was the childhood home of William E. Chilton II, a U.S. Senator from 1911 to 1917. Overlooking the Coal River, the two-story Gothic revival house is listed on the National Register of Historic Places.

Two brothers, Leroy and Richard Rashid, purchased the home in 1978 and completed a room-by-room restoration that had been started by the St. Albans Historical Society. Parts of the home could not be restored so materials from another mid-1800s house nearby were used. Now there are six intimate dining rooms with antiques and artwork as well as an authentic Shaker Room with signed furniture, a Cellar Lounge with antique stained-glass windows and a new banquet room, The Carriage Room.

**Hours**: Monday through Saturday 6:00–10:00 P.M.

**Directions**: From I-64 take the St. Albans Exit 44. Turn right on Rt. 35 South and left at the light on Rt. 60 East. Go one mile and turn right at the light onto B Street. Cross the railroad tracks, turn right on Sixth Street Loop and follow to number two. The restaurant is handicapped accessible. Phone: (304)722-2918.

# Scott Depot
## *Hamon Glass Studio*

In Scott Depot there is a small, family-run glassmaking company ideal for those who like to shop off the beaten path. Handmade and handblown glass has long been made in West Virginia, and its reputation for beauty and quality extends around the world. Each factory enjoys a certain specialty. (There are three others in this region. See also Blenko, Gibson and Pilgrim glassworks.) For Robert and Veronica Hamon, the husband-wife team of Hamon Glass Studio, their specialties are paperweights, blown art glass and glass sculpture. Robert, a second generation glassworker, began making glass at the age of ten. He gained experience with several other companies before beginning his partnership with Veronica in 1969.

**Hours**: Gift shop open Monday through Friday 9:00 A.M. to 4:00 P.M. and Saturday by advance appointment only. Tours of the studio are available by appointment as well. Phone: (304)757-9067.

**Directions**: From I-64, take Exit 39 (Route 34) toward Scott Depot. Go one half mile and turn left on Teays Boulevard, then turn left on Teays Valley Road. Proceed two miles to a right-hand turn on Scott Lane and then one mile to a right turn onto Hamon Drive. Hamon Glass is at 102 Hamon Drive. Finding the studio is nearly as much fun as gazing at one of the dazzling paperweights!

# South Charleston
## South Charleston Mound

A grass-covered, 35-foot-high, 175-foot-wide earthen pile protrudes mysteriously from the ground in South Charleston, challenging visitors to ponder its significance. The second largest remaining Indian burial mound in the state, it was erected as long as 2,000 years ago by a race of people known as Indians of the **Adena Culture.** No one is quite sure where the civilization came from. Some scholars believe they settled here from Mexico and Middle America via the Mississippi and Ohio rivers, while others believe they came from Europe. Even the dates of their existence are approximated. However, there is no denying the mounds they left behind—an official report by the Bureau of Ethnology in 1890–91 reported 50 mounds of varying sizes in this area—nor the artifacts uncovered in them that show both common cultural and physical traits as well as common burial customs.

From the mounds excavated archaeologists concluded that these mound builders were a broad-faced race of people due to their custom of flattening and reshaping their infants' heads with a cradle board. In addition the Adenans believed in cremation as indicated by charred bone fragments found in some mounds. When this South Charleston mound was excavated in 1883–84 by Colonel P. W. Norris of the Smithsonian Institution, a host of artifacts were found for study and speculation including 13 complete skeletons plus parts of another, a flint lance head, copper bracelets, arrowheads, tools and other metal and shell items. One of the skeletons wore a copper headdress and was centered between two semi-circles formed by the other skeletons. Some artifacts from the excavation are on loan to the Sunrise Museum in Charleston (see entry).

When you approach The Indian mound on MacCorkle Avenue (US Rt. 60 West) in the busy downtown business district, you will likely wonder why such an important historical site has suffered the fate of being surrounded by huge industrial operations. Union Carbide, The FMC Corporation and Volkswagen of America sprawl nearby. However, do what you can to block out the congestion and give thanks that at least this mound has been saved for us to marvel at. Many in areas of West Virginia, Ohio and Kentucky have been destroyed by land developers. Fortunately the only change to this mound occurred in the 1800s when its top was leveled for a horse race judge's stand.

**Directions**: The mound fronts Oakes and Seventh Avenue in Staunton Park. From I-64 west take Exit 56, Montrose Drive, turn left at light onto Rt. 60 west. Go a few blocks and the mound will be on left.

## West Virginia Belle

A delightful way to take in the historical sites and scenery of southwest West Virginia is from aboard any of the several sternwheelers that ply the broad waters of the Ohio and Kanawha rivers. You travel the same course the Indians took years ago when they named the waterway "Ohio" meaning "beautiful river." And you can do it from similar paddle-churning steamships just as westward-bound pioneers did. When you add the modern-day bonuses of the relaxed pace, site narration, as many as three meals a day, live music, dancing and entertainment, a boat excursion becomes a "must-do" experience.

There are several lines cruising the waterways (see *P.A. Denny* and *C.P. Huntington* sternwheelers). The largest one is the *West Virginia Belle*. It maintains docks in both South Charleston and Huntington. Christened in May 1988, the 200-foot-long, 742-ton vessel is U.S. Coast Guard registered to accommodate 1,200 passengers. It is handicapped accessible and has a total of five bar areas, a souvenir ship, two wooden dance floors, an elevator and three enclosed decks. The fourth deck is completely open for fun in the sun. Owned and operated by a sister and brother team, the ship is decorated in handsome Victorian style with velvet brass in the interior and gold-crowned stacks on the exterior.

River riders have many choices of cruises. There are day-long, 100-mile trips (complete with three meals and entertainment) between Huntington and South Charleston. There are also nine-hour, daytime cruises departing from and returning to South Charleston as well as popular evening-long dinner/dance cruises from both ports. On Sundays there are brunch outings, afternoon 90-minute sightseeing trips and dinner cruises.

Each year beginning in November and continuing through the Christmas season, the *West Virginia Belle* is transformed into

Accommodating 1,200 passengers, the sternwheeler West Virginia Belle cuts a pretty picture along the Kanawha River.

STEPHEN J. SHALUTA, JR.

Santa's Showboat. Bright lights and decorations topped by two 12-foot reindeer pulling a 22-foot sleigh carrying a 15-foot Santa Claus set the cheery stage. A hundred animated, costumed figures ranging from elves, penguins and bears to rabbits and happy boys and girls add to the fun. A Santa appears together with his helpers on every cruise, so be sure to bring a copy of your wish list for him. Not even Scrooge could resist this winter wonderland. Both day and evening cruises are offered for Santa's Showboat so call for a complete schedule.

**Tip**: The *West Virginia Belle* has docks in both South Charleston and Huntington, so you will need to check from which dock your cruise departs and to which one it returns.

**Admission**: From $8.00 for adults, $5.00 for children for the shortest sightseeing trips to $76. 95 for the day-long cruises. The *West Virginia Belle* also hosts dances, proms, weddings and other special charters. Toll-free phone numbers for more information: 1(800)543-0227 (inside WV) and 1(800)327-1381 (outside WV).

**Directions**: The South Charleston dock is located behind Krogers at 18 Riverwalk Plaza (to the left of MacCorkle Avenue) and may be reached by taking Exit 54 off I-64 and turning right at the light onto MacCorkle Avenue. The Huntington dock is at the Harris Riverfront Park. Take Exit 11 (Hal Greer Boulevard) off I-64, follow to 3rd Avenue and turn left. Fork right onto Veterans

Memorial Boulevard, turn right on 10th Street and follow to the park.

# Williamson
## *The Coal House*

In the courthouse square of Williamson, the county seat of Mingo County on the Tug River at the Kentucky border, sits an arresting monument to the importance of coal to the economic and social development of the area. Built during the Great Depression and now on the National Register of Historic Places, the square black building with its arched entryway is so shiny and clean it makes

*Sixty-five tons of coal blocks make up the walls of the Coal House, a monument to the mineral that shaped West Virginian history.* DAVID FATTALEH

one think it was built of cut stone and not coal. The townsfolk often find themselves reassuring visitors that this Coal House truly was made of coal.

Now housing the Tug Valley Chamber of Commerce and the Williamson Credit Bureau, the Coal House was the brainchild of

O.W. Evans, manager of the Norfolk and Western Railways Fuel Department in Williamson. Evans inspired local businesses and individuals to give all the materials, labor and cash necessary to bring it to completion in 1933.

Designed by H.T. Hicks, architect of Welch, WV, the Coal House used 65 tons of locally mined coal, cut into blocks, for its exterior walls. The blocks have remained in surprisingly good shape due to an every-other-year coating of weather-proofing varnish. In case you might worry, the building poses no major fire threat. It was insured without question by a national insurance company. Should you need more information, phone the Chamber of Commerce at (304)235-5240.

**Hours**: 9:00 A.M. to 5:00 P.M., Monday through Friday.

**Directions**: The Coal House is located in the courthouse square in downtown Williamson. From Huntington take I-64 to US Rt. 52 south. From Charleston, take I-64 to US Rt. 119 south.

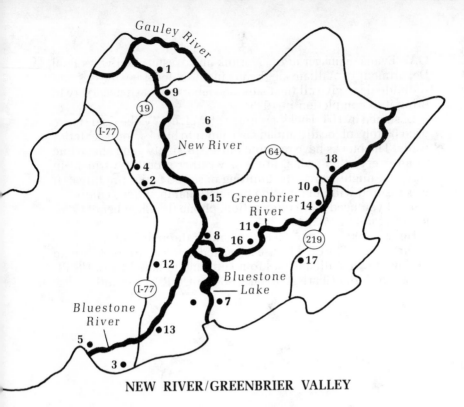

## NEW RIVER/GREENBRIER VALLEY

1. **Ansted**
   Contentment and Hawks Nest
   State Park

2. **Beckley**
   New River Park
   Theatre West Virginia
   Wildwood House Museum

3. **Bluefield**
   Area Arts and Crafts Center
   Eastern Regional Coal Archives

4. **Bradley**
   Blue Circle Ranch

5. **Bramwell (Historic District)**

6. **Clifftop**
   Midland Trail and Camp
   Washington Carver

7. **Forest Hill**
   Wakerobin Gallery

8. **Hinton**
   Bluestone Dam, Lake and
   Museum
   Historic District

9. **Lansing**
   Canyon Rim Visitor Center

10. **Lewisburg**
    Visitor Center and Walking Tour
    Lost World Cavern

11. **Pence Springs**
    The Graham House
    Pence Springs Hotel

12. **Pipestem**
    Pipestem Resort State Park

13. **Princeton**

14. **Ronceverte**
    Organ Cave

15. **Sandstone**
    Sandstone Jetboat

16. **Talcott**
    Big Ben Tunnel and John Henry
    Statue

17. **Union**

18. **White Sulphur Springs**
    The Greenbrier

# New River/
## ══Greenbrier Valley══

Pack your walking shoes and camera and hike a trail alongside a gorgeous, ageless waterway; throw in some old shorts and splash down a white-water river; bring a light jacket and go underground into a coal mine or cave; leave your worries behind and head to a state park where there's everything you need for a getaway; and bring an ear bent toward the interesting cultural mix that is coal country. That's what you'll need and can expect when visiting southern West Virginia.

Most activities in southern West Virginia center around the area's fascinating coal mining heritage and its uncommon, often unusual, natural beauty. The awesome New River, 52 miles of which is declared a National River, lures outdoor lovers of all interests (the Visitor Center in Lansing is not to be missed), and numerous resorts catering to year-round recreation attract many others—such as Pipestem Resort State Park, a treasure! White-water rafting, fishing and skiing top the list of favorite sports while the Beckley Exhibition Coal Mine offers an excellent, close-up look at the industry. There are other historical sites of special note such as the ideal one-day trip destination steeped in 19th-century charm, Lewisburg. The underground caves nearby, Lost World Caverns and Organ Cave, offer fascinating explorations of the hidden secrets of the earth.

The region is easily accessible to southwest Virginia vacationers traveling from bordering areas such as Lynchburg and Roanoke and is only a two- to three-hour drive from cities in north central North Carolina such as Winston-Salem. There are very few large cities in the region. Many entries are in remote areas—perfect escapes from the crowds.

For more information on New River/Greenbrier Valley, contact:

Bluestone Convention and Visitors Bureau, 500 Bland St., Bluefield, WV 24701, phone (304)325-8438.

Lewisburg Convention and Visitors Bureau, 105 Church St., Lewisburg, WV 24901, phone (304)645-1000.

Summers County Convention and Visitors Bureau, 206 Temple St., Hinton, WV 25951, phone (304)466-5420.

With nearly 2,000 miles of streams and rivers, West Virginia is considered by many as the whitewater capital of the world.

White Sulphur Springs Convention and Visitors Bureau, 102 Main St., White Sulphur Springs, WV 24986, phone (304)536-9440 or 1(800)284-9440.

# Ansted

## Contentment and Hawks Nest State Park

Just north of the Lansing Visitor Center on Rt. 60 in Ansted lies the three-building historic complex **Contentment**. Under the auspices of the Fayette County Historical Society, the site contains a pre-Civil War home, a museum and a restored one-room country school house.

Built around 1830, one year before the founding of Fayette County, the white frame house with its gray tin roof was purchased by Colonel George W. Imboden in 1872 when he came here to develop the area's coal interest. Imboden was well known during the Civil War as the Confederate Commander of the 18th Virginia Cavalry Regiment and was also the first Mayor of Ansted. His home, later named Contentment by his wife, still has the original walnut mantels in three rooms and interesting alternating walnut and oak flooring. You see many period antiques in the home including a "fainting sofa," a handmade desk once belonging to the family of West Virginia Governor Okey Patterson, a hand-cranking music box and children's toys.

Adjoining Col. Imboden's home, the historical society maintains a museum that displays Civil War artifacts and other Fayette County memorabilia. Of special interest are the many pieces from the home of county leader Morris Harvey, namesake of the Morris Harvey College in Charleston. Captured copper moonshine stills, pictures of mining camps, antique sewing machines and Mrs. Imboden's wedding gown and traveling trunk are favorites with visitors.

The small restored school house on the complex's grounds is one of only a few that remain of the nearly 1,000 school houses like it that once dotted West Virginia's countryside. It is packed with reminders of what it was like to go to school a century or more ago; a Burnside stove, benches and desks, copies of the standard texts (*McGuffrey Reader* and *Blue Back Speller*), handbells and photos. The one-room school house even has the names of dozens of former teachers inscribed on its walls.

**Admission**: Adults $2.00, children $1.00.

**Hours**: The Contentment complex is open Sundays during the month of May and on Monday through Sunday, June through September. Hours are 10:00 A.M. to 4:00 P.M. except Sundays when the complex is open 1:30 to 4:00 P.M. Phone: (304)465-0165 or 658-5695.

**Directions**: You will find Contentment on Rt. 60 one mile east of Hawks Nest State Park in Ansted.

**Hawks Nest Park** also in Ansted is not to be missed (see entry on State Parks). In an area first popularized in the early 1800s by Chief Justice John Marshall who spoke about the high peaks where fish hawks nested, the park boasts among its many amenities an aerial tramway running from clifftops to the river's edge. When you take this ride, popular since its beginning in 1970 three years after the opening of the park, consider some of the local legends who made the same trip but by different means. Mad Anne Bailey, the wild Indian scout, purportedly rode her horse Liverpool off Hawks Nest cliff in an effort to escape Indians. You will no doubt prefer your method of descent aboard the tramway to hers.

Ansted is remembered also for its **Westlake Cemetery**. Here rest the remains of Stonewall Jackson's mother, Julia Neale Jackson.

**Directions:** Near the center of the town of Ansted turn on Cemetery Street (Revco Drug Store on the corner). Approximately a half block on the left is Westlake Cemetery.

# Beckley

## *New River Park*

If you were allowed only one choice for a day-trip destination in southern West Virginia, you should pick the New River Park in Beckley. No other spot in the region offers the variety of things to do, so many opportunities to learn about the area's culture and lore and the prospect of just plain fun. Plan to make a full day of it here.

Topping the long list of sites located at the park is the **Beckley Exhibition Coal Mine**, the only historically preserved coal mine in the state. Here you can see and trace what it was like to work in a low-seam coal mine beginning with the 1890s hand-loading era on through today's modern mechanization. The mine was once part of 29 acres of coal fields owned by the Phillips family. Only 10 to 11 acres were actually mined. In 1962, following careful safety preparations, 1,500 feet of curving passageways were opened for public tour. Now, 30 years later, ex-miners continue to guide visitors aboard clanking "man trip" rail cars into the dark depths. The 45-minute tour shows you all about the various techniques and tools used. The mood is light and entertaining including often-heard jokes like "arrangements can be made to leave a mother-in-law down in the mine." But when the guide turns out all the lights to reveal the blackest darkness your eyes have likely ever seen—a darkness miners had to deal with about seven or eight times each work day when their lamps went out—the realism inspires profound respect for an incredibly hard, challenging job. The guides' stories about their experiences is more than worth the price of admission. You will want to bring along a light jacket both to keep warm in the 58-degree underground mine and to guard against a drop or two of water that may fall. Provided no one in your group is claustrophobic, this is a most fascinating, enjoyable tour.

A small coal museum, located in the building where you purchase tickets for the exhibition mine, displays interesting artifacts and memorabilia. And a gift shop offers reminders of your visit.

**Admission**: Adults $5.00, children $3.00.

**Hours**: Tours are available 10:00 A.M. to 5:30 P.M. from Easter weekend through November 1. More information may be obtained by calling (304)256-1747.

Also at the park, and both adjacent and related to the Exhibition Coal Mine, is the **Coal Company House**. If the coal mine shows you how miners worked, a tour of the small Coal Company House shows you how they lived. It was common practice for coal companies to build coal camps near mines they operated.

The camps generally consisted of company-owned stores, schools, churches and houses. Some coal camps even had their own live-in doctors. The companies issued their own money, called "scrip," which miners used to pay for their rent and living expenses. Thus the coal companies made profits not only from the coal their workers mined but from the workers themselves. Rent for the houses, most of which were from three to six rooms in size depending on the size of a miner's family, ranged from $8.00 to $20.00 per month. An example of such a home, previously owned and used by the New River Coal Company in Sprague, West Virginia, from 1925 through the 1940s, has been restored by the City of Beckley for you to see. The three-room house reflects the time when it was lived in and includes many items used by early mining families.

**The Youth Museum** of Southern West Virginia is on the park's grounds as well. Designed to inspire curiosity in young people, it features a combination of permanent, changing and hands-on exhibits housed in a novel space built from four railroad boxcars. The on-going attractions are a planetarium and The Peace Totem, an eye-catching art work. Of special interest too is an outstanding assemblage of 100 folk-art wood carvings that tells the story of John Henry, the great steel-driving man who personified early railroad construction (see entry). Past exhibits have included a mechanical yet life-like Dinosaurs Alive show that roared and stomped its way through the museum in conjunction with dinomite events like Dino-Snores, an overnight camp-in, and a week-long Dinosaur Camp.

**Admission**: For information on events, exhibits and corresponding admission fees (which are reasonable—the Dinosaurs Alive exhibit costs $3.00 to see) call the museum at (304)252-3730.

**Hours**: The museum is open daily, May 1 through Labor Day from 10:00 A.M. to 6:00 P.M. The rest of the year it is open Tuesday through Saturday 10:00 A.M. to 5:00 P.M. Closed Sunday and Monday.

Behind the Youth Museum you can see what it was like living on the West Virginia frontier by viewing the **Mountain Homestead** exhibit. The one-acre complex, complete with a circa 1844 four-room log house, barn, one-room school house, blacksmith shop, moonshine still and tools, depicts the day-to-day lifestyle of early mountaineers. There are demonstrations of open-hearth cooking including the use of a spider, a three-legged iron skillet popular in the late 1800s. The transition to more modern living is noted in a 1930s kitchen. Of interest is that these newer structures were simply added on to the old in lieu of the expensive prospect of tearing down and rebuilding altogether. A nominal entrance fee applies for the exhibit. Use the same number as the

The story of John Henry, the great steel-driving man of railroad fame, is told in the Youth Museum's folk art carvings.   Ron Snow

Youth Museum for more information on the Mountain Homestead, including a schedule of Pioneer Day Camps and special heritage days. The Mountain Homestead operates at the same hours as the Youth Museum.

If all of the above isn't enough to satisfy your interests then consider what else the park boasts: an olympic-size swimming pool complete with showers and changing rooms, a water slide, tennis courts, horseshoes, basketball courts and a playground. You can even plan a picnic to savor in a nice picnic area or camp out at the park's campground. There are 17 full hook-up sites.

**Directions**: New River Park is reached by taking Exit 44 off I-77. Turn east on Rt. 3 (Harpers Road) and go 1½ miles to Ewart Avenue where you will turn left by the gas station and drive ¼ mile to the park's entrance. There is plenty of free parking.

### Theatre West Virginia

Each summer from mid-June through August, Grandview Park's Cliffside Amphitheatre, just outside Beckley, hosts an outdoor repertory theater called **Theatre West Virginia.** At an elevation of 2,500 feet the day-use park offers a gorgeous setting on 892 acres in which to enjoy the performances with a "grand view" of where the New River Gorge winds to form Horseshoe Bend.

Drama productions began here in 1961 when the West Virginia Historical Drama Association gave the first performance of Kermit Hunter's epic of West Virginia's birth during the Civil War, *Honey in the Rock*. (The title stems from the unusual natural gas wells Indians found when first settling here. Frightened by them, they called them "Honey in the Rock.") Ten years later, Billy Edd Wheeler's portrayal of the famous feuding families, *Hatfields and McCoys*, began its long run, making the theater company the first in the country to stage two outdoor dramas in repertory. In 1992, having enjoyed one of the most protracted careers in the industry, *Honey in the Rock* was temporarily on hold. Another wonderful production, *Stonewall, Old Blue Light*, which premiered in 1992, tells the life story of West Virginia's favorite son, Stonewall Jackson, through song, narrative and dance.

The *Hatfields and McCoys* continues to pose questions of how the Tug River, which divided not only Kentucky and West Virginia but the two families as well, was made to run red by the bitter 40-year-long dispute. Did it begin over a $1.00 debt? Or did it start when Johnse Hatfield ran off with Rose Ann McCoy but didn't marry her? Perhaps it was because Floyd Hatfield wrongfully claimed Rands McCoy's hog as his own? Find out for yourself or take in one of the other dramas or musicals instead. By 1994 all three historical productions will be in repertory. Each year one contemporary musical is performed by the theatre.

Grandview Park, now a part of the **New River Gorge National River Park** run by the National Park Service, makes a delightful destination even when Theatre West Virginia is not in residence. On land once owned in 1855 by Joseph Carper, the famous rifle maker, the park is especially popular in the spring when large, plentiful rhododendron bloom. The park also features picnic areas, game courts, a playground, gift shop and hiking/cross-country ski trails.

**Admission**: Ticket prices range from around $12.00 for adults and $6.00 for children Sunday through Thursday to $15.00 for adults and $7.00 for children on Friday and Saturday.

**Hours**: All performances begin at 8:30 P.M. at Cliffside Amphitheatre. Call (304)256-6800 or 1(800)666-9142 for information on the revolving schedule.

**Directions**: From I-64 East take Exit 129B and follow signs six miles to the park entrance.

## Wildwood House Museum

The historic home of General Alfred Beckley, the founder of both the City of Beckley and Raleigh County, has been preserved as a museum and is available to tour on weekends May through September.

Known first as Park Place before being named Wildwood House, the large two-story double log cabin resting on a stone foundation was built for Beckley and his family by John Lilly, Sr., in 1836 and placed on the National Register of Historic Places in 1971.

Alfred Beckley left behind a successful military career in Pittsburgh, Pennsylvania, when he came to this largely uninhabited area to develop a huge plot of 170,038 acres of land willed to him by his father, John, for whom the town is named. He drew up plans for the town's 1838 founding complete with streets and alleys, a courthouse, church, burial grounds, school, tavern and stores. He donated his own land for the streets, half of the building lots and cemetery. He even later gave two acres of land for the courthouse square provided **Beckley** be named and remain the county seat. By 1850, with the first business, a blacksmith shop, in place and his proposed bill approved by the Virginia General Assembly, General Beckley got his wish. Raleigh County, named for Sir Walter Raleigh, was created with Beckley as its county seat. General Beckley had by then returned to the military, first in 1849 when the General Assembly commissioned him a Brigadier General of Militia and later, from 1861, when he served in the Civil War. After the War Between the States, Beckley returned to his work of making Beckley the best it could be. He served as a lawyer, engineer, preacher, teacher, politician and peacemaker until his death on his birthday in 1888.

General Beckley's home is much as it was when he lived here including a dining room, kitchen and porches as well as clapboard siding and white paint that were added around 1850. Old, wavy glass windows leave little doubt as to the building's age. A brick walkway, constructed of brick removed from Neville Street in downtown Beckley, now extends from the square front porch to a white picket fence. Inside, many furniture pieces owned by the Beckley family, who occupied the house until 1901, are on display. Beckley's family is still represented at the home. His great-granddaughter, Mrs. M. M. Ralsten, is among those looking after the property.

**Admission**: Adults $2.00, children $1.00.

**Hours**: The museum is open to the public May through September from 10:00 A.M. to 4:00 P.M. on Saturdays and from 2:00 to 4:00 P.M. on Sundays. For more information call (304)252-8614.

**Directions**: Continue east on Rt. 3 from the New River Park and turn left on F Street. Follow the signs to the Laurel Terrace parking lot.

# Bluefield

## *Bluefield Area Arts and Crafts Center*

Before the advent of the huge coal mining industry in southern West Virginia in the 1880s, **Bluefield** existed as little more than a small farming community. Known as Higgenbotham Summit, the area had been owned by two families descended from Revolutionary War veterans who had built a fort there 200 years ago. But when the Norfolk and Western Railroad forged its tracks through the East River Valley to connect vast amounts of the economical fuel with widespread energy-hungry markets, new towns like Bluefield soon developed. Laborers, including southern blacks and European immigrants, came to dig millions of tons of the "black diamond" out of the deep, dark mines. Early miners made about 25 cents for each ton of coal they hauled out. Boys lied about their age for the privilege of making even less. Women, thought to be bad luck, were forbidden in the mines.

Shrewd entrepreneurs, mostly from the north, seized the opportunity to make fortunes. They built company towns next to mines they purchased and deducted all living expenses, including supplies bought from their company stores, from their workers' paychecks. The cultural mix that poured in was unlike anything these hills had known before. "People came from all over to work," one ex-miner said. "That's why you now have so many different dialects in West Virginia. Back then, sometimes you couldn't understand the person working next to you."

No other state was so strongly tied socially and economically to coal mining. Unfortunately, very little of the profits stayed inside West Virginia. As could be expected, the labor-intensive industry spawned many famous confrontations. The many differences among miners, coal companies and the government festered until lives were lost over the right to join the United Mine Workers of America in the 1920 Battle of Matewan.

In 1921, the Battle of Blair Mountain saw 10,000 armed miners rise up against their bosses. It was the largest revolt since the Civil War and had to be quelled by federal troops. (To see what it was like to lead the hard life of a miner, visit the exhibition mines in Pocahontas, VA, and Beckley.) Even in the midst of such difficulties, the industry boomed from the 1890s into the 1920s due in large part to an enormous 900-square-mile coal bank near Pocahontas, VA. The coal found here became the standard by which all other bituminous coal was measured. "Smokelessly" pure, highly volatile and low in sulphur content, it fueled the industrial revolution worldwide. Pocahontas fuel was also the choice of the U.S. Navy for its steam-powered battleships in both the Spanish-American War and First World War.

With the coal industry riding this high tide of buoyancy, Bluefield quickly distinguished itself as the corporate center of southern West Virginia's coalfield. Its new name came from the area's prevalent chicory, which has a dark blue flower. People used the train to come to Bluefield for both business and pleasure. Most of its venerable buildings, the city hall, Daily Telegraph building, opera house, bank, law and commerce buildings and hotel, stem from coal mining's early successful days, the turn of the century to the mid-1920s. A planning commission, the first in the city, supervised their construction to make sure all were compatible in style. The buildings still stand as a reminder of the area's heritage and may be viewed on a self-guided walking tour prepared by the Bluestone Visitors and Convention Bureau (VCB).

Free copies of the tour are available at the VCB office located on the second floor of the Old City Hall, 500 Bland Street, now the **Bluefield Area Arts and Crafts Center**. You should begin your trip to Bluefield here. The tour takes in nine historic buildings in a manageable seven-block area and is easily covered in an hour. The VCB also offers guided coach tours of nearby attractions for groups of 16 or more. Normally operating on weekends, the two- to three-hour tours can include lunch and a choice of sites and activities. The range covers meeting veteran coal miners underground at the Pocahontas Show Mine and touring Settlers Fort in Tazewell, VA, hiking the Bluestone Gorge Canyon Rim Trail and exploring Bluefield's shops. At least 48 hours notice is required. The cost is about $10.00 per person. Lunch is extra.

Of interest at the three-story **Old City Hall** are the jail cells that now contain a "History of Transportation" exhibit. The building itself, in Classical revival style, was designed by Wilbur Mills and is now on the National Register of Historic Places. It also boasts an art gallery in the space once occupied by the public library, a theater that produces six plays each year, a restaurant and curio shop. As you leave the Old City Hall for the walking tour, take note of **Ramsey School**, the oldest school in the city, on your left. Its curious seven entrances on seven different levels landed it in *Ripley's Believe It or Not!* collection of oddities.

**Tip**: Cool valley breezes have earned Bluefield the nickname "Nature's Air-Conditioned City." On the infrequent days when the temperature climbs above 90, head for the Greater Bluefield Chamber of Commerce (located across from the Old City Hall) and take them up on their offer to serve free lemonade.

**Hours**: Monday through Friday 9:30 A.M. to 4:30 P.M. and Saturday by appointment. Call the VCB office at (304)325-8438 for more information on the coach tours and other happenings at the Old City Hall.

**Directions**: Downtown Bluefield is easily accessible off I-77 via Rt. 52. Follow the signs from the interstate to the downtown area along Rts. 52 and 460. Rt. 52 becomes Bland Street. The VCB will be on your left.

## The Bluefield Orioles

Bluefield is also home to the Bluefield Orioles, a minor league baseball team affiliated with the big league Baltimore Orioles. The birds play a short season from mid-June through August at Bowen Field located on Stadium Drive. But baseball isn't the only game here. The ballpark is part of a City Park operated by the City of Bluefield Parks and Recreation Department. Open to the public, it also features a playground, softball field, football stadium, Youth Center with recreation equipment including pool and Ping-Pong tables and tennis courts. Those wishing to make an entire day of it at the park will be glad to know there is also a picnic area with four pavilions including tables, grills and covered sheds. On Tuesday nights you can play bingo.

For more information on the park, as well as a schedule of when the Orioles are in town, call (304)327-2448.

**Tip**: Don't be alarmed when you cross into Virginia at the park. Remember that the Bluefield area is comprised of twin cities, one in Virginia and one in West Virginia.

**Directions**: From I-77 take Rt. 460 west. Take the Bluefield College Exit and fork left onto Stadium Drive at the light.

## Eastern Regional Coal Archives

The downtown Bluefield walking tour takes you to Commerce Street where the Eastern Regional Coal Archives is perched on the second level of the **Craft Memorial Library** (600 Commerce Street). Whether you choose to interrupt the tour or come back to the Archives later, don't miss this excellent, large collection of coal mining history. Should archivist Stuart McGehee be in attendance when you visit, consider yourself lucky. He, like the research facility he maintains, is proof that history need not be dull. Says the energetic McGehee, "History needs to be utilized." He feels that "coal mining history is under-appreciated." It's a pity it is so often neglected by history books because "people do want to know about it."

All of the materials stored here are available for your viewing. Artifacts, blueprints, company records, company store account books, correspondence, diaries, films, ledgers, maps, miner's tools, newspapers, oral history tapes, more than 50,000 photographs, railroad memorabilia, rare books, scrapbooks, scrip and secondary research materials neatly line the walls and fill the display tables of the two-room Archives. The bulk of the memorabilia was initially gathered for the 1983 Pocahontas Coal-field Centennial Celebration. Following the event, the materials were taken to the Craft Memorial Library where funding from the A.R. Mathews Foundation, together with support service from the public library, made possible the present day Archives. McGehee and his staff continue to preserve and augment their collection, keeping alive a history so important to the region's heritage. The Archives welcomes materials related to coal mining that may benefit future generations' study and understanding.

**Hours**: 9:30 A.M. to 5:00 P.M. Monday through Friday. Researchers should call in advance, (304)325-3943, for an appointment.

**Directions**: Take I-77 to Exit 1 Bluefield. Follow signs for Rt. 52 North to downtown Bluefield. Turn right on Commerce Street. The Library is located at 600 Commerce, one block on the right. The Coal Archives is located on the second floor of the red-brick Craft Memorial Library. For more information write Eastern Regional Coal Archives, Craft Memorial Library, 600 Commerce St., Bluefield, WV 24701.

# Bradley

## *Blue Circle Ranch*

Families with a love of horses will want to stop north of Beckley at the Blue Circle Ranch. Here you can take hour-long guided trail rides on gentle horses through the serene southern West Virginia countryside. Picnic rides and overnight trips are available as well.

Ida Crookshanks of the ranch quickly admits "horse fever is a serious addiction," so you are right to assume that more than just the popular trail excursions are offered. You can take part in a lesson program, outfit yourself and your horse with either Western or English wear and equipment from the tack shop, board your horse and benefit from various clinics and schooling shows. The ranch stands at stud American Paint Horse and American Quarter Horse stallions and offers for sale several of the foals born each year in its stables.

**Admission**: The one-hour trail rides cost $12.00 plus tax per person. Children must be at least school age (six) to ride. For information on all the other goings on at the ranch—including how to bring the ranch's pony to your child's birthday party—call from inside West Virginia (800)870-3174 or from outside the state (304)877-3174.

**Directions**: From I-64 or I-77 take Exit 48 onto Rt. 19 North. Go three miles and turn right at the ranch's sign. For more information write Blue Circle Ranch, PO Box 225, Bradley, WV 25818.

# Bramwell

## *Historic District*

During the early 1900s, Bramwell was considered to be the most wealthy town of its size in America. The Flat Top Land Association, the largest land holder in the Pocahontas coalfields, had taken root here in 1885, and the town was incorporated three years later by special charter. Coal magnates, profiting from an explosive demand for coal, built their Victorian and Tudor-style mansions here, five miles from Bluefield. As many as 14 millionaires purportedly called Bramwell home during its heyday. In 1910 a fire took much of the town's business block, and brick replacement buildings were built into the 1920s. One of these, the old Bryant and Newbold Pharmacy, was believed to be the third drug store in the country to stock the popular perfume, Chanel No. 5. Like so many communities, Bramwell fell from grace during the Depression. With the coal industry especially hard hit, Bramwell's once-prosperous bank closed in the early 1930s. The town's buildings survived, nevertheless, and the town itself was placed on the National Register of Historic Places in 1983.

You can enjoy a self-guided walking/driving tour, of 21 of Bramwell's structures. Prepared by the Bramwell Millionaire Garden Club, the tour features two of the town's oldest buildings, the **McGuffin House** and the **Town Hall**, built in 1885 and 1888 respectively, and two of the most opulent, the **Thomas House** and the **Freeman House**. Copies of the tour brochure may be picked up at the Bluestone Visitors and Convention Bureau in Bluefield (hours Monday–Friday, 9:00 A.M.–4:00 P.M.; call (304)325-8438 for more information), or at either of Bramwell's bed-and-breakfast establishments, the Bluestone Inn on Main Street and Three Oaks and a Quilt on Duhring Street. The Garden Club offers two guided tours of the mansions: a spring tour and a candlelight Christmas tour. For more information call the Garden Club at (304)248-7114.

**Directions**: From I-77 take West Virginia Exit 1 (Rt.52) and travel north 15 miles to Bramwell. Follow the signs to the Historic District.

# Clifftop

## *Midland Trail and Camp Washington Carver*

On Rt. 60 east, you can travel along the **Midland Trail**, the same route used by those who had re-fortified themselves at Colonel Stockton's stagecoach stop. A 120-mile-long east-west route curving from White Sulphur Springs to Charleston, the Midland Trail was first cut by herds of buffalo and later expanded by pioneers. The trail was authorized by the Virginia Assembly as the State Road in 1790. By stagecoach, or "snakeguts," as coaches were known in the early 1800s, it took two long dusty days to traverse. By car today it is a mere two and one-half to three-hour ride. You'll want to take some extra time to linger along the way at sites like Camp Washington Carver located on Rt. 60 in Clifftop next to Babcock State Park. (For more information on the Midland Trail call (800)822-US60).

Named for Booker T. Washington and George Washington Carver, the **Camp Washington Carver** was built between 1939 and 1942 by the Civilian Conservation Corps (CCC). It was run by the West Virginia State College as the nation's first black 4-H Camp before the Department of Culture and History took over its operations as a Mountain Cultural Center in 1979 to keep alive its rich mountain heritage. The facility now offers a regular schedule of weekend entertainment ranging from a dinner theater series, a Golden Oldies Festival to a four-day Appalachian String Band Music Festival, a national old-time competition.

Entertainment runs from May through September. Nearly all the events are outdoors so remember to bring lawnchairs or blankets to sit on. Concession stands and dining room provide traditional food. No alcoholic beverages are permitted.

The camp also provides fun for daytime enjoyment. Check out the camp's centerpiece, the **Great Chestnut Lodge** (the largest log building of its kind in the world), savor lunch in a pleasant picnic area, trek the two-mile-plus Manns Creek Gorge Hiking Trail and/or shop in the Country Store.

**Admission**: Ticket prices range from $2.00 to $10.00 depending on the event.

For a schedule of events call (304)438-6429.

**Directions**: From Rt. 60 take Rt. 41 into Clifftop.

# Forest Hill
## Wakerobin Gallery

Lovers of fine, handmade Appalachian crafts will want to take about a ten-mile detour south from Talcott and visit the Wakerobin Gallery in Forest Hill. At the junction of Seminole Road and Rt. 12, the gallery is known best for its stoneware pottery, but it also specializes in paintings, weavings, stained glass and wooden toys.

Marcia Springston, the resident potter, deserves the credit for the lovely, high-fired, lead-free pieces found here. Her pottery is also dishwasher, oven and microwave safe. Well-trained at the Cayahoga Valley Art Center, John C. Campbell Folk Art School, University of Northern Colorado and Indiana University, Springston has exhibited her work throughout the United States. Many of us would feel lucky to create just once in our lives a piece equal in beauty to one of Springston's. She turns out magnificent ware again and again, and her talent is even more impressive and special because she has been blind since birth.

**Hours**: 10:00 A.M. to 4:00 P.M. everyday except Wednesday and Sunday. The phone is (304)466-2053.

**Directions**: Junction of Seminole Road and Rt. 12. For more information write Wakerobin Pottery, HC65, Box 112C, Forest Hill, WV 24935.

# Hinton

## *Bluestone Dam and Bluestone Lake*

Just south of Hinton on Rt. 20, the massive Bluestone Dam holds back the waters of the New River and its nearby tributary, the Bluestone River. Free guided tours of the concrete facility are offered by the dam's manager, the Army Corps of Engineers, from Memorial Day weekend through Labor Day weekend. The tours are about one hour long and are handicapped accessible.

The parking area at the dam provides an excellent vantage point. You'll often see fishermen working the dam's tailwaters, a popular, productive spot.

The dam itself does not seem as old as it is. Work began on it in January 1942 but had to be put off until January 1946 because of World War II. Operational in 1949, the dam was finally completed in 1952 and carried a price tag of about $30 million. Complete with penstocks for future hydroelectrical use if needed, the dam closes a 2,048-foot gap between opposing mountain sides and rises 165 feet above the river bed. It has also created one of the state's largest lakes, the 2,040-acre Bluestone Lake. For more information on the dam as well as tour reservations, call (304)466-1234 or write Bluestone Lake, 701 Miller Avenue, Hinton, WV 25951. The same number may be used for information on boating, fishing, water skiing and other recreation on Bluestone Lake.

Still more recreation opportunities flank either side of Bluestone Lake. To the east, the 20,000-acre Bluestone Wildlife Management Area, (304)466-3398, beckons outdoors people. And to the west, Bluestone State Park, (304)466-2805, offers 25 deluxe cabins, 87 campsites, snack bar, swimming pool, boat rental, hiking trails, game courts, picnic areas and nearby golf course.

**Hours**: Office hours at Bluestone Lake: Monday-Friday from 7:30 A.M. to 4:00 P.M.. Top of dam open seven days a week Memorial Day through Labor Day, 8:00 A.M.–7:30 P.M. (closes at 4:00 P.M. Monday and Tuesday).

**Directions**: On I-64 take Exit 139 Sandstone. Travel south approximately 13 miles on Rt. 20. On I-77 take Exit 14 Athens. Travel on Rt. 7 to Rt. 20 and go north approximately 27 miles.

## Bluestone Museum

Those interested in fish and game taxidermy will want to stop at the Bluestone Museum before leaving the area. Built by a 20-year veteran of Alaskan big game guiding and taxidermy, the small museum features dozens of displays of mounted fish, large and small game and reptiles.

Remember this spot if you're lucky enough to land a big fish or other trophy and want to have it mounted before heading home. There is a taxidermy shop in the museum's basement. A gift shop complete with T-shirts and souvenirs rounds out the offering.

**Admission**: $1.00

**Hours**: 10:00 A.M. to 6:00 P.M. daily except during January and February when it is closed. Phone: (304)466-1454.

**Directions**: On Rt. 87 in Hinton.

## Historic District

From Rt. 3 you can connect with Rt. 20 North to visit the historic town of Hinton where many of the attractions center around the uncommon beauty of Bluestone Lake and the southern beginning of the magnificent **New River Gorge National River**. Hinton serves as a gateway community to the National River which was added to the National Park System in 1978 to preserve 53.5 miles from here to Fayetteville, of the fascinating, ancient, northwestwardly-flowing New River. In 1988 **Gauley River National Recreation Area** and the **Bluestone National Scenic River** were also included in the National Park System, making for an ideal, one-of-a-kind stretch loaded with opportunities for white-water rafting, boating, hunting, fishing, hiking and camping.

To get your bearings and help narrow your choices for activities, begin your day trip to Hinton at either the **Hinton Visitors Center**, located on the banks of the New River on Rt. 3 Bypass, or at the **Summers County Visitors Center**, located in town at 206 Temple Street (which is Rt. 20 North; Phone: (304)466-5420). The Hinton Visitor Center will be of most help with activities directly related to the New River Gorge National River. Staffed by park rangers, the small center features a short slide show about the river and offers information on guided hikes, canoe trips, bus tours, evening programs, youth programs and more; open only seasonally. The phone is (304)466-0417. (See the entry on the Canyon Rim Visitor Center at the other extreme of the National River in Lansing for year-round operation.)

The Summers County Visitors Center will lead you to Hinton's historic sites and is an attraction in and of itself. Under the same roof as the Visitors Center lies a small Railroad Museum detailing Hinton's 1870s beginning on the coat tails of the C&O Railroad Company. For nearly 75 years Hinton served as a main terminal for the railway. Artifacts from the period are on display in the museum. Admission is $2.00 for adults and $1.00 for students. The Crafters Gallery, a not-for-profit outlet for handmade arts and crafts, tempts visitors here as well. All the pieces you see are made by West Virginians and are on consignment.

When you are at the Center, remember to pick up a free copy of the Historic **Hinton Walking Tour** brochure and follow its lead for an up-close look at Hinton's past and its best-loved buildings. The self-guided tour takes you over several original brick streets to an historic district of 21 buildings. This entire district was placed on the National Register of Historic Places in 1984. An eclectic mix of architecture makes the tour especially fun and interesting. You can see examples of American Gothic, Classical and Greek revival architecture in the tour's numerous churches while other influences, including Classical revival, High Victorian, American Four Square and Second Empire, can be seen in the tour's homes, banks, opera houses and stores.

For those with kids in tow, watch for the **City Sidetrack Park**, located just off the tour's path on Front Street. The park has a 267-foot long waterslide and is open from Memorial Day through Labor Day. The phone is (304)466-1600.

**Hours**: The Visitors Center is open 10:00 A.M.–7:00 P.M. Memorial Day to Labor Day.

# Lansing
## *Canyon Rim Visitor Center*

All the attractions between Glen Jean and Lansing center around the awe-inspiring **New River Gorge.** Even though the National Park Service maintains its New River Gorge National River Headquarters in Glen Jean, the best starting place for day-trippers is the new Canyon Rim Visitor Center, opened in 1991, on Rt. 19 on the north side of the river in Lansing. Having perhaps the best view anywhere of the gorge, both through its floor-to-ceiling windows inside, and outside from its terrace and boardwalk, the large, modern center features an 11-minute slide-show orienta-

Sitting 876 feet above the river, the New River Gorge Bridge is the world's longest single-arch steel span—1,700 feet long.

LARRY BELCHER

tion. Handsome, large exhibits detail the gorge's geological and cultural history, and touch-screen information stations show the area's major industries and recreational opportunities. On weekends and holidays during the summer, bus tours take sightseers to the bottom of the gorge, and any number of marked nature trails await hikers year-round. This is also the place for information on a wealth of activities and interpretative programs conducted by park rangers. From guided hikes and evening storytelling to bird walks and star gazing, something is happening most of the time.

Some facts you will learn at the Visitor Center may surprise you. The **New River** is approximately 65 million years old and flows northwestwardly, falling rapidly to create one of the most exciting white-water rivers in the east. Average depth of the gorge is 1,000 feet. Perhaps the most impressive fact about the New River is its age. Geologists have confirmed that it was once much longer when it was part of the ancient Teays River system that flowed through what is now the center of North America. Advancing glaciers during the ice age caused it to turn into other newly created rivers, the Ohio and the Kanawha. Yet a remnant of the original river still exists and flows across the Appalachian Plateau unlike other area rivers. Thus the powerful New, one of the all-time great misnomers, could have been in place before the Appalachian Mountains took shape.

The New's modern history and folklore are rich and colorful. Transportation via the river in this area had proven difficult for early settlers; its currents, depths and widths being prohibitive. Ferries were often the only means of crossing it. Not until the railroad arrived in 1873 did the inaccessible area become reachable—and its prizes, coal and timber, connected to world-wide markets. Communities sprang up nearly overnight to meet the demand, and when mines and forests were played out, the towns were abandoned just as quickly.

One way to absorb the area's rich culture is out on one of the many hiking trails maintained by the National Park Service. Recommendations and maps as well as ranger-guided scheduled treks are available at the Visitor Center. You can recount in your mind many colorful legends, some no doubt exaggerated over time but most true. Trails range from ¼ mile to more than 10 miles in length and vary in difficulty from flat to steep terrain. Do be a conscientious nature hiker: stay on the trails, keep pets on a leash and maintain the trails by remembering if you pack something in, pack it out.

One trail to consider is the **Kaymoor Mine Trail**. It takes you to several remaining historic mine structures where thousands of miners lived and worked, beginning with the first shipment of coal in 1899 and ending with closure in 1962. You must look only and not enter the dangerous mining structures. The 2.1-mile trail begins 10 minutes away from the Visitor Center on Rt. 82 also known as Fayette Station Road. The predecessor to the New River Gorge Bridge, the Rt. 82 bridge is no longer safe and is now closed, remaining only as a reminder of the times. The trail crosses a secure foot bridge over Wolk Creek and later hugs the rim of the gorge, offering wonderful views from 400 to 500 feet above the river.

Still another hike well-suited for the mind, heart and feet is the **Mary Ingles Trail**, also known as the Thurmond-Minden Trail. The easy trail, 3.2 miles in length one-way, begins at trail heads either off the Minden Road or off Rt. 25 near Thurmond. Following an old railroad bed complete with five trestles but with its ties taken up, the trail passes McKinley Rock, a waterfall and views of Thurmond and Minden. While no one can be certain, it is possible that Mary Ingles used this course—or one similar to it—in her famous escape from Shawnee Indians. Captured with her two sons in 1755 in Drapers Meadow, Virginia, Ingles was taken as far away as present day Cincinnati. Later, after being separated from her boys, she was moved to Big Bone Lick, Kentucky, to gather salt. Soon thereafter, together with an old Dutch woman and against all odds, Ingles began her remarkable escape from her abductors, covering more than 500 miles of rugged Ohio, Kanawha and New River terrain in 42 days to return home to Virginia. Her one surviving son was returned ten years later. A testament to individual courage, Ingles's legend reminds us of the many difficulties faced by our country's pioneers.

While on the Mary Ingles Trail, pause at the view of the sleepy town of **Thurmond** to consider its rowdy former life. Incorporated in 1900 with a population of 300, Thurmond became the commercial and social center of the New River Coal industry. So strongly linked and dependent on the railway system was Thurmond that it had no streets—the only such town in America. It nevertheless produced as much as 20 percent of all C&O Railroad revenues by 1910. With two banks, two drugstores, two jewelry stores, a meat distributor, a movie theater and grocery stores, Thurmond also had the lively Dun Glen Hotel where social life roared and a famous 14-year-long poker game took place. The game might still be in progress in "Little Monte Carlo" had the hotel not burned. The town became so wild that residents were warned not to walk along the tracks at night—and surely not to carry a lantern for danger of being seen and shot. By the 1950s with the expanded use of automobiles, much of Thurmond had been abandoned leaving behind colorful memories and, now, one of the smallest incorporated towns in the state.

Outdoor activities get a lot of attention at Canyon Rim, especially the ever-popular and exhilarating white-water rafting (see entry). Try some of the nature walks and learn about the area's flora and fauna. Many guided, interpretive programs begin at the Visitor Center. Mountain biking is also popular; there are miles of trails throughout the 52-mile-long New River Gorge. Rock climbers have a choice of 1,400 courses of climbing surface in the gorge. Should your visit coincide with the third Saturday in October, don't miss Bridge Day, a day-long festival that celebrates both the technology of the bridge and the natural beauty that surrounds it. Bands, jugglers and dancers entertain, delicious smelling foods tempt visitors, and parachuters and rappelers do their tricks on the only day of the year you may walk across the bridge. The opposing side of traffic is kept open, one lane each way.

A crossing by car that once took 40 minutes via winding mountain roads and a narrow bridge now takes a mere 60 seconds. At 1,700 feet long, the **New River Gorge Bridge** is the world's longest single-arch steel span and sits 876 feet above the river (or 325 feet higher than the Washington Monument). The total length of the roadbed is 3,030 feet. Designed by the Michael Baker, Jr., Company and constructed by the American Bridge Division of the U.S. Steel Corporation, the ten-year-long project, completed in 1977, cost $37 million. Cor-Ten steel, which does not need painting, was hoisted into place on record-size three-inch-diameter cables which in turn were stretched 3,500 feet to matching pairs of 330-foot-tall towers secured on opposite ends of the gorge. The completed four-lane bridge is 69 feet four inches wide, its heaviest erected section weighs 184,000 pounds, and its largest joint contains 23,000 bolts!

**Hours**: The Visitor Center is open daily 9:00 A.M. to 5:00 P.M. during the winter and 9:00 A.M. to 8:00 P.M. Memorial Day through Labor Day. Handicapped accessible, the center has restrooms and lots of parking. It also features an exhibit area and sales publication section. For more information on activities near to and sponsored by the Visitor Center call (304)574-2115.

**Directions**: On Rt. 19 between Glen Jean and Lansing.

# Lewisburg
## Visitor Center and Walking Tour

Lewisburg is a day-tripper's kind of town. More than 200 years old with dozens of well-preserved 18th- and 19th-century buildings and actively brimming with new life, Lewisburg represents a pleasant mix of the old and new. There is more than enough here to meet the various needs of history buffs, nature lovers and those eager for a weekend escape. A former mayor of Lewisburg often said, "Only two kinds of people ever leave Lewisburg—those who will return and those who wish they could."

Named for Andrew Lewis, a surveyor who set up camp in 1751 near the spring behind today's courthouse, the town struggled to survive before finally being chartered in 1782. The white men's presence was not accepted when Lewis first came. Though Indians had not settled here, the area was a productive hunting ground of theirs. They wiped out two early white settlements in 1763 killing nearly all the men and capturing the women and children. A new, fortified camp known as Fort Savannah tried again to inhabit the area, then called Lewis Spring, in 1770. Four years later, from this successful camp, a group of militiamen commanded by General Lewis marched 160 miles to Point Pleasant and defeated Chief Cornstalk and a band of Shawnees, Mingos, Ottawas and Delawares in a bloody battle that, because of its decisiveness, put an end to Indian aggression in the area. (See entry on Point Pleasant Monument.) In honor of Lewis's service the Lewis Spring camp was renamed Lewisburg. The town prospered as a farming and trading center, stagecoach stop, education, government and law center with several courts serving Virginians. Patrick Henry practiced here, once winning acquittal for a man accused of murder. Spas and resort hotels sprang up next to popular, healthful mineral springs, and by the mid-1800s most other new buildings, including those you see today, were made from red brick instead of the outdated log.

The Civil War had a direct impact on the area when the Battle of Lewisburg was fought here on May 23, 1862. Union leader George Crook, who was to become famous later for his defeat of the great Geronimo, led his forces to victory over Confederate Henry Heth and his men. Even so, Lewisburg remained a southern outpost most of the war. Many of the town's buildings were used as hospitals and barracks by both North and South. In 1978, a 236-acre area of Lewisburg was designated a National Register Historic District, and many individual structures were listed on the National Register of Historic Places.

One of the best ways to take in this district is on an excellent self-guided walking tour. Starting at the town's **Visitor Center** at 105 Church Street, it includes 72 sites and takes about 2½ hours. An alternate tour of 39 sites takes about one hour. Be aware that not all of the buildings on the tour are public. Some continue as private residences. You can pick up the free walking-tour booklet as well as brochures about all kinds of area attractions at the Visitor Center. Copies are available after hours too in a box outside the center. For additional help, see John McIlhenny, the center's director. He is as knowledgeable as he is helpful in leading you to specific points of interest. Comfortable walking shoes are a must. Lewisburg's small, concentrated size is one of its appealing strengths. Nearly all sites can be reached on foot.

Of the many public buildings and attractions you may enter on the walking tour, several are noteworthy including your starting place, the Visitor Center, housed in **Carnegie Hall**. Built in 1902 when it was home to the Lewisburg Female Institute (known later as Greenbrier College), the building is now the town's educational and cultural center complete with fine art, music, dance, pottery and weaving studios. Carnegie Hall frequently presents drama and musical performances as well as public lectures. The **Old Stone Church**, one of Lewisburg's best-loved landmarks, is the oldest church in continuous use west of the Alleghenies. With early settlers interred in its cemetery, the limestone church looks much as it did when it was built in 1796.

Inside the **North House** you get a look at intricately carved woodwork. Now the Museum of the Greenbrier Historical Society exhibiting period china, furniture, clothing and legal documents, this was the tavern where jurists were once lodged when serving the Virginia court. Open April through October, the North House was built in 1820. The **Greenbrier County Library** is one of the few buildings still operating as first planned. Built in 1834 by James Frazier, it was the library for jurists rooming across the street and the library and study for the Court of Appeals. It did, however, double first as a hospital during the Civil War and later as a Masonic Lodge following the conflict before being purchased by the city in 1939 and revitalized as a library once again in 1941. Of intriguing note is a part of an old plaster wall with the inscribed signatures of Civil War soldiers still visible. A two-story Library Annex, built in 1835 as slave quarters and kitchen of the Johnston Reynolds Mansion, was moved to adjoin the library in 1978. A popular get-together at the annex is children's story hour.

The Lewisburg spring where Andrew Lewis set up camp, is also preserved. Covered by a limestone springhouse now more than 200 years old, the spring wet the whistles of the area's first settlers as well as those at Fort Savannah. You may venture to the **Greenbrier County Courthouse**, erected in 1837 and aptly placed on Court Street. It is the last remaining of several court-houses built in Lewisburg, large and brick and only ornamented by columns and an octagonal cupola. The walking tour passes the **Confederate Cemetery** on McElhenny Road. Of special interest is the cross-shaped common grave of 95 unknown Confederate soldiers lost in the Battle of Lewisburg. These unclaimed men were first buried at the Old Stone Church before being moved here a few years following the battle.

Last but not least is the site where you may want to spend the most time indoors. The **General Lewis Inn**, at 301 East Washington Street, is a full-service inn and an especially good choice for meals and overnight stays. Here you are assured of a brush with history—none of the beds is less than 100 years old. The inn's collection of antique glass, china, kitchen utensils, tools and firearms is fascinating enough to wake up the most latent love for history. The east wing is the oldest part of the inn, built in 1834 when it was known as the John Withrow House. Subsequent additions of a lobby and west wing added in 1928 completed the handsome structure you see today. Call the inn at (304)645-2600 to reserve one of its 26 guest rooms.

Should you want to avoid touring on foot, the **Lewisburg Carriage and Horse Service** provides the answer. One-hour-long narrated tours of the historic town, including a stop at the General Lewis Inn, are available. You can take in the sites while comfortably riding in an authentic 100-year-old Amish buggy pulled by Belgian draft horses. Tours run May through October, 9:00 A.M. to 5:00 P.M. Monday through Saturday and 1:00 to 5:00 P.M. Sunday. Special arrangements can often be made for tours at other times. Costs range from $12.00 per person for adults and $10.00 per person for groups of four or more to $6.00 per person for senior citizens and children under 12. Call the Visitor Center for more information and reservations.

Still another alternative are "back roads" auto tours available free at the Visitor Center. To scenic and historic areas in and around Lewisburg and ranging in length from 10 to 30 miles, the well-prepared, self-guided tours are perfect for those who want to go to out-of-the-way places at their own pace.

When in Lewisburg you will also want to shop in the historic district's numerous antique and specialty shops. Selling quality—not kitschy—crafts, art and antiques, the attractive shops may be numerous enough to satisfy even die-hard shopping addicts. Pick up a detailed list, complete with a map, of 28 merchants at the Visitor Center.

Lewisburg hosts the **State Fair of West Virginia** held in August. More than 250,000 people visit this annual celebration featuring many agricultural events, including horse and livestock shows, goat-milking competitions, sheep shearings, draft horse pulls and harness races, as well as carnival rides, ice shows, circus presentations, fireworks and performances by national stars. A complete listing of events is available by late June if you send a stamped, self-addressed envelope to Program of Events, State Fair of West Virginia, Drawer 986, Lewisburg, WV, 24901. Further information may be obtained at (304)645-1090.

Following a day of sightseeing, taking in a performance at the **Greenbrier Valley Theatre** may be just the ticket. Broadway musicals, classical and modern drama and Children's Theatre matinees are presented mid-June through early August on Thursday, Friday, Saturday and Sunday. You will find the theatre in the Old Barn at the Greenbrier Valley Airport, located four miles north of Lewisburg on Rt. 219. Phone (304)645-3838 for reservations and ticket information.

If you are bent on experiencing as much as you can of an area when traveling, then you must search out and sample a **ramp dinner** when in Lewisburg. It is called variously "haute cuisine," "a regional specialty" or simply "good old country cooking." Ramp, the lively vegetable from which it takes its name, is similar to a cross between a leek and garlic (see section). It grows wild in the woods and is harvested in the spring. Many groups—volunteer fire departments, churches and schools—schedule ramp dinners as fund raisers. Don't worry: other foods like ham, chicken, beans and desserts are included in the ramp dinner, and you can expect it to be plentiful and moderately priced. The Visitor Center can direct you to this springtime gastronomical delight.

**Hours**: The Visitor Center is open year-round Monday through Saturday 9:00 A.M. to 5:00 P.M. May through October it is also open on Sundays, 1:00 to 5:00 P.M. The phone is (304)645-1000.

**Directions**: From I-64 take Rt. 219 south to Lewisburg. Turn right on Washington Street and left on Church Street. The Visitor

Center will be on your right. For more information write the Lewisburg Visitor and Convention Bureau, Carnegie Hall, 105 Church Street, Lewisburg, WV 24901.

## Lost World Caverns

As you drive along the gently curving, rising and falling country roads surrounding Lewisburg, pay special attention to the quiet landscape. There is more here than meets the eye. Under these rolling hills are about 100 named caves, up to 1,500 known but unnamed others, plus more being discovered by spelunkers every day. Two famous, huge caves, **Organ Cave** (see separate entry) and Lost World Caverns, are commercial and available for tour. After visiting these fascinating natural wonders, you may be so taken with what can happen underground that you may never look at a rise in an open field again without speculating about what could lie below.

Lost World Caverns were discovered by Virginia Polytechnic Institute explorers in 1942 when they bravely descended 120 feet through a grapevine-covered opening to the cave's floor. Known then as Grapevine Cave in honor of its source, it was continuously explored and mapped until 1970 when it was renamed Lost World Caverns and a new, more accessible horizontal entrance was opened into its largest part. It was named a Registered Natural Landmark in 1977. Following extensive improvements, including another new entrance, new walkways and a new, large reception center and gift shop, the underground wonderland was opened again for public tour in 1981. Lost World Caverns is especially large, with many rooms rivaling Western caverns.

Of the fascinating formations you see on your well-lighted, guided 35-minute tour, notice the hex blocks, which cover the majority of the cavern floor. About 300 million years old, these interesting patterns were created when ancient oceans lowered and limestone, formed from the sediment, was exposed and dried. You can also see the Ice Cream Wall, complete with natural shades of vanilla, chocolate and butterscotch, and the caverns' mammoth flowstone column, Goliath, measuring 40 feet high and 25 feet around. The Snowy Chandelier is noteworthy too. An especially good example of brilliantly white calcite, it is one of the largest compound stalactites in the nation, tipping the scales at about 30 tons. And if you have ever felt like doing nothing more than sitting on a rock for a long time, you will have to be very patient to beat the record of Parkersburg's Bob Addis. He is in the *Guinness Book of World Records* for lighting atop the caverns' 500,000-year-old War Club Stalagmite in 1971. He built a platform with ropes fastened to the top of the 28-foot-tall War Club and stayed there for 15 days, 23 hours and 22 minutes to set the stalagmite sitting record.

**Admission**: Adults $6.00, children 6–13 $3.00.

**Hours**: Summer: 9:00 A.M.–7:00 P.M. Winter: 9:00 A.M.–5:00 P.M. Closed on Thanksgiving, Christmas, New Year's Day and Easter. For the regular tour nothing more than a light jacket and comfortable shoes are needed. Lost World Caverns offers three-hour-long wild tours that take strong-bodied explorers away from the commercial walkways and lights. Extra fees and reservations are required for wild tours and children must be at least 14 years old. For more information phone (304)645-6677 or write Lost World Caverns, Rt. 6, Box 308, Lewisburg, WV 24901.

**Directions**: From Lewisburg, travel north on Rt. 219. After crossing I-64, turn left on Arbuckle Road and left on Fairview Road. The entrance will be on your right.

# Pence Springs

## The Graham House

Now on the National Register of Historic Places, Graham House is one of West Virginia's oldest log homes having been built by Colonel James Graham between 1770 and 1772. An unusually large building for its time, it offers an excellent look at how well-to-do settlers lived. Save for a new wing at the rear, the house authentically depicts the era. While it was a home for his family, the Graham House also served as a defense post, sheltering other settlers from frequent Indian raids. You can see the holes in the walls through which settlers fired against Indians. One Shawnee attack in 1777 killed both Colonel Graham's ten-year-old son and a friend of the family and led to Graham's other child, his seven-year-old daughter Elizabeth, being abducted. For the next eight years Graham searched for his daughter. He finally won her release in exchange for blankets and trinkets near Maysville, Kentucky. Popular local lore says Graham turned the shoes around on his horses to prevent being followed home with his newly freed daughter.

While the furniture is not original, it is indigenous to the area around the 1800s. Furnishings include rope beds, spinning wheel, trunks, Graham family pictures and other primitive pieces. The house is now maintained by the Graham House Preservation Society.

**Admission**: Adults $1.00, children $.50.

**Hours**: Saturday 11:00 A.M. to 5:00 P.M. and Sunday 1:00 to 5:00 P.M., Memorial Day through Labor Day. Call (304)466-4362 or 3321 for more information including how you can schedule a meeting, reunion or reception at the log house.

**Directions**: Pence Springs is between Hinton and Lewisburg on Rts. 3 and 12. The Graham House is 3 miles south of Pence Springs Hotel on Rt. 3. For more information write Graham House, HC 73, Box 158, Pence Springs, WV 24962.

## *Pence Springs Hotel*

When approaching the small area of Pence Springs, first-timers may feel that the lovely drive is reason enough for a visit. Rt. 3 curves and winds its way around rocky river beds and over steep hills. New visitors ask what could there possibly be to do here. If you're among the doubters, look more closely. The answer is plenty. Pence Springs offers one discovery after another, often where least expected, making this an ideal one-day trip destination.

The center of activities is the newly revitalized Pence Springs Hotel. Beginning in 1918, when it first opened, and on through the 1920s, the three-story brick hotel was a vacationer's paradise. As many as 14 trains a day brought people here to revel in the peaceful summers, play golf on the biggest course in the region and—above all—drink the famous water for which the town is named. Some said drinking 10 cups each day of the spring water would cure anything; others claimed it gave longevity. The 1904 World's Fair had awarded it a silver medal. Whatever the reason, upwards of 125 people a day were lodging here in the hotel's first year. By 1926 it was considered to be West Virginia's best retreat, commanding a stiff $6.00 per day including all meals. The good times rolled even during Prohibition when the liquor continued to pour as freely as the spring water. This was a government-sanctioned watering hole. Early hotel brochures described a "modern billiard room" where women were not permitted. The room was actually where men came to drink. You can see the secret rooms today in the hotel's basement, including the space where the hard stuff was hidden.

A double-edged sword, the Depression and the rising use of private automobiles, slashed into the hotel's future hopes. Guests no longer came by train. Following numerous slow years, the hotel closed in 1935. The property was not used again until 1947 when it was purchased by the state and transformed into a women's prison. But the hotel's days as a prison came to an end in 1983 when rising costs together with required improvements, such as a gymnasium and law library, could not be met. The hotel was soon thereafter condemned.

Ashby Berkley, a Pence Springs businessman, came to the hotel's rescue. Like many from the area with fond memories of the hotel's glory days, Berkley wanted to return it to its former grandeur. He bought the property in 1987 and undertook an ambitious major historic restoration. It was one of the largest individually

255

held restoration projects in the United States at the time. A year and a half later after the hotel was rescued from its prison confinement and problems such as eight inches of water standing in the basement were resolved, two floors were made ready and the hotel re-opened on Thanksgiving Day to the delight of locals.

It is hard to imagine this was once a prison. The restored parts of the inn are clean and attractive. "We're not posh," warns Berkley, but still the tall ceilings, hardwood floors (many of which had been covered by concrete during the prison days), flowered carpets and mix of antiques in the 26 guest rooms please the eye. All three meals are served at the inn, either in the formal dining room or on the long, enclosed airy sun porch. There are conference rooms for meetings held in what used to be a casino, a music room, a basement pub that features marble from the old prison showers as well as occasional performances by jazz groups, a big wrap-around front porch ideal for lollygagging and ample lawns for croquet. All of the hotel's 28 acres are deemed a National Register Historic site. In the summer months, the hotel puts on free light theater productions on a small stage adjoining the porch.

**Rates**: From $60.00 for a double room.

**Season**: April through December. Reservations are a must; call (304)445-2606. There are phones in the guest rooms but no TVs. For more information write PO Box 90, Pence Springs, WV 24692.

**Directions**: Pence Springs is between Hinton and Lewisburg on Rts. 3 and 12.

Venture down the hill from the inn for a drink from the famous **spring**. The gazebo that covers the spring ranks as one of the oldest structures in the county. The old bottling house adjacent to the spring bottled more water than any other place in the area in the early 1920s. It now houses an antique shop, but you can still see how the water was bottled. The shop is open Wednesday through Sunday and at other times by special request.

Every Sunday from April through October, Pence Springs hosts one of the largest **flea markets** in the state right across the road from the spring, a tradition of more than 20 years. There is no telling what you may find here.

# Pipestem
## *Pipestem Resort State Park*

The creme de la creme of resorts among West Virginia's state parks is Pipestem, sitting pretty in the Bluestone Dam recreation area. On over 4,000 acres of scenic plateau, the park is a playground for daytrippers as well as those staying longer in the deluxe overnight accommodations. Recreational opportunites for virtually all outdoor enthusiasts account for the large number of visitors, from both out of state and West Virginia, who return year after year: two golf courses, two swimming pools, (one indoor and heated), lighted tennis and basketball courts, paddle boating, horseback riding and bicycling rentals. Long Branch Lake and nearby **Bluestone River and Lake** tempt the boaters and fishermen to linger til sundown along the peaceful waters. In winter, cross-country skiing and sledding draw snow lovers to the miles of trails in the surrounding mountains. For those prefering sedentary entertainment, an amphitheater in the forested hills hosts summer weekend musicals, concerts and plays, and an arts and crafts center sells quality handcrafted items typical of West Virginia. Year-round, park personnel sponsor various nature programs.

The 113 rooms in the main lodge, which sits on the lip of beautiful Bluestone River Gorge, overlook a spectacular canyon. For overnighters seeking seclusion, the **Mountain Creek Lodge** is tucked near the river at the base of the canyon and is reached only by an aerial tramway. Families may prefer one of the 25 heated, deluxe cabins that come with decks, television, fireplaces, modern kitchens and baths. To round out the choices, there is a campground of 82 sites with hot showers and laundry facilities.

One of the biggest pluses to a family stay at Pipestem (named after the local bush used by Indians in the making of pipes), is the availability of the Honey Bear Lodge Child Care Center. Children ages 2 through 12 can stay for the day or the hour and participate in a full program of exercise, crafts, drama and games designed for the development of learning skills. This is a gem of a park where families can play together or apart without feeling guilty about leaving anyone at home.

**Admission**: All recreational facilities can be enjoyed by daytrippers at nominal rates. Rooms (for two) in main lodge are under $70 and at the Mountain Creek Lodge (open May 1 to October 31) for under $60.

**Hours**: Park is open for public from 6:00 A.M. to 10:00 P.M. The front desk at main lodge is open 24 hours a day.

**Directions**: 20 miles north of Princeton and 12 miles south of Hinton of Rt. 20. From the west take the Athens Road Exit from I-77 to Rt. 20. For reservations or more information call 1(800)CALL-WVA or (304)466-1800 or write Pipestem Resort State Park, Pipestem, WV 25979.

# Princeton

Nearly 25 years before the Civil War, Mercer County and the town of Princeton were founded and named in honor of the Revolutionary War hero General Hugh Mercer who was mortally wounded in battle in Princeton, New Jersey. The area's founders could not have foreseen the diverse attractions that years later would entertain Princetonians, but they would be happy nonetheless that their quiet community would be full of one-day trip possibilities.

Centrally located within 30 minutes of Bluefield, Pipestem Resort State Park, Winterplace Ski Resort and Bluestone Lake, Princeton offers the down-home **Crafters Mall** and **West Virginia Antique Mall**. A conglomerate of some 70 shops all under one roof, the two malls are especially noted for their bonafide handmade West Virginia crafts. Look for them off Rt. 20, one mile north of town on Athens Road. They are open seven days a week and the phone is (304)425-5199. Princeton is also home to **Artifacts**, an unusual gallery/museum located on Mercer Street and specializing in art in miniature. Mostly watercolors, the works range from postage-stamp size to five by seven inches. The mix of artifacts for sale includes World War I and II pieces, tomahawks, clothes and post cards. A small entrance fee admits you to Artifacts, which is open only Thursday through Saturday, 4:00 to 8:00 P.M. The phone is (304)425-2697.

The **Princeton Raceway Park** offers excitement that is everything but quiet. Mini-stock, street-stock, modified and superstock race cars roar by on a 4/10-mile oval clay speedway; cars and motorcycles speed to the finish line on an 1/8-mile IHRA-sanctioned dragway. There is seating for 3,000 people at the speedway and 2,000 at the dragway.

**Admission**: Adults $6.00, chidlren $3.00 and $10.00 for a pit pass.

**Hours**: Races begin at 7:30 P.M. Friday and Saturday evenings, April through October. Phone: (304)425-4804.

**Directions**: Off I-77 Exit 14. Follow the sign to Rt. 19 for 1/4 mile, turn right on Corn Bread Ridge Road, the rough, gravel-and-dirt road that takes you to the track.

Of the 200 American cities hosting minor and major league baseball teams, Princeton is the smallest. So, if you relish a relaxed, small-town atmosphere and want to see young ball players hungry to succeed, then head for a **Princeton Reds** game at Hunnicutt Field located behind the Mercer County Vocational Center. A rookie league arm of the Cincinnati Reds, the Reds play a short season from mid-June through August.

**Hours**: The team's schedule and ticket information is available at (304)487-2000.

**Directions**: Off I-77 Exit 9. Take US 460 west, turn right at the second traffic light and left at the next.

# Ronceverte
## *Organ Cave*

Organ Cave has been known since 1704 when pioneers used it for shelter. In 1791 Thomas Jefferson walked into its depths and purportedly came across the bones of a prehistoric dinosaur, the remains of which stand today in Philadelphia. The cave was also a haven for weary Civil War soldiers. Eleven hundred of Robert E. Lee's men were known to have taken part in religious services inside the cave. As important as this respite was, the cave became a source of something even more powerful and helpful to their cause: gunpowder. Water collected here, ladened with potassium nitrate, could be evaporated to produce saltpetre, a main ingredient of gunpowder. Of the original 52 wooden saltpetre hoppers used for this process, 37 are well preserved for you to see in the cave.

Opened commercially in 1835, Organ Cave contains more than 40 miles of mapped passageways, no two alike, and more are being found every day. The one-hour-plus guided tour leads you on well-lighted pathways past magnificent calcite formations created millions of years ago, including the cave's namesake, a "rock organ," which resembles the pipes of a church organ. If you strike that formation with a wooden mallet, it does produce a tone which reverberates in this huge cathedral-like underworld. Remember to bring a light jacket (the temperature underground remains a constant, brisk 55 ), your favorite walking shoes and your camera. We all know nature works in mysterious, wonderful ways and you will want a snapshot of this outstanding example.

**Tip**: The town name Ronceverte, meaning "Greenbrier" in French, is a reminder that there were French settlers in this area.

**Admission**: Adults $6.00, children $3.00.

**Hours**: Tours are available year-round, rain or shine, November 15 through March 14, 9:00 A.M. to 5:00 P.M. and all other times 9:00 A.M. to 7:00 P.M. No reservations are needed. More adventuresome explorers wishing to delve deeper into the cave's unchartered depths should consider a Wild Tour. For extra fee information and reservations on these, as well as any other questions you may have about the cave, call (304)647-5551.

**Directions**: From Lewisburg take Rt. 219 south and turn left on Rt. 63 (north) in Ronceverte. The entrance is well-marked. For more information write Organ Cave, Rt. 2, Box 381, Ronceverte, WV 24970.

# Sandstone
## *Sandstone Jetboat*

Don't miss the Sandstone Jetboat, *Miss M. Rocks*. It will take you up the New River, around shoals and small rapids, to a wonderful vantage point beneath Sandstone Falls. You will want to have your camera in hand for a picture of the river-wide falls.

If you don't care to take the boat tour, you can still see **Sandstone Falls** from a National Park Service overlook on Rt. 20, north of Hinton or south of the Sandstone I-64 Exit. On the other side of the gorge you can also see Irish Mountain, named for the Irish railmen who settled here in the mid-1800s.

**Admission**: Adults $10.00. Children accompanied by a paying adult ride free.

**Hours**: Trips run daily—except Wednesdays 10:00 A.M. to 6:00 P.M., Memorial Day through Labor Day. During the month of May, trips are available on weekends. You need not make reservations or bring special clothes. *Miss M. Rocks* is covered to guard against bad weather.

**Directions**: You will find the boat dock off I-64 at the Sandstone Exit 139. After exiting, take a left turn at the stop sign, go 30 yards and turn right to the railroad underpass. The dock is ¼ mile down this gravel road.

# Talcott
## *Big Bend Tunnel and John Henry Statue*

On Rt. 3 in Talcott, pause atop the **Big Bend Tunnel** to see the monument dedicated to the memory of John Henry, the great steel-driving man. As you look out from the roadside perch high on Big Bend Mountain, you can see the railroad tracks disappear into the hillside under your feet. It is hard to imagine the bravery of the men who drove steel by hand to break away more than a mile of red shale for this tunnel. But in 1870 the C&O Railroad Company enlisted many men to undertake the dangerous task and thereby expand their rail lines. Completing the job took three years. One in five men lost their lives in the process as the tunnel caved in around them!

Tradition says one worker was **John Henry,** but researchers say the man did exist. Louis Chappell, author of the 1933 book *John Henry: A Folklore Study*, interviewed men in Talcott who had worked on the tunnel as boys. Many of them had known the six-foot-tall, 200-pound Henry who was thought to have been a freed slave from the south. They said he was fun-loving and a good singer and banjo picker. And many said the well-known story from the popular ballad that pitted Henry with a hammer in each hand racing to beat a steam drill is true too. Some said the hammers weighed nine pounds each, others contend 40. Historian Lester N. Lively reports that Henry's hammer and steel were found years later in the number 3 shaft in 1932 when a concrete floor was poured in the tunnel. Supposedly, superstition had kept anyone from picking up the tools. Other questions still fuel the legend. Was a bet placed on Henry's win over the steam drill? How did he die and when? Was it right after the race? Or later that night after dinner when he was going to sleep? Or could it have been much later when rocks crushed him as they had so many of his fellow workers?

Perhaps the answers will come to you when you see the large statue of Henry at the site. It is as big, bold and proud as Henry must have been. Erected by the Hilldale-Talcott Raritan Club 100 years after the completion of the tunnel, it serves as a wonderful reminder of an important page of West Virginia history.

**Directions**: The plaques commemorating the Big Bend Tunnel, now a twin tunnel, and the John Henry Statue are located on a sharp curve of Rt. 3 in Talcott. Parking is available.

## White Sulphur Springs/Union

Numerous attractions in and around White Sulphur Springs are mentioned elsewhere in this guide, including the Greenbrier State Forest (see entry on State Parks and Forests) and the Federal Fish Hatchery (see entry on Trout Hatcheries). The Greenbrier River Trail, a 75-mile long old railroad grade stretching from nearby North Caldwell in Greenbrier County to Cass in Pocahontas County, will interest hikers, bikers and skiers (see entry). Phone (304)536-1944 for more information. **The Coal House**, located two miles east of White Sulphur Springs on Rt. 60, appeals to West Virginia souvenir shoppers. Made of blocks of cannel coal shaped by a hatchet and joined together by black mortar, the shop features handmade coal jewelry, figurines and other crafts. Open Monday through Saturday 9:00 A.M. to 5:30 P.M. and Sunday 11:00 A.M. to 5:00 P.M., the shop's phone is (304)536-3288. Golfers may want to play a round at the Valley View Country Club in White Sulphur Springs on Rt. 60. Near the site where the first golf club in America was organized in 1884, the course is open to the public. Call (304)536-1600 for a tee time.

Returning to Rt. 219 South, you can visit a gristmill in operation by the same family since the 1790s, **Reeds Mill**, and purchase a bag of water-ground flour. On the National Register of Historic Places, the mill is located 12 miles south of Lewisburg and one and one-half miles east at Second Creek Bridge. Phone: (304)772-5665.

Continuing south on Rt. 219 you come to **Union**, the seat of Monroe County. In an area seemingly forgotten by the onslaught of civilization—not a traffic light, fast-food restaurant, movie theater or mall can be found in the county–Union is loaded with history and is perfect for a quiet getaway. Head first to the Monroe County Historical Society Museum and Tourist Information Center located on Rt. 219 and Main Street. Among the information you can pick up here is a free, well-prepared, self-guided walking tour of 47 of Union's venerable 19th-century buildings. From the attractive view of the town at Green Hill Cemetery (where both Revolutionary and Civil War soldiers are buried) to the Greek revival Watchman Office and Print Shop (where a newspaper has been printed for more than 120 years) and the Romanesque Monroe County Court House and Jail (with its original shutters where 200 years' worth of records are still kept), the tour offers a delightful view of the past. The museum and Tourist Information Center is open free of charge June 1 through October 1, Monday through Saturday 10:00 A.M. to 4:00 P.M. and Sunday 1:00 to 4:00 P.M. The phone is (304)772-5317.

Although not on the walking tour, the **Old Rehoboth Church** should not be missed. Located about two miles east of Union on Rt. 3, the log church is one of the oldest church buildings west of the Allegheny Mountains, having been dedicated in 1786 and even once serving as an Indian defense fort. On the National Register of Historic Places, it is one of ten designated Methodist shrines in the country. A small museum with no admission charge located at the church is open April 15 to October 15, Tuesday through Saturday 9:00 A.M. to 5:00 P.M. and Sunday 1:00 to 5:00 P.M. The phone is (304)772-3387.

When in Greenville, stop at the **Old Mill**, a living museum and working mill on Rt. 122. On the National Register of Historic Places, it features craftspeople practicing age-old crafts as well as exhibits on steam and gas engines. Crafts, herbal products and tasty ice cream are available at the adjacent Company Store. The Old Mill is open on weekends only, May until cold weather. The hours are 10:00 A.M. to 5:00 P.M. on Friday and Saturday and NOON to 5:00 P.M. on Sunday. Call (304)832-6775 for more information.

## The Greenbrier

The pinnacle of lavish resort hotels, The Greenbrier, is located on 6,500 acres of woodland in White Sulphur Springs. Scoring the highest marks possible with Mobile Travel Guide, AAA and others, the famous resort has hosted most U.S. Presidents, royalty and heads of state from all points of the globe. Manicured grounds give way to sparkling white, columned buildings with grand entryways adorned with chandeliers. Porters in white gloves and waiters in formal clothes speak in hushed tones while stretch limousines and expensive European imports shine in the parking lots. Seven hundred luxury rooms together with three championship golf courses, outstanding har-tru and dyna turf tennis facilities, horseback riding, trout-stocked streams, trap and skeet-shooting fields, indoor and outdoor pools, afternoon tea, excellent dining and an unrivaled, pampering spa and mineral bath program are presented for guests year-round. A strict dress code applies for all activities. "For more than two centuries," goes the slogan, "The Greenbrier has been ladies and gentlemen being served by ladies and gentlemen . . .it still is."

The opulence contrasts almost incongruously with the simple beginnings. Ailing people travelled long distances, sleeping in tents or wagons along the way, for the opportunity to bathe in the area's purported health-giving, sulfurous waters. Indians had earlier discovered the strange water, deciding anything that smelled and tasted so foul must be good for them. In 1750 Nicholas and Kate Carpenter and their daughter Frances built a log home here on Howard's Creek. Kate Carpenter lost her husband in an Indian raid and later married Michael Bowyer. Bowyer's daughter, Mary, married James Calwell, and the young couple inherited their parents' property and built a small tavern near a spring, the beginning of a planned resort. An enclosure around the spring was built in the early 1830s, and the Calwells next added a cottage in 1835. The cottage became known later as the **President's Cottage** because it doubled as a summer White House for many presidents, including Martin Van-Buren, the first chief executive known to have stayed there.

During the Civil War the hotel was caught between the North and the South with both sides occupying it at different times. After the conflict, with a railroad to White Sulphur Springs complete and distinguished guests like Robert E. Lee enjoying the spas, the hotel flourished. In 1910 the C&O Railway Company acquired the resort, adding a new building that is the center wing of today's Greenbrier Hotel. The U.S. Army later purchased the hotel in 1942 and transformed it into Ashford General Hospital where more than 20,000 soldiers were treated. Following World War II, the C&O again purchased the hotel and together with internationally known interior decorator Dorothy Draper brought the resort back to life. More than $11 million was spent over a two-year period on the resort's rejuvenation. The resort has prospered ever since. For reservations and more information call 1(800)624-6070 or (304)536-1110 or write The Greenbrier, White Sulphur Springs, WV 24986.

**Directions**: The Greenbrier is located just off I-64 at White Sulphur Springs.

# Covered Bridges

West Virginia's picturesque covered bridges, many weathered with the character only time brings, are special sites, well worth venturing out of your way to see and photograph. Beginning in the mid-1800s they were an integral part of the state's turnpike system, patterned after popular German, Swiss and Austrian designs. Covered to protect the all-wood, hand-hewn, intricate supporting truss system, the bridges were both the pride of excellent craftsmen and the prize of Civil War battles fought for control of a specific area.

Stretching across small, gentle creeks and powerful rivers, the state's bridges utilized seven different truss types often named after the winning designer/bidder who led the crafting of the bridge. You can see examples of Long, Howe, Warren, Kingpost, Queenpost, Multiple Kingpost and Multiple Kingpost with Burr Arch trusses. All arrive at the same idea of creating a support made stronger by joining together small triangles of timber; however, some, like the aptly named Long type (after designer Stephen Long), used on the Philippi Covered Bridge in Barbour County, needed to be adjusted to meet certain needs—in this case, length. The Philippi Bridge is the oldest and longest in the state (at 285 feet, 10 inches) still in use, having been built by the master builder Lemuel Chenoweth and his brother, Eli, in 1852. The bridge enhanced traffic to and from important areas like Richmond and Norfolk and was the site of the first land confrontation of the Civil War on June 2 and 3, 1861.

Even though West Virginia's mountainous and river-laden remote areas were difficult to reach for turnpike and bridge builders, the state did have nearly 90 covered bridges in use as late as 1947. The arrival of the railroad years in 1873 had doomed the covered bridges to eventual obsolescence. Railroad bridges could be made quickly and economically from sections of prefabricated, weather-resistant iron that did not require the maintenance nor pose the threat of fire of wood bridges. Railroad bridges didn't even need to be covered. Thus an era of artful style marked by individual craftsmen gave way to a calculated science of bridge engineering. Today only 17 covered bridges remain standing in the state.

Use the list that follows to find a covered bridge near your intended day trip. Like the other attractions special to West Virginia, (including white-water rafting, wildlife management areas, state parks and glassmaking), covered bridges are precious and unique legacies. Most in this state are located in the Mountaineer Country and New River/Greenbrier Valley regions and are short, ranging from 30 to 40 feet to about 100 feet in length. The smallest is the Laurel Creek Covered Bridge outside of Lillyville, measuring a quaint 24 feet, 5 inches long. Be aware that you may drive across most but not all bridges. Some are open to pedestrians only, and some are on private property.

## Mountaineer Country

### Fish Creek Covered Bridge

Directions: Travel east on Route 250 from Hundred. Turn right on Secondary Route 13.
Stream: Fish Creek
Truss: Kingpost
Builder: Unknown
Date: 1881
Length: 36 feet
Condition: Fair, in use

### Dents Run Covered Bridge

Directions: Take Route 19 south from Westover and turn right on Secondary Route 43. Turn left on Secondary Route 3.
Stream: Dents Run
Truss: Kingpost
Builder: W.A. Loar
Date: 1889
Length: 40 feet
Condition: Good, in use

### Barrackville Covered Bridge

Directions: The bridge is located in Barrackville on Secondary Route 21 at the junction of Routes 250 and 32.
Stream: Buffalo Creek
Truss: Multiple Kingpost with Burr Arch
Builder: Lemuel and Eli Chenoweth
Date: 1853
Length: 145 feet, 9¾ inches
Condition: Fair, in use

### Center Point Covered Bridge

Directions: The bridge is located 12 miles north of Route 50 in Center Point on Route 23.
Stream: Pike Fork of McElroy Creek
Truss: Long
Builder: John Ash and S.H. Smith
Date: 1888
Length: 42 feet, 1 inch
Condition: Good, in use

### Fletcher Covered Bridge

Directions: Travel west on Route 50 from Wolf Summit. Turn right on Secondary Route 5 and north on Secondary Route 5/29.
Stream: Righthand fork of Ten Mile Creek
Truss: Multiple Kingpost
Builder: Solomon Swiger

Date: 1891
Length: 58 feet, 4 inches
Condition: Good, in use

### Simpson Creek Covered Bridge
Directions: Take Exit 121 off I-79 south. Go .2 miles on Secondary
  Route 24 north to the bridge.
Stream: Simpson Creek
Truss: Multiple Kingpost
Builder: Asa S. Hugill
Date: 1881
Length: 75 feet, 2 inches
Condition: Good, in use

### Philippi Covered Bridge
Directions: The bridge is on Route 250 in Philippi.
Stream: Tygart River
Truss: Long
Builder: Lemuel and Eli Chenoweth
Date: 1852
Length: 285 feet, 10 inches
Condition: Good, in use

### Carrollton Covered Bridge
Directions: From Philippi travel south on Route 119 to Secondary
  Route 36. Turn left. The bridge is .8 miles ahead in Carrollton.
Stream: Buckhannon River
Truss: Multiple Kingpost with Burr Arch
Builders: Emmett J. and Daniel O'Brien
Date: 1855–56
Length: 140 feet, 9 inches
Condition: Good, in use

## Mountain Lakes

### Walkersville Covered Bridge
Directions: The bridge is located one mile south of Walkersville on
  Route 19.
Stream: Right fork of West Fork River
Truss: Queen Post
Builder: John G. Sprigg
Date: 1903
Length: 39 feet, 4 inches
Condition: Good, in use

## Mid-Ohio Valley

### Staats Mill Covered Bridge
Directions: The bridge is located at the FFA-FHA State Camp,
  southeast of Ripley.
Stream: Pond

Truss: Long
Builder: Henry F. Hartley
Date: 1888
Length: 97 feet
Condition: Excellent, open to pedestrians only

**Sarvis Fork Covered Bridge**
Directions: Travel on Secondary Route 21 north from Sandyville.
    Turn right onto Secondary 21/15.
Stream: Left fork of Sandy Creek
Truss: Long
Builder: R.B. Cunningham
Date: 1889
Length: 101 feet, 3½ inches
Condition: Fair, in use

### Metro Valley

### Milton Covered Bridge
Directions: The bridge is at the junction of Route 60 and Secondary
    Route 25 in Milton.
Stream: Mud River
Truss: Howe
Builder: R.H. Baker
Date: 1876
Length: 108 feet, 5 inches
Condition: Fair

### Potomac Highlands

### Locust Creek Covered Bridge
Directions: From Hillsboro travel south on Secondary Route 31 about
    6.3 miles to the bridge.
Stream: Locust Creek
Truss: Warren Double Intersection
Builder: Unknown
Date: 1870s
Length: 113 feet, 9 inches
Condition: Good, in use

### New River/Greenbrier Valley

### Hokes Mill Covered Bridge
Directions: Use Route 219 south from Ronceverte. Turn right on
    Secondary Route 48. After 3.6 miles turn south on Secondary
    Route 62 and follow to Hokes Mill.
Stream: Second Creek
Truss: Long
Builder: Unknown
Date: 1897–99

Length: 81 feet, 6 inches
Condition: Fair, in use

### Herns Mill Covered Bridge

Directions: Take Route 60 west from Lewisburg 2.6 miles. Turn left
on Secondary Route 60/11 and left again on Secondary Route 40.
Follow Route 40 2.2 miles to the bridge.

Stream: Milligans Creek
Truss: Queenpost
Builder: Unknown
Date: 1884
Length: 53 feet, 8 inches
Condition: Good, in use

### Indian Creek Covered Bridge

Directions: The bridge is six miles south of Union on Route 219
across from St. John's Church.

Stream: Indian Creek
Truss: Long
Builders: Ray and Oscar Weikel and E.P. and A.P. Smith
Date: 1903
Length 49 feet, 3 inches
Condition: Fair, open to pedestrians only

### Laurel Creek Covered Bridge

Directions: From the Indian Creek Covered Bridge, return north on
Route 219. Turn left on Secondary Route 219/7 to Lillydale. Turn
right on 219/11 and follow through Lillydale to the bridge.

Stream: Laurel Creek
Truss: Queenpost
Builder: Robert Annott
Date: 1911
Length: 24 feet, 5 inches
Condition: Fair, in use

# Skiing

Many of the attractions detailed in this guide are best enjoyed during the warm-weather months. This is not to say there is less to do in West Virginia in the winter. In fact, each winter more than one-half million people visit the state in their favorite season. Most come, often with their families, to ski the well-groomed slopes of the Mountain State's snow-covered peaks.

Numerous resorts cater to skiers' needs, offering complete facilities for any level of competence, from the beginner to the expert, for a short or extended getaway: comfortable (and deluxe) lodging, dining, lifts, rentals, instruction and snow-making equipment all at the same location. So popular is skiing in West Virginia that the state's Division of Tourism and Parks even maintains a daily-taped skiing condition report, available November through March at 1(800)CALL-WVA. Use the same number for help with lodging and skiing reservations. Visitors can choose between fast and exciting downhill (also known as Alpine) skiing or go-at-your-own-pace cross-country (Nordic) skiing. Both offer excellent exercise and the opportunity to savor one of West Virginia's best assets, its natural beauty.

Skiing can be expensive; however, most resorts offer week-day reduced rates and/or numerous special packages. One of our favorites, the Snowshoe Mountain Resort in the Potomac Highlands region, has mid-week three-day packages for two with a room in their lodge and lift tickets for around $350.00 With a one-bedroom condo the cost of the package rises to a little more than $520.00. Meals in the resort's restaurants are extra. Weekend lift tickets/skiing rates can cost nearly double the week-day price.

Without the expense of the lifts, cross-country skiing is much more affordable and is very popular at Canaan Valley where the average snowfall is 150 inches a year. Three-day mid-week packages at another favorite, the Elk River Touring Center in Slatyfork in the same region, range from around $130.00 per person for economy accommodations to around $170.00 per person for deluxe accommodations. Both rates are based on double occupancy and both include eight meals, three trail-use fees and two lessons. Cross-country equipment rental fees generally run around $10.00 per day.

With such a wide variety of packages, services and rates available, it is a good idea to request a brochure from a resort in advance so you can tailor a trip to suit your needs. Depending on the time of your trip, reservations may be necessary months in advance.

Use the chart that follows to help locate a resort to your liking. All are in the eastern, mountainous half of the state with the largest concentration centered in Potomac Highlands.

# DOWNHILL (ALPINE)

## POTOMAC HIGHLANDS

| | Season | Lifts | Lodging/Dining | Snowmaking | Instruction | Night Skiing | Other |
|---|---|---|---|---|---|---|---|
| **Canaan Valley Resort** Rt. 1, Box 330 Davis, WV 26260 (304) 866-4121 | Dec.-Mar. | 2-4 | ● | ● | ● | ● | Top elevation 4,280 feet. 21 slopes. |
| **Timberline Four Seasons Resort** Box 625 Canaan Valley, WV 26260 (304) 866-4801 | Nov. 30-Apr. | 2 | ● | ● 100% | ● | | 1,000-foot vertical drop. 16 slopes, one 2 miles long. |
| **Silver Creek Ski Resort** P.O. Box 83 Snowshoe, WV 26209 (304) 572-4000 | Dec.-Mar. | 2-4 | ● | ● 100% | ● | | 663-foot vertical drop. One 4,700 foot run. |
| **Snowshoe Mountain Resort** P.O. Box 10 Snowshoe, WV 26209 (304) 572-5252 | Nov.-Apr. | 6 | ● | ● 100% | ● | | 4,848' elevation. 1,500-foot vertical drop. One 1.5 mile run. |

## MOUNTAINEER COUNTRY

| | Season | Lifts | Lodging/Dining | Snowmaking | Instruction | Night Skiing | Other |
|---|---|---|---|---|---|---|---|
| **Alpine Lake Resort** Rt. 2, Box 99-D2 Terra Alta, WV 26764 (304) 789-2481 | Dec. 26-Mar. 1 | 2 | ● | | ● | ● Sat. | Weekends only. |

## NORTHERN PANHANDLE

| | Season | Lifts | Lodging/Dining | Snowmaking | Instruction | Night Skiing | Other |
|---|---|---|---|---|---|---|---|
| **Oglebay Resort** Wheeling, WV 26003 (304) 243-4000 | Dec.-Mar. | 3 | ● | | ● | ● | Runs from 900-1,600 feet. 330-foot vertical drop. |

## NEW RIVER/GREENBRIER VALLEY

| | Season | Lifts | Lodging/Dining | Snowmaking | Instruction | Night Skiing | Other |
|---|---|---|---|---|---|---|---|
| **Winterplace Resort** Box 1 Flat Top, WV 25841 (304) 787-3221 | Dec.-Mar. | 4 | ● | ● 100% | ● | ● | 21 slopes. |

# CROSS COUNTRY (NORDIC)

## POTOMAC HIGHLANDS

| | Lodging/Dining | Instruction | Rental | Night Skiing | Length of Trails | Other |
|---|---|---|---|---|---|---|
| **Blackwater Nordic Center** Blackwater Falls State Park Davis, WV 26260 (304) 259-5511 | • | • | • | | 25 km | Rope tow |
| **Canaan Valley Resort Ski Touring Center** Rt. 1, Box 330 Davis, WV 26260 (304) 866-4121 | • | • | • | | 18 miles | Guided tours |
| **Elk River Ski Touring Center** Slatyfork, WV 26291 (304) 572-3771 | Nearby | • | • | • | 50 km | Snow-boarding |
| **Blackwater Outdoor Center** Box 325 Davis, WV 26260 (304) 259-5117 | Nearby | • | • | | 30 km | Equipment repair |
| **White Grass Ski Touring Center** Rt. 1, Box 299 Davis, WV 26260 (304) 866-4114 | Day lodge | • | • | • | 50 km | Cafe |

## MOUNTAIN LAKES

| | Lodging/Dining | Instruction | Rental | Night Skiing | Length of Trails | Other |
|---|---|---|---|---|---|---|
| **Richwood Nordic Ski Rental** 6 Main Street Richwood, WV 26261 (304) 846-6790 | Nearby | By prior arrange-ment | • | | numerous miles | Weekends only |

## MOUNTAINEER COUNTRY

| | Lodging/Dining | Instruction | Rental | Night Skiing | Length of Trails | Other |
|---|---|---|---|---|---|---|
| **Terra Alta Ski Touring Center** Rt. 2, Box 99-D2 Terra Alta, WV 26764 (304) 789-2481 | • | • | • | | 10 miles | Weekends only |

## NEW RIVER/GREENBRIER VALLEY

| | Lodging/Dining | Instruction | Rental | Night Skiing | Length of Trails | Other |
|---|---|---|---|---|---|---|
| **Pipestem Resort State Park** P.O. Box 150 Pipestem, WV 25979 (304) 466-1800 | • | | • | | 12 miles | Sled run with rope tow |

# Whitewater Rafting

Arguably the most exciting and popular activity in West Virginia is whitewater rafting. With nearly 2,000 miles of mountain streams and rivers available, many people regard the state as the whitewater capital of the world.

Much of the lure of whitewater rafting lies in its variety. You have many choices of rivers, degrees of difficulty, types of rafts, lengths and kinds of trips and licensed outfitters. However one constant does exist: this is a thrilling experience which takes you to unrivaled natural beauty.

You can make your run as action-packed and water-splashing or quietly-calm and relaxing as you wish. Rapids are classed by their difficulty, ranging from I, the most tranquil, to VI, the most challenging and severe. Total beginners can run class I and II riffles even without guides; however fast-moving water rated above class II requires professional, skilled outfitters.

Depending on the difficulty of the water, you can expect to see several kinds of boats. The most common, an inflatable raft, ranges from 12 to 16 feet in length and accommodates four to 10 riders. A duckey, an inflatable kayak-like craft, is for those who lean toward solo navigation, although two-person models are available. More stable and more easily controlled than a kayak (and requiring only a few minutes of instruction time), a duckey is about three feet wide and nine feet long. The kayak can be easily tipped over, but after a day or two of guidance, the advantages of the small, lightweight, water-tight plastic or fiberglass kayak become apparent. It's very maneuverable, can glide over water surges and even roll over without sinking. The dory, another kind of boat, offers a comfortable alternative well-suited for rafters who like to fish as they float. Common first on western rivers and oceans, the flat-bottomed dories are made of fiberglass, wood or aluminum and have a sharp prow, angled sides and a triangular stern.

Most outfitters stick to a pattern of the kinds of trips they offer based on the nature of the water they run, their experience, their facilities and, of course, safety. Most operate during the spring, summer and fall. If you don't see what you want from one guide, it may be a good idea to check with another. You might start by asking about half- or full-day float trips. Of special interest to beginners, young children and seniors, they are run on quiet stretches of rivers with rapids ranging from class I to III. Full-day trips generally include meals.

Combination fish and float trips must not be overlooked. Because you will have a guide with you, he could make the important difference of finding fish or not. You will reach waters unattainable by any other means while searching for large and smallmouth bass, muskie, walleye, catfish and panfish. Overnight trips, another option, attract river riders who enjoy camping. Many outfitters have their own campsites or camping facilities. Along the way of an overnight trip you can swim, practice paddling different kinds of boats, fish, hike or simply work on your sun tan. Some outfitters concentrate their offerings on instruction, including operating duckies and kayaks, reading rapids, choosing courses and learning rescue and safety procedures. Others combine rafting with specific horseback or mountain bike riding forays. You might also rock climb one day and raft the next or hike special trails before heading to the river for a ride.

The difficulty of some segments of rivers requires outfitters to place age limits on the passengers they take. Be sure to check if your children are permitted on the ride of your choice. You can expect to pay around $42.00 per person for a Saturday half-day guided outing. It can be as much as $10.00 less on weekdays. Full-day guided treks complete with breakfast and lunch run around $52.00 per person on Saturdays. Camping packages, including two river trips, two nights camping and meals such as steak dinners, are around $135.00 per person on weekends and $110.00 per person Monday through Thursday. Whitewater rafting is especially popular in West Virginia and many outfitters are quickly booked up. It is a good idea to secure reservations up to four or five months in advance, especially on longer, more involved trips.

The best whitewater is concentrated in the eastern half of the state, the most famous being found on the New and Gauley Rivers. The New features three main sections: the calm upper, well-suited for gentle float and fishing outings; the middle, with class II and III rapids good for gaining nerve; and the boisterous lower section with class II to V rapids. Don't worry, there's often plenty of time between rapids with names like "Sunrise," "Double Z" and "Thread the Needle" for you to fully absorb your guide's instructions. Whitewater rafting on the Gauley River in central West Virginia is controlled by Summersville Dam when the Summersville reservoir is lowered each spring and fall. A very brief season in high demand is created over especially difficult class III to V + rapids where the river drops 668 feet through 28 miles. More than 100 rapids that demand solid technique challenge riders. You must be at least 16 years old to paddle through stretches named "Shipwreck," "Mash" and "Lost Paddle" on the river's upper reaches. The lower section, still similar to a carnival ride, is often used as a practice route before tackling the upper parts.

As challenging as whitewater rafting on the Gauley River is, it's even more fun when you know something about its source, the Summersville Dam and Lake. Built by the U.S. Army Corps of Engineers between 1960 and 1966 at a cost of $48 million, the rock-fill type dam rises 390 feet high and stretches 2,280 feet wide. Water is released from the dam via a 1,555-foot-long, 29 foot-wide tunnel controlled by three nine-foot-wide valves. The long-standing tradition of naming a project after the name of the town nearest it had to be broken when this huge dam was finished because the nearest town was Gad. "Gad Dam" never came to be.

Other rivers to consider include the Tygart, not as crowded as some but offering rapids from class I to V+; the Bluestone, Meadow and Big Sandy Creek, all with whitewater that is short-lived following spring rains (Big Sandy Creek swells to include class II and IV rapids as well as large drops and waterfalls); and the lovely Shenandoah that meanders through Harpers Ferry and other small towns loaded with history. The Greenbrier, and the South Branch of the Potomac lure canoeists with their gentle water, ample wildlife and changing terrain.

Use the list of licensed whitewater companies that follows to find out more about scheduling a trip.

**Tip**: Most companies require that you wear tennis or other rubber-solded shoes. It is also a good idea to bring sunglasses, sunscreen, a light windbreaker and a change of dry clothes, shoes and socks. In the cooler months polypropelene clothing as well as wool socks and sweaters are advisable. In the summer you'll see most riders in shorts or swimsuits and T-shirts. Outfitters provide helmets, lifejackets and paddles, and some offer wet suits.

### New River/Greenbrier Valley

Ace Whitewater (American Canadian Expeditions Ltd.)
P.O. Box 1168, Oak Hill, WV 25901
Phone: (304)469-2651 or (800)223-2641
Rivers: New, Gauley

Adventure Expeditions, Inc.
P.O. Box 249
Glen Jean, WV 25846
Phone: (304)469-2955 or (800)223-2641
Rivers: New, Gauley

Adventures, Inc.
Drawer 39
Lansing, WV 25862
Phone: (304)574-3834 or (800)CALL-WVA
Rivers: New, Gauley, Greenbrier, Cheat, Bluestone

American Whitewater Tours, Inc.
Route 1, Box 430

Fayetteville, WV 25840
Phone: (304)574-3655 or (800)346-RAFT
Rivers: New, Cheat, Gauley

Cantrell Canoes & Rafts, Inc.
504 Summers St.
Hinton, WV 25951
Phone: (304)466-0595
Rivers: New, Bluestone, Greenbrier

Class VI, Ltd.
P.O. Box 38
Lansing, WV 25862
Phone: (304)574-0704 or (800)CLASS-VI (800)252-7784
Rivers: New, Gauley

Class VI River Runners
Box 78, Ames Heights Rd.
Lansing, WV 25862
Phone: (304)574-0704, (800)CLASS-VI (800)252-7784 or (800)CALL
  WVA
Rivers: New, Gauley, Greenbrier, Shavers Fork

Drift-A-Bit, Inc.
P.O. Box 885, Old Route 38
Fayetteville, WV 25840
Phone: (304)574-3282 or (800)633-RAFT
Rivers: New, Gauley

Mountain River Tours, Inc.
P.O. Box 88, Sunday Rd.
Hico, WV 25854
Phone: (304)658-5269 or (800)822-1FUN
Rivers: New, Gauley, Greenbrier, Meadow, Bluestone

Mountain State Outdoor Center, Inc.
P.O. Box 128
Lansing, WV 25862
Phone: (304)574-0704 or (800)CLASS-VI, (800)252-7784
Rivers: New, Greenbrier, Shavers Fork

New and Gauley River Adventures
Box 44, Lansing Rd.
Lansing, WV 25862
Phone: (304)574-3008, 3011 or (800)759-RAFT
Rivers: New, Gauley, Meadow, Bluestone, Greenbrier, Cherry

New Gauley Expeditions, Inc.
P.O. Box 264
Fayetteville, WV 25840
Phone: (304)574-3679, (800)472-RAFT or (800)CALL WVA
Rivers: New, Gauley, Greenbrier

New River Scenic Whitewater Tour
Box 637, Hinton Bypass
Hinton, WV 25951
Phone: (304)466-2288, (800)292-0880 (outside WV) or (800)CALL
    WVA
Rivers: New, Gauley, Greenbrier, Bluestone

North American River Rafters, Inc.
P.O. Box 231
Hico, WV 25854
Phone: (304)658-5276 or (800)950-2528
River: Gauley

North American River Runners
P.O. Box 81
Hico,WV 25854
Phone: (304)658-5276, (800)950-2585 or (800)CALL WVA
Rivers: New, Cheat, Gauley

Passages to Adventure, Inc.
P.O. Box 71
Fayetteville, WV 25840
Phone: (304)574-1037 or (800)634-3785
Rivers: New, Cheat, Gauley, Bluestone, Big Sandy, Meadow

The Rivermen
P.O. Box 360
Fayetteville, WV 25840
Phone: (304)574-0515 or (800)545-7238
Rivers: New, Gauley

Rivers II, Inc.
P.O. Drawer 39, Fayette Mine Rd.
Lansing, WV 25862
Phone: (304)574-3834 or (800)879-7483
Rivers: New, Gauley, Greenbrier, Bluestone

Songer Whitewater, Inc.
P.O. Box 300
Fayetteville, WV 25840
Phone: (304)658-9926 or (800)356-RAFT
Rivers: New, Gauley, Meadow, Greenbrier, Bluestone

West Virginia River Adventures
P.O. Box 95
Hico, WV 25854
Phone: (304)658-5241 or (800)950-2585
Rivers: New, Gauley

West Virginia Whitewater
Box 30
Fayetteville, WV 25840

Phone: (304)574-0871
Rivers: New, Gauley

Whitewater Information/New River Dories
P.O. Drawer 243
Glen Jean, WV 25846
Phone: (304)465-0855, (800)782-RAFT or (800) CALL WVA
Rivers: New, Gauley, Bluestone, Greenbrier

Wildwater Expeditions Unlimited, Inc.
P.O. Box 155
Lansing, WV 25862
Phone: (304)658-4007 or (800)WVA-RAFT
Rivers: New, Cheat, Gauley, Bluestone, Greenbrier

## *Potomac Highlands*

Appalachian Wildwaters, Inc.
P.O. Box 277
Rowlesburg, WV 26425
Phone: (304)454-2475 or (800)USA-RAFT
Rivers: New, Cheat, Gauley, Big Sandy, North Fork of the South
   Branch of the Potomac, Bluestone, Meadow, Greenbrier, Shavers
   Fork

Blackwater Outdoor Center
Box 325
Davis, WV 26260
Phone: (304)259-5117
Rivers: Cheat, North Branch of the Potomac

Blue Ridge Outfitters
P.O. Box 650
Harpers Ferry, WV 25414
Phone: (304)725-3444
Rivers: Potomac, Shenandoah

Cheat River Outfitters, Inc.
P.O. Box 134
Albright, WV 26519
Phone: (304)329-2024
Rivers: North Branch of the Potomac, Cheat, Shenandoah

Cheat Whitewater World, Ltd.
Star Route 903, HC 2, Box 2245
Jim Thorpe, PA 18229
Phone: (717)325-3656
River: Cheat

Expeditions, Inc.
P.O. Box 277C
Rowlesburg, WV 26425

Phone: (304)454-2475 or (800)USA-RAFT
Rivers: Cheat, Gauley

Laurel Highlands River Tours, Inc.
P.O. Box 107
Ohiopyle, PA 15470
Phone: (412)329-4501 or (800)4-RAFTIN
Rivers: Cheat, Tygart

Mountain Streams and Trails Outfitters
Box 106
Ohiopyle, PA 15470
Phone: (412)329-8810 or (800)245-4090
Rivers: Cheat, Gauley, Tygart

Rough Run Expeditions
P.O. Box 277D
Rowlesburg, WV 26425
Phone: (304)454-2475 or (800)USA-RAFT
Rivers: Cheat, Tygart

Whitewater Adventures of Cheat River Canyon, Inc.
P.O. Box 31
Ohiopyle, PA 15470
Phone: (412)329-8850 or (800)WWA-RAFT
Rivers: Cheat, Tygart, Big Sandy

Youghiogheny Outfitters, Inc.
P.O. Box 21
Ohiopyle, PA 15470
Phone: (412)329-4549
River: Cheat

### Eastern Gateway

Precision Rafting Expeditions of the Gauley River
P.O. Box 185
Friendsville, MD 21531
Phone: (800)447-3723
River: Gauley

River and Trail Outfitters
604 Valley Rd.
Knoxville, MD 21758
Phone: (301)695-5177
Rivers: Shenandoah, Potomac

River Riders, Inc.
Rt. 3, Box 1260
Harpers Ferry, WV 25425
Phone: (304)535-2663
Rivers: Shenandoah, Potomac, Greenbrier

# Fishing/Hunting Guides

Many outdoors people know that information on the hottest fishing holes and best hunting spots is hard to come by—especially for outsiders. So, if you don't trust your own instinct and skill to find fish and game on waters and land you don't know, enlisting the services of a guide may be the answer. Use the fishing guide list that follows and call a pro. It can make a difference between fish in the bucket and clean hands.

Some are obviously also white-water rafting guides (see white-water rafting entry for a complete listing of outfitters). An asterisk (*) denotes those locations that offer fishing/hunting vacation packages. For fly fishing novices, the Fastwater Fly Fishing School in the Potomac Highlands Region may be the place to start. Their address is Rt. 3, Box 200, Harman, WV 26270, (304)227-4565.

## Mountaineer Country
Appalachian Wildwaters, Inc., PO Box 277, Rowlesburg, WV 26425, (304)454-2475

## Mountain Lakes
Fraley Stables*, Econolodge, PO Box 737, Summersville, WV 26651, (304)872-5151

Kilmarnock Farm Retreat*, Rt. 1, Box 91, Orlando, WV 26412, (304)452-8319

West Fork Inn*, Rt. 2, Box 212, Rt. 2, Box 212, Jane Lew, WV 26378, (304)745-4893

## Potomac Highlands
Blackwater Outdoor Center, Box 325, Davis, WV 26260, (304)259-5117

Cheat Mountain Club*, Rt. 1, Box 115, Elkins, WV 26241, (304)636-2301

Smoke Hole Lodge*, PO Box 953, Petersburg, WV 26847, no phone

## New River/Greenbrier Valley
Cantrel Canoes and Rafts, Inc., 504 Summers St., Hinton, WV 25951, (304)466-0595

Class VI River Runners, PO Box 78, Ames Heights Rd., Lansing, WV 25862, (304)574-0704

Drift-A-Bit, PO Box 885, Fayetteville, WV 25840, (304)574-3282

New River Scenic Whitewater Tours, Inc., PO Box 637, Hinton, WV 25951, (304)466-2288

Whitewater Information, Ltd./Home of New River Dories, PO Drawer 243, Glen Jean, WV 25846, (304)465-0855

North American River Runners, PO Box 81, Hico, WV 25854, (304)658-5276

Appalachian Outdoor Adventures*, PO Box 655, Fayetteville, WV 25840, (304)574-3559

# State Parks and Forests

Lovers of the outdoors, take note. West Virginia's State Parks and Forests are the state's most popular leisure-time destinations. Easily accessible, well managed and with many open year-round, each has its own unique appeal and recreational opportunites.

The parks are divided into four descriptive categories: Resort Vacation Parks, Vacation Parks, Day Use/Natural Areas and Historical Parks. The state's four Resort Vacation Parks boast everything you need at one site for either a short getaway or an extended stay. They feature overnight accommodations in a large lodge, separate cottages, cabins and campsites, ranging from rustic to posh. During the high summer season you can expect to pay around $520.00 for a weekly rental of a two-bedroom cottage. One-night and weekend rentals are available as well, as are larger three- and four-bedroom cottages. Main lodge rates are about $60.00 per night for two persons. Resort Vacation Parks also have amenities such as good restaurants, championship golf courses, tennis courts, horseback riding, swimming pools, skiing trails and fishing lakes as well as nature programs (three of the parks have professional naturalists on staff), crafts shops and museums. One of our favorites, Pipestem Resort State Park in the New River/Greenbrier Valley region, offers overnight trips on horseback to remote areas, dances and dinner theater performances. Twin Falls Resort Park in the same region, is another favorite because of its novel "rent-a-camp" program. Including fully-equipped campsites, the program is great for those who want to camp out but don't have all of the gear. An interpretive nature trail for the blind and a restored 19th-century Pioneer Farm/Museum also score high marks at Twin Falls. Open year-round, the Potomac Highland region's Canaan Valley Resort Park excels during the winter when skiers enjoy complete facilities including chairlifts, snow-making equipment and ski rentals.

Vacation Parks differ only slightly. They are a bit smaller with less of an emphasis on lodges, golf and tennis, yet their natural beauty equals that of the resorts. Many Vacation Parks have naturalists on staff, familiarizing visitors through hikes, lectures, and hands-on programs with their region's plants and animals. Cabins and campsites are the rule of thumb for overnight stays, but North Bend (Mid-Ohio Valley region), Tygart Lake (Mountaineer Country), Hawks Nest (New River/Greenbrier Valley) and Blackwater Falls parks (Potomac Highlands) do have small modern lodges. Prices are comparable to Resort State Parks. The largest state park, Watoga, covering more than 10,000 wooded acres in the Potomac Highlands region, treats visitors to nearly the same recreational facilities as a resort park.

Though smaller still, the Day Use/Natural Areas should not be overlooked. Well-known outdoor drama productions, including *Honey in the Rock* and *Hatfields and McCoys*, are staged alongside Broadway shows at Grandview Park's Cliffside Amphitheatre in the New River/Greenbrier Valley region. Not to be outdone, the Metro Valley region's Chief Logan Park features summer musicals as well as *The Aracoma Story*, a play about local Indian legend.

Because of their importance in preserving the history of the state, all of the Historical Parks are popular and well visited. For this reason many are detailed in separate entries in this guide.

Use the chart that follows to match your interests with the facilities state parks and forests offer. For cabin and cottage rentals we recommend reservations as much as a year in advance—they are very popular. Remember that hunting is not permitted in state parks but is allowed in state forests.

# West Virginia
# State Parks and Forests

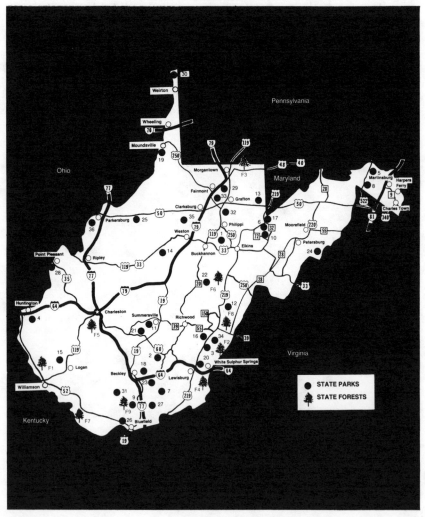

COURTESY WV DIVISION OF TOURISM AND PARKS

| PARKS | ACRES | Deluxe Cabins | Standard Cabins | Economy Cabins | Rustic Cabins | Lodge Rooms | Tent/Trailer Sites | Restaurant | Refreshments | Groceries | Golf Course | Swimming | Boat Rental | Boat Launch Ramp | Fishing | Horseback Riding | Picnicking | Game Courts | Playgrounds | Hiking Trails | Natural Interest | Nature/Rec. Program | Museum | Historical Interest | Souvenir Shop | Hunting | Map Reference |
|---|---|---|---|---|---|---|---|---|---|---|---|---|---|---|---|---|---|---|---|---|---|---|---|---|---|---|---|
| Audra | 355 | | | | | | 65 | ■ | N | | | S | | | ■ | | ■ | ■ | | | | | | | | | 1 |
| Babcock | 4,127 | | | 18 | 8 | | 50 | ■ | ■ | ■ | N | P | ■ | | ■ | ■ | ■ | ■ | ■ | ■ | | | | ■ | | | 2 |
| Beartown | 110 | | | | | | | | | | | | | | ■ | | | ■ | ■ | | | | | | | | 3 |
| Beech Fork | 3,981 | | | | | | 275 | ■ | ■ | N | | | ■ | ■ | ■ | | ■ | ■ | ■ | ■ | | | | | ■ | | 4 |
| Berkeley Springs | 4 | N | N | N | | N | | N | N | N | N | P | | | | | | | | | | | ■ | ■ | ■ | | 5 |
| Blackwater Falls | 1,688 | 25 | | | | 55 | 65 | ■ | ■ | N | N | L | ■ | | N | ■ | ■ | ■ | ■ | ■ | ■ | ■ | | | ■ | | 6 |
| Blennerhassett Island Hist. | 500 | | | | | | | | ■ | | | | | | ■ | | ■ | | | | | | ■ | ■ | ■ | | 36 |
| Bluestone | 2,155 | 25 | | | | | 87 | N | ■ | N | N | P | ■ | ■ | | ■ | ■ | ■ | ■ | | | | ■ | | ■ | | 7 |
| Cacapon Resort | 6,115 | 11 | 13 | 6 | | 50 | | ■ | ■ | N | ■ | L | ■ | | ■ | ■ | ■ | ■ | ■ | ■ | | | | ■ | | | 8 |
| Camp Creek | 500+ | | | | | | 12 | | | | | | | | ■ | | ■ | ■ | ■ | ■ | | | | | | | 9 |
| Canaan Valley Resort | 6,015 | 15 | | | | 250 | 34 | ■ | ■ | N | ■ | P | | | ■ | N | ■ | ■ | ■ | ■ | | | | ■ | | | 10 |
| Carnifex Ferry Battlefield | 156 | | | | | | | N | N | ■ | | | | | | | ■ | ■ | ■ | ■ | | | ■ | ■ | | | 11 |
| Cass Scenic Railroad | 1,089 | 12 | | | | | | N | ■ | N | N | | | | | | ■ | ■ | ■ | | | | ■ | ■ | ■ | | 12 |
| Cathedral | 132 | | | | | | | | | | | | | | | | ■ | | | ■ | ■ | | | | | | 13 |
| Cedar Creek | 2,443 | | | | | | 48 | ■ | ■ | | | P | ■ | | ■ | | ■ | ■ | ■ | ■ | | ■ | | | ■ | | 14 |
| Chief Logan | 3,303 | | | | | | 25 | ■ | ■ | N | | P | | | ■ | | ■ | ■ | ■ | ■ | | | | | | | 15 |
| Droop Mountain Battlefield | 287 | | | | | | | | | | | | | | | | ■ | ■ | ■ | | | | ■ | ■ | | | 16 |
| Fairfax Stone | 4 | | | | | | | | | | | | | | | | | | | | | | | ■ | | | 17 |
| Grandview | 891 | | | | | | | | ■ | | | | | | | | ■ | ■ | ■ | ■ | | | | ■ | | | 18 |
| Grave Creek Mound | 2 | | | | | | | | ■ | ■ | | | | | | | ■ | | | | | | ■ | ■ | ■ | | 19 |
| Greenbrier River Trail | 950 | | | | | | | | | | | | | | | | | | | ■ | | | | | | | 20 |
| Hawks Nest | 276 | | | | | 31 | | ■ | ■ | N | | P | ■ | ■ | N | | ■ | ■ | ■ | ■ | | | ■ | ■ | ■ | ■ | 21 |
| Holly River | 8,292 | | 9 | | | | 88 | ■ | ■ | ■ | | P | | | ■ | | ■ | ■ | ■ | ■ | ■ | | | ■ | ■ | ■ | 22 |
| Little Beaver | 562 | | | | | | 30 | | N | N | | | ■ | | ■ | | ■ | ■ | | | ■ | | | | | | 23 |
| Lost River | 3,712 | 9 | 15 | | | N | | ■ | ■ | N | | P | | | | ■ | ■ | ■ | ■ | ■ | ■ | | ■ | ■ | ■ | | 24 |
| North Bend | 1,405 | 8 | | | | 29 | 80 | ■ | ■ | N | N | P | | | ■ | | ■ | ■ | ■ | ■ | ■ | | | | ■ | | 25 |
| Pinnacle Rock | 245 | | | | | | | | | | | | | | ■ | | ■ | ■ | | | | | | | | | 26 |
| Pipestem Resort | 4,023 | 25 | | | | 143 | 82 | ■ | ■ | N | ■ | P | N | N | ■ | ■ | ■ | ■ | ■ | ■ | | | ■ | | ■ | | 27 |
| Pt. Pleasant Monument | 4 | | | | | | | | | | | | | | | | | | | | | | ■ | ■ | | | 28 |
| Pricketts Fort | 188 | | | | | | | | | | ■ | ■ | | | ■ | | | | | | | | ■ | ■ | ■ | | 29 |
| Tomlinson Run | 1,398 | | | | | | 50 | ■ | ■ | | | P | ■ | | ■ | | ■ | ■ | ■ | ■ | | | | | ■ | | 30 |
| Twin Falls Resort | 3,776 | | 13 | | | 20 | 50 | ■ | ■ | N | ■ | P | | | ■ | ■ | ■ | ■ | ■ | ■ | ■ | ■ | | ■ | ■ | | 31 |
| Tygart Lake | 2,134 | 10 | | | | 20 | 40 | ■ | ■ | N | N | L | ■ | ■ | ■ | | ■ | ■ | ■ | ■ | ■ | | | | ■ | | 32 |
| Valley Falls | 1,145 | | | | | | | | | | | | | | ■ | | ■ | ■ | ■ | ■ | | | | | | | 33 |
| Watoga | 10,100 | 8 | 25 | | | | 88 | ■ | ■ | N | P | ■ | ■ | | ■ | ■ | ■ | ■ | ■ | ■ | ■ | | | | ■ | | 34 |
| Watters Smith Memorial | 532 | | | | | | | | ■ | | | P | | | ■ | ■ | ■ | ■ | | | | | ■ | ■ | ■ | | 35 |
| **FORESTS** | | | | | | | | | | | | | | | | | | | | | | | | | | | |
| Cabwaylingo | 8,123 | | 13 | | | 34 | | N | | N | | | | | N | | ■ | ■ | ■ | | | | | | | ■ | F1 |
| Calvin Price | 9,482 | | | | | | | | | | | | | | ■ | | | | | | | | | | | ■ | F2 |
| Camp Creek | 5,300+ | | | | | | | | | | | | | | ■ | | | | ■ | | | | | | | ■ | F9 |
| Coopers Rock | 12,713 | | | | | | | ■ | | | | | | | ■ | | ■ | ■ | ■ | | | | ■ | ■ | ■ | ■ | F3 |
| Greenbrier | 5,130 | | 12 | | | 16 | | N | N | N | N | P | | | N | | ■ | ■ | ■ | | ■ | | | ■ | | ■ | F4 |
| Kanawha | 9,302 | | | | | 46 | | ■ | N | | P | | | | ■ | ■ | ■ | ■ | | | | | | | | ■ | F5 |
| Kumbrabow | 9,474 | | | | 5 | 15 | | | | | | | | | ■ | | ■ | ■ | ■ | | | | | | | ■ | F6 |
| Panther | 7,810 | | | | | 6 | | ■ | | | | P | | | ■ | | ■ | ■ | ■ | | | | | | | ■ | F7 |
| Seneca | 11,684 | | | | 7 | 10 | | | N | | | | | | ■ | | ■ | ■ | ■ | | | | | | | ■ | F8 |

N-Nearby   P-Pool   L-Lake   S-Stream                Refer to West Virginia Tourist and Highway Map for exact routes.

# Wildlife Management Areas

Most outdoor sportspeople will tell you that even a bad day hunting or fishing is better than a day in an office. So one-day trippers who are hunting and fishing enthusiasts will be delighted to know that the West Virginia Division of Natural Resources maintains 46 public areas throughout the state that are open year-round and are loaded with excellent hunting and fishing opportunities. Called Wildlife Management Areas, these include areas owned by the Division, national and state forests and lands leased by the Division from the U.S. Army Corps of Engineers, private companies and corporations. The Areas are maintained with funds derived from the sale of hunting and fishing licenses and from taxes paid by sportspeople when they buy hunting and fishing equipment.

Few states can boast such a well-run and successful program. Coupled with West Virginia's natural beauty and wide variety of fish and game, these Wildlife Management Areas are hard to beat for finding a back-to-nature escape away from the crowds. Interestingly enough, there are more Areas in the populated Metro Valley region—the area in which you would least expect to find them—than in any other. The lands are for your use and enjoyment, and their management benefits all wildlife. The Division of Natural Resources asks visitors to respect the lands and use them wisely. (A word to the uninitiated: These are not areas where you should take a brand-new fancy car as many of the roads are not paved and require a four-wheel-drive vehicle. Nor are these places where you should expect to find the comforts of home. Many have no developed facilities at all. Also these areas are not the best for hiking, or walking your dog. Trails in the state and national forests are better suited for that. If you must hike, wear bright colored clothing and be well aware of the dates of the hunting season calendar.)

A typical Wildlife Management Area ranges in size from 2,000 to 12,000 acres. Burches Run Lake WMA south of Wheeling is only 54 acres, and both Sleepy Creek WMA near Berkeley Springs and East Lynn Lake WMA outside of Wayne sprawl across 22,928 acres. The terrain varies from densely forested hillsides to open fields, mountainous ranges to wetland expanses. Game may include deer, bear, turkey, raccoon, grouse, squirrel, rabbit and even wild boar. Trapping for muskrat, fox, mink, beaver and other animals is permitted at some locations. Various limits on firearms are enforced; at some locations only bowhunting is permitted. Fishing is enjoyed from the bank or by boat on lakes, ponds, streams and rivers. Some trout waters enforce fly-fishing only. You can try your luck on everything from spotted, large and smallmouth bass, panfish, catfish and walleye to stocked and native trout, pike, muskie, striped bass and hybrids. Boat launching is available with some areas placing limits on motor horsepower. You can also camp for a nominal fee or use ballfields in some of the Areas. Others have only picnic tables, well water and pit toilets.

You will need to secure the proper licenses and become aware of official state regulations before you hunt or fish. It's a good idea to check signs and posters at each site for specific rules. Be sure to respect "No Trespassing" signs on contiguous private property. Resident and non-resident licenses are available at about 800 places throughout the state, or you may order your license in advance by mail. An application form may be obtained from the West Virginia Division of Natural Resources, State Capitol Complex, Building 3, Room 812, Charleston, WV 25305, Attention Hunting and Fishing License Section. Additional information, including a written guide with directions and lists of the many wildlife species found in each Wildlife Management Area, is available from the same address. Phone (304)348-2771.

Use our chart to find a Wildlife Management Area in the region of your trip. Thirteen Wildlife Management Areas located in the state's three national forests, the Monongahela, the George Washington and the Jefferson National Forest, are included in this chart, and all are in the Potomac Highlands. You will need a national forest stamp, available at license offices for a nominal charge, to hunt or fish on national forest lands. These Areas are especially large and remote. Call the number given for directions. (Additional Wildlife Management Areas can be found in state forests. You may also fish—but not hunt—in state parks.) When a mailing address and phone number for a Wildlife Management Area is not available, the address and phone number of the nearest Division District Office is listed instead.

# EASTERN GATEWAY

Nearest Division District Office:
1 Depot St., Romney,
WV 26757, (304) 822-3551

| | fishing | hunting | trapping | campsites | picnic tables | toilets | showers | drinking water | boat ramp | boat rental | rifle range | HC access |
|---|---|---|---|---|---|---|---|---|---|---|---|---|
| **Edwards Run** Acres: 397 FOB, Capon Bridge, Division District Office | • T FF | • | | | | • | | | | | | |
| **Fort Mill Ridge** Acres: 217 FM, Romney, Division District Office | • | • | | | | | | | | | | |
| **Nathaniel Mountain** Acres: 8,875 FM, Romney, Division District Office | • T | • | | • 8 | | • | | • | | | | |
| **Shannondale Springs** Acres: 623 FOB, Charles Town, Rt. 2, Box 109F, Hedgesville, WV 25427, (304) 754-3855 | • | • | | | | | | | | | | |
| **Short Mountain** Acres: 8,005 FM, Kirby, Division District Office | • T | • | | • 6 | | | | • | | | | |
| **Sleepy Creek** Acres: 22,928 F, Berkeley Springs, Rt. 2, Box 109F, Hedgesville, WV 25427, (304) 754-3855 | • | • | | • 75 | | • | | • | | • 2 | | |
| **Springfield** Acres: 9,459 FM, Springfield, Division District Office | | • | | | | | | | | | | |
| **Widmeyer** Acres: 422 F, Berkeley Springs, Division District Office | | • | • | | | | | | | | | |

# POTOMAC HIGHLANDS

| | fishing | hunting | trapping | campsites | picnic tables | toilets | showers | drinking water | boat ramp | boat rental | rifle range | HC access |
|---|---|---|---|---|---|---|---|---|---|---|---|---|
| **Handley** Acres: 784 O, Edray, Rt. 2, Box 320, Marlington, WV 24954, (304) 799-6317 | • T | • | | • 13 | | • | | • | | | | |

LEGEND: F–Forested, O–Open, M–Mountainous, W–Wetlands, B–Brush, T–Trout, FF–Fly-fishing Only, L–Limited, B–Bow-hunting Only, N–Nearby

## Monongahela National Forest
200 Sycamore St., Elkins, WV 26253, (304) 636-1800

| | fishing | hunting | trapping | campsites | picnic tables | toilets | showers | drinking water | boat ramp | boat rental | rifle range | HC access |
|---|---|---|---|---|---|---|---|---|---|---|---|---|
| **Beaver Dam** Acres: 36,574 FM | • T | • | • | • 17 | | • | | • | | | | |
| **Blackwater** Acres: 58,978 FOM | • T | • | • | • 85 | • | • | | • | | | | |
| **Cheat** Acres: 80,771 FM | • T | • | • | • | | | | | | | | |
| **Cranberry** Acres: 160,990 FM | • T | • | • | • | | | | | | | | |
| **Little River** Acres: 124,483 FM | • T | • | • | • N | | | | | | | | |
| **Neola** Acres: 97,928 F | • T | • | | • | | | | | | | | |
| **Otter Creek** Acres: 68,553 FM | • T | • | | • N | | | | | | | | |
| **Potomac** Acres: 135,096 FM | • T | • | | • | | | | | | | | |
| **Rimel** Acres: 64,185 FM | • T | • | | • | | | | | | | | |
| **Tea Creek** Acres: 64,854 FM | • T | • | | • | | | | | | | | |

## George Washington National Forest
Rt. 1, Box 31A, Edinburg, VA 22824, (703) 984-4101

| | fishing | hunting | trapping | campsites | picnic tables | toilets | showers | drinking water | boat ramp | boat rental | rifle range | HC access |
|---|---|---|---|---|---|---|---|---|---|---|---|---|
| **Shenandoah** Acres: 49,316 FM | • T | • | | • | | | | | | | | |
| **Wardensville** Acres: 50,852 FM | • T | • | | • | | | | | | | | |

## Jefferson National Forest
Rt. 5, Box 15, Blacksburg, VA 24060, (703) 522-4641

| | fishing | hunting | trapping | campsites | picnic tables | toilets | showers | drinking water | boat ramp | boat rental | rifle range | HC access |
|---|---|---|---|---|---|---|---|---|---|---|---|---|
| **Potts Creek** Acres: 18,211 FM | • T | • | | | | | | | | | | |

## MOUNTAIN LAKES
Nearest Division District Office: Box 38, French Creek, WV 26218, (304) 924-6211

| | fishing | hunting | trapping | campsites | picnic tables | toilets | showers | drinking water | boat ramp | boat rental | rifle range | HC access |
|---|---|---|---|---|---|---|---|---|---|---|---|---|
| **Big Ditch** Acres: 388 O P.O. Box 595, Cohen, WV 26206, (304) 226-5885 | • | • B | | | | • | | | • | | | |

|  | fishing | hunting | trapping | campsites | picnic tables | toilets | showers | drinking water | boat ramp | boat rental | rifle range | HC access |
|---|---|---|---|---|---|---|---|---|---|---|---|---|
| **Burnsville Lake** Acres: 12,579 OMB Burnsville 16 Laurel Heights, Sutton, WV 26601, (304) 924-6211 | • | • |  | • |  |  |  |  | • | • |  | • |
| **Elk River** Acres: 18,216 FMB Sutton Rt. 2, Box 100, Sutton, WV 26601, (304) 765-5692 | • T | • |  | • |  |  |  |  |  |  | • 2 |  |
| **Stonecoal Lake** Acres: 3,000 FB Horner Division District Office | • T | • |  | • N |  |  |  |  | • 2 |  |  |  |
| **Stonewall Jackson Lake** Acres: 20,818 FO Weston Division District Office | • T | • |  | • N |  |  |  |  | • 5 |  |  |  |
| **Summersville Lake** Acres: 5,650 FM Summersville Division District Office | • T | • |  | • N | • | • | • | • |  |  |  |  |
| **Wallback** Acres: 6,713 M Wallback Division District Office |  | • |  |  |  |  |  |  |  |  |  |  |

## MOUNTAINEER COUNTRY

|  | fishing | hunting | trapping | campsites | picnic tables | toilets | showers | drinking water | boat ramp | boat rental | rifle range | HC access |
|---|---|---|---|---|---|---|---|---|---|---|---|---|
| **Briery Mountain** Acres: 1,000 F Terra Alta Division District Office 1304 Goose Run Rd., Fairmont, WV 26554, (304) 366-5880 |  | • |  |  |  |  |  |  |  |  |  |  |
| **Pleasant Creek** Acres: 3,373 FMW Rt. 3, Box 180, Philippi, WV 26416, (304) 457-4336 | • | • | • | • 48 |  | • |  | • |  |  | • |  |
| **Teter Creek Lake** Acres: 136 FO Belington c/o Audra State Park Rt. 4, Box 564, Buckhannon, WV 26201, (304) 457-1162 | • T | • L |  | • 20 |  | • |  | • |  |  |  |  |

Nearest Division District Office:
1304 Goose Run Rd., Fairmont,
WV 26554, (304) 366-5880

| | fishing | hunting | trapping | campsites | picnic tables | toilets | showers | drinking water | boat ramp | boat rental | rifle range | HC access |
|---|---|---|---|---|---|---|---|---|---|---|---|---|
| **Bear Rocks Lakes** Acres: 285 FO, Triadelphia Division District Office | • T | • L | • | | | • | | • | | | | • |
| **Burches Run Lake** Acres: 54 F, Pleasant Valley Division District Office | • T | • L | | | • | • | | • | | | | |
| **Castleman's Run Lake** Acres: 343 FO, Bethany Division District Office | • T | • L | | | | • | | • | | | | |
| **Conaway Run Lake** Acres: 630 FB, Alma, Box 244, Middlebourne, WV 26149, (304) 758-2681 | T | | | 10 | | • | | | • | 2 | • | |
| **The Jug** Acres: 1,830 FO, Middlebourne Division District Office, 6321 Emerson Ave., Parkersburg, WV 26101, (304) 420-4550 | • | • | | | | | | | | | | |
| **Lewis Wetzel** Acres: 12,498 FM, Rt. 1, Box 8, Jacksonburg, WV 26377, (304) 889-2233 | • T | • | | 20 | • | • | • | • | | | • | |

## MID-OHIO VALLEY

Nearest Division District Office: 6321 Emerson Ave., Parkersburg, WV 26101, (304) 420-4550

| | fishing | hunting | trapping | campsites | picnic tables | toilets | showers | drinking water | boat ramp | boat rental | rifle range | HC access |
|---|---|---|---|---|---|---|---|---|---|---|---|---|
| **B.J. Taylor** Acres: 141, Left Hand Division District Office | | • L | | | | | | | | | | |
| **Frozen Camp** Acres: 1,500 FOM, Marshall Division District Office | • | • | | | | | | | • | | | |
| **Hughes River** Acres: 10,000 FOM, Cisco Division District Office | • | • | | | | | | | | | | |

**LEGEND:** F–Forested, O–Open, M–Mountainous, W–Wetlands, B–Brush, T–Trout, FF–Fly-fishing Only, L–Limited, B–Bow-hunting Only, N–Nearby

| | fishing | hunting | trapping | campsites | picnic tables | toilets | showers | drinking water | boat ramp | boat rental | rifle range | HC access |
|---|---|---|---|---|---|---|---|---|---|---|---|---|
| **Ritchie Mines** Acres: 1,731 W Mellin Division District Office | | • | | | | | | | | | | |
| **Woodrum** Acres: 1,700 FOM Kentuck Division District Office | • | • | | | | | | | • | | | |

## METRO VALLEY
Nearest Division District Office: Rt. 1, Box 484, Pt. Pleasant, WV 25550, (304) 675-4380

| | fishing | hunting | trapping | campsites | picnic tables | toilets | showers | drinking water | boat ramp | boat rental | rifle range | HC access |
|---|---|---|---|---|---|---|---|---|---|---|---|---|
| **Beech Fork Lake** Acres: 7,531 FM Lavalette Division District Office | • | • | | •<br>275 | | • | | | •<br>2 | | | |
| **Big Ugly** Acres: 6,421 FOM Leet Box 195, Harts, WV 25524 (305) 675-4380 | | • | | •<br>11 | | • | | • | | | | |
| **Chief Cornstalk** Acres: 10,776 F Box 225, Cornstalk Rd., Southside, WV 25187, (304) 675-4380 | •<br>T | • | • | •<br>25 | | • | | • | | | | |
| **East Lynn Lake** Acres: 22,928 FM East Lynn Division District Office | •<br>T | • | | •<br>174 | • | • | | • | | | | |
| **Fork Creek** Acres: 9,000 F Nellis 340 Wilson St., Madison, WV 25130, (304) 675-4380 | •<br>L | • | | •<br>20 | | • | | • | | | | |
| **Green Bottom** Acres: 836 FOW Lesage Division District Office | • | •<br>B | | | | | | | | | | |
| **Hilbert** Acres: 243 FM Sod Division District Office | | • | | | | | | | | | | |

LEGEND: F–Forested, O–Open, M–Mountainous, W–Wetlands, B–Brush, T–Trout, FF–Fly-fishing Only, L–Limited, B–Bow-hunting Only, N–Nearby

| | fishing | hunting | trapping | campsites | picnic tables | toilets | showers | drinking water | boat ramp | boat rental | rifle range | HC access |
|---|---|---|---|---|---|---|---|---|---|---|---|---|
| **Laurel Lake** Acres: 12,854 FM, Lenore, Box 626, Lenore, WV 25676, (304) 475-2823 | •T | •B | | •25 | | • | • | • | | | | |
| **McClintic** Acres: 2,787 FOWB, Pt. Pleasant, Division District Office | • | • | • | •9 | | • | | • | | | • | • |
| **Mill Creek** Acres: 751 FM, Milton, Division District Office | • | | | | | | | | | | | |

## NEW RIVER/GREENBRIER VALLEY
Nearest Division District Office: General Delivery, MacArthur, WV 25873, (304) 256-6947

| | fishing | hunting | trapping | campsites | picnic tables | toilets | showers | drinking water | boat ramp | boat rental | rifle range | HC access |
|---|---|---|---|---|---|---|---|---|---|---|---|---|
| **Berwind Lake** Acres: 18,000 F, War, Box 38, Warriormine, WV 24894, (304) 875-4412 | •T | • | | | | | | | | | | |
| **Bluestone Lake** Acres: 17,512 FOM, Hinton, Rt. 1, Box 91, Indian Mills, WV 24949, (304) 466-3398 | • | • | • | •N | | | | | •4 | | | |
| **Meadow River** Acres: 1,430 OW, Rupert, Division District Office | | •B | | | | | | | | | | |
| **Moncove Lake** Acres: 755 F, Gap Mills, Rt. 4, Box 72A, Gap Mills, WV 24941, (304) 772-3450 | • | • | | •50 | | • | • | • | | | | |
| **Plum Orchard Lake** Acres: 3,201 F, Scarbro, Rt. 1, Box 186, Scarbro, WV 25917, (304) 469-9905 | • | • | | •44 | | • | | | • | •4 | • | |
| **R. D. Bailey Lake** Acres: 17,280 FM, Justice, HCR 67, Box 20 Simon, WV 24882, (304) 682-8633 | •T | •B | • | •169 | | • | | | • | | • | |

# Calendar of Events

## JANUARY

**Early:**

Lewisburg, *Shanghai Parade*, (304)645-1000 or 833-2068.
Flat Top, *New WinterPlace Pro-Am Race*, (304)787-3221.

**Mid:**

Berkeley Springs, *Winter Festival of the Waters*, (304)258-9147.
Charleston, *Martin Luther King, Jr.* Holiday Celebration, (304)558-0220.
Mullens, *Senior Fling*, (304)294-4000 or 1(800)CALL-WVA.

**Late:**

Snowshoe, *Jose Cuervo's "Games of Winter"*, (304)572-1000.
Davis, *Blackwater Falls Cross Country Ski Workshop*, (304)259-5216 or 1(800)CALL-WVA.
Davis, *Mountain State Cross-Country Marathon*, (304)866-4114.

## FEBRUARY

**Early:**

Snowshoe, *N.F.L. Celebrity Ski Challenge*, (304)572-6744 or 1(800)523-6329.
Parkersburg, *West Virginia Special Olympics Winter Games*, (304)422-1868 or 1(800)926-1616.
Richwood, *Richwood Winterfest*, (304)846-6790.

**Mid:**

Mullens, *Sweetheart Weekend Getaway*, (304)294-4000 or 1(800)CALL-WVA.
Pipestem, *Sweetheart Weekend*, (304)466-1800 or 1(800)CALL-WVA.
Berkeley Springs, *Washington's Birthday Weekend Celebration*, (304)258-9147.
Williamstown, *Fenton Glass February Gift Shop Sale*, (304)375-7772.

**Late:**

Helvetia, *Fasnacht, Swiss ethnic celebration*, (304)924-6435.
Snowshoe, Molson *"Ski Challenge"*, (304)572-1000.
Berkeley Springs, *"Toast to the Tap"*, International Water Tasting and Competition, (304)258-9147.
Davis, *Winter Carnival*, (304)866-4121, Ext. 2682 or 1(800)CALL-WVA.

## MARCH

**Early:**

Flat Top, *Spring Fling*, (304)787-3221.

Davis, *Governor's Cup Ski Race*, (304)259-5315 or 1(800)782-2775.

Flat Top, *New WinterPlace Triathlon*, (304)787-3221.

Davis, *"March Madness"*, month-long ski activities, (304)866-4121, Ext. 2682 or 1(800)CALL-WVA.

**Mid:**

Pipestem, *Appalachian Culture Weekend*, (304)466-1800 or 1(800)CALL-WVA.

Snowshoe, *Jimmie Heuga Ski Express*, (304)572-4000 or 523-6329.

**Late:**

Snowshoe, *"Crazy March"*, (304)572-1000.

Pickens, *West Virginia Maple Syrup Festival*, (304)924-5096.

Lewisburg, *Annual Choir Festival*, (304)645-1000 or 833-2068.

Berkeley Springs, *"A Taste of Our Town"*, local cuisine sampling, (304)258-9147 or (304)447-8797.

Moundsville, *Spring Craft Show*, (304)845-8659 or 3980.

## APRIL

**Early:**

Huntington, *Easter Egg Hunt*, (304)696-5954.

Wheeling, *Antique Show and Sale*, (304)242-7272 or 1(800)624-6988.

Wheeling, *Good Egg Treasure Hunt*, (304)243-4028.

Berkeley Springs, *Easter Celebration*, (304)258-1022 or 1(800)CALL-WVA.

Cairo, *Easter Weekend Celebration*, (304)643-2931 or 1(800)CALL-WVA.

**Mid:**

Charleston, *West Virginia Dance Festival*, (304)558-0220.

Elkins, *Randolph County International Ramp Festival*, (304)636-2717 or 1(800)422-3304.

Richwood, *"Feast of the Ramson" ramp festival*, (304)846-6790.

**Late:**

Salem, *Green Tree Fair*, (304)782-5245.

Elkins, *Spring Dulcimer Festival*, (304)696-1903.

Marlinton, *Great Greenbrier River Race*, (304)653-4722 or 1(800)336-7009.

Clay, *Clay County High School Ramp Dinner*, (304)587-4226.

Martinsburg, *House and Garden Tour*, (304)535-2627 or 1(800)848-8687.

Mullens, *Wildflower Walk*, (304)294-4000 or 1(800)CALL-WVA.

Huntington, *Dogwood Arts and Crafts Festival*, (304)696-5990.

## MAY

**Early:**

Romney, *Potomac Eagle Scenic Rail Excursions*, (304)422-6069 or 1(800)CALL-WVA.

Point Pleasant, *Antique Steam and Gas Engine Show*, (304)675-5737.

Parkersburg, *"Rendevous on the River"*, frontier life re-creation, (304)428-3000 or 1(800)CALL-WVA.

Richwood, *Cranberry Mountain Spring Nature Tour*, (304)846-6790.

Grafton, *Mother's Day Observance and Celebration*, (304)265-1589.

**Mid:**

South Charleston, *Freedom Festival*, (304)744-0051

Buckhannon, *West Virginia Strawberry Festival*, (304)472-9036

**Late:**

Fairmont, *Three Rivers Coal Festival*, (304)363-2625

Bluefield, *Telescripps Mountain Festival*, (304)327-7184

Charleston, *Vandalia Gathering*, (304)558-0220

White Sulphur Springs, *West Virginia Dandelion Festival*, (304)536-1755 or 1720

Wheeling, *National Pike Festival*, (304)233-5900, ext. 224

## JUNE

**Early:**

Moundsville, *Fostoria Glass Society Convention/Show & Sell Exhibit*, (304)843-1410

Philippi, *Blue and Gray Reunion*, (304)457-3700

New Martinsville, *River Heritage Days*, (304)455-3366

South Charleston, *Rhododendron State Outdoor Art & Craft Festival*, (304)744-4323

Ravenswood, *Ohio River Festival*, (304)273-5703

Charles Town, *Spring Mountain Heritage Arts & Crafts Festival*, (304)725-2055 or 1(800)624-0577

Lewisburg, *Lewisburg Lions Club Antique Show & Sale*, (304)645-1000 or 1(800)833-2068

Star City, *Mountaineer Country Glass Festival*, (304)599-3407

Ronceverte, *Ronceverte River Festival*, (304)645-7911 or 645-2049

**Mid:**

Oak Hill, *Whitewater Wednesday*, (304)465-5617 or 927-0263

Glenville, *West Virginia State Folk Festival*, (304)462-7361

Davis, *"Blackwater 100"*, motorcycle/ATV race, (304)259-5315 or 1(800)782-2775

**Late:**
Summersville, *Bluegrass-Country Music Festival*, (304)872-3145
Point Pleasant, *Pt. Pleasant Sternwheel Regatta*, (304)675-3844
Princeton, *Princeton Summerfest*, (304)487-1502
Cass, *Dinner Trains*, (304)456-4300 or 1(800)CALL-WVA
Hillsboro, *Pearl S. Buck Birthday Celebration*, (304)653-4430
Ripley, *Mountain State Art and Craft Fair*, (304)372-7008

## JULY

**Early:**
Elkins, *Annual Auto Extravaganza*, (304)636-9976
Cass, *Dinner Trains*, (304)456-4300 or 1(800)CALL-WVA
Weirton, *Weirton International Food and Arts Festival*, (304)748-7212
Wheeling, *Fourth of July Celebration*, (304)232-6191
Burnsville, *Civil War Reenactment*, (304)853-2371
Richwood, *Scenic Mountain Triathlon*, (304)846-6790
Elkins, *Summer Concert and Dance series*, (304)636-1903

**Mid:**
Wheeling, *Jamboree in the Hills*, (304)232-1170 or 1(800)624-5456
Mineral Wells, *West Virginia Interstate Fair & Exposition*, (304)489-
    2940 or 1301
Clifftop, *Doo-Wop Saturday Night*, Camp Washington Carver,
    (304)558-0220
Snowshoe, *Snowshoe Chili Cookoff*, (304)572-1000

**Late:**
Wheeling, *Upper Ohio Valley Italian Festival*, (304)233-1090
Beverly, *Beverly Days*, (304)636-5032
Moorefield, *State Poultry Festival*, (304)538-2725

## AUGUST

**Early:**
Logan, *"The Aracoma Story"*, (304)752-0253
Clifftop, *Appalachian String Band Music Festival*, (304)558-0220
Hinton, *West Virginia State Water Festival*, (304)466-5400
Charleston, *"MultiFest"*, (304)776-5669
Monongah, *Monongahfest*, (304)534-3320
Richwood, *Cherry River Festival*, (304)846-6790
New Martinsville, *Town & Country Days*, (304)386-4444

**Mid:**
Elkins, *Augusta Festival*, (304)636-1900
Lewisburg, *State Fair of West Virginia*, (304)645-1090
Snowshoe, *"Mountain Bike Challenge"*, (304)572-1000

Charleston, Fox 11 "Kids Expo", family festival, (304)757-0011
Clifftop, Old-Time Day, Camp Washington Carver, (304)558-0220
Weirton, Turn-of-the-Century Festival, (304)797-1604

**Late:**
Beckley, Appalachian Arts & Crafts Festival, (304)252-7328
Parkersburg, American Indian Heritage Weekend, (304)428-3000 or
 1(800)CALL-WVA
Snowshoe, Snowshoe "Symphony Weekend" concert, (304)572-1000
Charleston, Charleston Sternwheel Regatta, (304)348-6419

## SEPTEMBER

**Early:**
South Charleston, Rose Show, (304)744-1486
Clarksburg, West Virginia Italian Heritage Festival, (304)622-7314
Weston, Stonewall Jackson Heritage Arts & Crafts Jubilee, (304)269-
 1863
Summersville, Nicholas County Potato Festival, (304)872-1588

**Mid:**
Pipestem, Annual Mountain Music Festival, (304)466-0626
South Charleston, The Mound Festival, (304)746-5552 or 744-4197
Helvetia, Helvetia Fair, (304)924-6435
Huntington, Hilltop Festival, (304)529-2701
Parkersburg, West Virginia Honey Festival, (304)428-1130
Romney, Hampshire County Heritage Days, (304)822-5013
Davis, Milk and Honey 10K Run, (304)866-4121, ext. 2682 or
 1(800)CALL-WVA
Franklin, Treasure Mountain Festival, (304)358-7918
Sistersville, West Virginia Oil & Gas Festival
Morgantown, Mason-Dixon Festival of West Virginia, (304)599-1104
 or 1(800)458-7373
Huntington, Bavarian Festival, (304)696-5954
Keyser, Founder's Day Celebration, (304)788-3679
Parkersburg, Harvest Moon Arts & Crafts Festival, (304)422-7121
Summersville, Carnifex Ferry Reenactment, (304)872-3773

**Late:**
Winfield, Encampment and Living History Trail, (304)757-6511
Arnoldsburg, West Virginia Molasses Festival, (304)655-8374
Rivesville, Paw Paw Festival, (304)278-7335
Charles Town, Fall Mountain Heritage Arts & Crafts Festival,
 (304)725-2055 or 624-0577
Summersville, Gauley River Festival, (304)574-0482
Davis, Leaf Peepers Festival, (304)259-5315 or 1(800)782-2775

Moorefield, *Hardy County Heritage Weekend*, (304)538-6560
Waverly, *Volcano Days Festival*, (304)679-3611
Kingwood, *Preston County Buckwheat Festival*, (304)329-0021

## OCTOBER

**Early:**

Elkins, *Fiddlers' Reunion*, (304)636-1903
Harpers Ferry, *Election of 1860 Celebration*, (304)422-6069 or
   1(800)CALL-WVA
Milton, *West Virginia Pumpkin Festival*, (304)743-9222
Wheeling, *Oglebayfest*, (304)243-4000 or 1(800)624-6988
Burlington, *Old Fashioned Apple Harvest Festival*, (304)289-3911
Hundred, *Octoberfest*, (304)775-7455
Point Pleasant, *Country Festival/Antique Steam & Gas Engine Show/
   Quilt Show*, (304)675-5737
Salem, *Harvest Festival*, (304)782-5245
Elkins, *Mountain State Forest Festival*, (304)636-2717
Barboursville, *Barboursville Oktoberfest, Inc.*, (304)736-9820
Salem, *Salem Apple Butter Festival*, (304)782-3565
Weston, *Octoberfest*, (304)269-2608
Lewisburg, *"Taste of Our Town"*, local cuisine sampling, (304)645-
   7917
Berkeley Springs, *Apple Butter Festival*, (304)258-3738 or 1(800)447-
   8757
Mullens, *Lumberjackin' Bluegrassin' Jamboree*, (304)294-4000 or
   1(800)CALL-WVA
Point Pleasant, *"Battle Days"* reenactment, (304)675-3844

**Mid:**

Spencer, *West Virginia Black Walnut Festival*, (304)927-1780
Martinsburg, *Mountain State Apple Harvest Festival*, (304)263-2500
Morgantown, *Mountaineer Balloon Festival*, (304)296-8356
Fayetteville, *New River Gorge Bridge Day*, (304)465-5617 or 927-0263
Hinton, *Railroad Days Festival*, (304)466-5420
Huntington, *New River Train Ride*, (304)453-1641

**Late:**

Cass, *Halloween Train*, (304)456-4300 or 1(800)CALL-WVA
Huntington, *Winterscapes*, (304)696-5522

## NOVEMBER

**Early:**

Wheeling, *City of Lights Festival*, (304)233-2575
Wheeling, *Winter Festival of Lights*, (304)243-4000 or 1(800)624-6988
Cairo, *Arts and Crafts Show*, (304)643-2931 or 1(800)CALL-WVA

Point Pleasant, Old Fashioned "Pig Pickin'", (304)675-5737
Wheeling, Christmas at the Mansion, (304)242-7272 or 1(800)624-6988

**Mid:**

Charleston, Capitol City Art and Craft Show
Wheeling, Fantasy of Light Parade, (304)233-2575

**Late:**

Fairmont, 18th Century Christmas Market, (304)363-3030
Charleston, "Trees of the Nations" museum exhibit, (304)344-8035
Mullens, Christmas Crafts Show & Sale, (304)294-4000 or 1(800)CALL-WVA
South Charleston, "Christmas on the Kanawha" boat parade, (304)746-5552 or 1(800)238-9488

### DECEMBER

**Early:**

Morgantown, Lighting of Woodburn Hall/Holiday Gala, (304)293-8499
Lewisburg, First Night Christmas Celebration, (304)645-1000 or 1(800)833-2068
Harpers Ferry, Old Tyme Christmas, (304)725-8019 or 1(800)848-TOUR
Parkersburg, Christmas Open House, (304)428-3000 or 1(800)CALL-WVA
Salem, Spirit of Christmas at Fort New Salem, (304)782-5245
Sheperdstown, Old Time Christmas, (304)876-0669

**Mid:**

Parkersburg, "Margaret's Birthday Party", (304)428-3000 or 1(800)CALL-WVA
Pipestem, Christmas Bird Count, (304)466-1800 or 1(800)CALL-WVA

**Late:**

Huntington, "First Night Celebration", (304)696-5522
Cairo, New Year's Eve Dinner and Dance, (304)643-2931 or 1(800)CALL-WVA
Davis, New Year's Eve Party, (304)866-4121, ext. 2682 or 1(800)CALL-WVA
Mullens, New Year's Eve Watch, (304)294-4000 or 1(800)CALL-WVA

# Index

# Acknowledgments

In addition to all the kind West Virginians who so patiently pointed us in the right direction, we wish to thank in particular:

Cindy Harrington, Dan Le Roy, Kevin Struthers, Michelle Bailey and Libby White, WV Division of Tourism & Parks, Charleston;

David Fattaleh, and Stephen J. Shaluta, Jr., Photo Lab, West Virginia Division of Tourism & Parks, Charleston, who so kindly furnished most of the photographs in the book;

Ray Swick, Blennerhassett Island Historical State Park, Parkersburg;

Felice Jorgeson, Smoot Theatre, Parkersburg;

Jon McIlhenny, Director, Lewisburg Convention and Visitors Bureau;

Mary McNabb, Administrator WV State Capitol, Charleston;

Sylvia Miller, The Old Stone House, Morgantown;

David Perry, Watoga State Park;

Sidney A. Rosenbluth, Ph.D., Dean of the School of Pharmacy, West Virginia University, Morgantown;

Kelly Stewart, Executive Director, Southern WV Convention and Visitors Bureau, Beckley;

Stacey Vavrek, Northern WV Convention and Visitors Bureau, Morgantown;

Dianne Wilkey, Halliehurst, College of Davis & Elkins, Elkins;

The WV Division of Tourism & Parks, and the WV Division of Natural Resources, for the use of maps, lists, charts and photos;

And a very special thank you to Janet Nelson for her patience, humor, guidance and organizational brilliance.

# About the Authors

A writer and editor for EPM Publications, Suzanne Lord owns a cabin on the Shavers Fork of the Cheat River at the edge of the Monongahela National Forest, where the slopes of the Alleghenies rise to meet Otter Creek Wilderness and the Potomac Highlands. When not exploring mountain inns and the wonders of West Virginia described herein, she lives in McLean, Virginia, with her husband, Peter, and Jessie, their Chesapeake Bay retriever.

Jon Metzger first joined EPM when he was in high school. He has worked in office management and sales and helped to research and write the popular *Inns of the Blue Ridge*. He is also a jazz vibist of note, having developed an international following through extensive touring, recording and lecturing. An avid tennis player and fisherman, Metzger, 33, lives with his wife, Linda, and their basset hound.